# STRATEGIC CONCEPTS

## That Clarify A Focused Life

**A Self-Study Manual Defining and Applying Focused Life Concepts to Leaders Today**

by Dr. J. Robert Clinton

ISBN 0-9710454-3-7

**TABLE OF CONTENTS**

## TABLE OF CONTENTS

**TABLE OF CONTENTS**

<u>Page</u>   <u>Contents</u>

**TABLE OF CONTENTS**

<u>Page</u>    <u>Contents</u>

### Section III.  Proactively Moving Toward The Focused Life

# Preface

**For Ezra had prepared his heart to seek the law of the Lord, and to do it, and to teach in Israel statues and judgments.** Ezra 7:10

**And it came to pass, when the time was come that he should be received up, he steadfastly set his face to go to Jerusalem.** Luke 9:51

Clearly some Bible characters led focused lives. There was purpose in what they did. Disciplined minds followed through on decisions that continually led to that purpose. What can we learn about lives that are extremely focused? Do they just happen? Is it possible to learn lessons from their lives? Can such lessons help other leaders[1] who are not so focused to have more proactive, deliberate, effective ministries that contribute to a purposeful life? The thesis of this manual gives a resounding **YES!!!**

> **Leaders, must make decisions about life and ministry which flow from their understanding of who God has made them to be and for what God is shaping them. These decisions will lead them to effective purposeful lives, which in retrospect will be seen to have been focused lives. But it is not a self-seeking individualistic choice of life but a seeking of what a SOVEREIGN GOD is doing—His purposes. All of the focused life thinking must be done in light of a strong understanding of the Sovereignty of God.**

What is a focused life? What are the factors that help a leader make decisions about life and ministry so as to focus them? My studies of leaders' lives have uncovered some answers to these questions. Let me briefly share with you the process of my discovery and then some answers to these questions.

In 1982 I begin to do individual case studies of leaders. These studies included Biblical characters, historical characters, and contemporary Christian leaders. I have continued to collect data and compare these cases up to the present. Currently I have over 3000 of these cases. Eventually a framework developed for explaining how leaders emerged. I have written up this framework in a coherent set of ideas, which I call leadership emergence theory.[2] The central idea of the theory concerns the integration of findings around a time-line. We have identified shaping processes and patterns, which help us understand God's work in a life. We have identified some major leadership lessons.[3] These leadership lessons have helped us evaluate leaders' lives.

---

[1] I am directing this manual to full time Christian leaders, that is, those who have opted for a vocation, which allows them to fully operate in terms of their ministry gifts. I am not suggesting that non-full time workers cannot have a focused life. Indeed I think they can. However, my research has focused only on full time Christian leaders so I don't have the data base to define the concepts with certainty for lay leaders or even bi-vocational workers. Though I do think much of what I am stating will fit. In fact, I think that these concepts can be adapted (contextualized) for secular careers of committed Christians.

[2] I wrote a popularization of the theory in **The Making of A Leader** published by NavPress. I did my Ph.D. Dissertation, giving the formal results of my research up to 1989. I published in 1989 a manual, **Leadership Emergence Theory** by Barnabas Publishers for use in classes and workshops. Since then I have done many spin-off publications including books and manuals on mentoring and giftedness as well as position papers on various facets of my continuing research (Boundary Processing, Social Base Processing, Paradigm Shifts, Destiny Processing, etc.).

[3] Seven important ones include: Effective leaders maintain a **learning posture** all their lives. Effective leaders view **spiritual authority** as a primary power base for their ministry. Effective leaders view present ministry in terms of a **lifetime perspective**. Effective leaders have a **dynamic ministry philosophy** which

Very recently I made a special comparative study of eight highly effective leaders. I used my criteria about the leadership lessons to evaluate their ministries. In addition to being very effective leaders, they finished well.[4] The purpose of this study was to trace the working of God to focus these leaders toward their life work and realization of that work. In short, the purpose was to study the concept of **focus** in the lives of these great leaders. These eight leaders included:

| Leader | Time | Brief Description |
|---|---|---|
| **Charles Simeon** | (1759-1836) | The Strategic Mentor—Effective Change Through Mentoring (an Anglican pastor) |
| **A. J. Gordon** | (1836-1895) | A Study in Ultimate Contribution (a Baptist Minister) |
| **Samuel Brengle** | (1860-1936) | Public Saint—A Study in Consistency (a Salvation Army worker) |
| **G. Campbell Morgan** | (1863-1945) | World Class Bible Teacher (a British pastor who also did parachurch work in the United States) |
| **Robert Jaffray** | (1873-1945) | Missionary Pioneer Who Exemplifies Major Life Achievement After Age 55 (Christian and Missionary Alliance worker) |
| **R. C. McQuilkin** | (1886-1952) | A Life Dominated by a Three Fold Thrust (founded Columbia Bible College) |
| **Henrietta Mears** | (1890-1963) | A Destiny for Challenging Emerging Leaders (Staff worker at First Presbyterian Church of Hollywood with broad influence all over the United States) |
| **L. E. Maxwell** | (1895-1984) | The Deeper Life—the Central Hub of this Focused Life (founded Prairie Bible Institute). |

I will refer to examples from these lives many times throughout this manual.

---

changes due to growth in Biblical understanding, giftedness development, and different leadership contexts. Effective leaders see **relational empowerment** as both a means and an end. Effective leaders view **leadership selection and development** as a priority in their ministry. Effective leaders evince a growing awareness of their **sense of destiny**. Normally a given effective leader will have 4 or so of the above. Very effective leaders will have nearly all.

[4]While there are probably a number of criteria that could be used to evaluate a lifetime of ministry we have developed the following. Leaders who finish well: 1) maintain a <u>personal vibrant relationship</u> with God right up to the end; 2) maintain a <u>learning posture</u> and can learn from various kinds of sources—life especially; 3) portray <u>Christ-likeness in character</u> as evidenced by the fruit of the Spirit in their lives; 4) <u>live out truth</u> in their lives so that convictions and promises of God are seen to be real; 5) leave behind one or more <u>ultimate contributions</u> (saint, stylistic practitioners, mentors, public rhetoricians, pioneers, crusaders, artists, founders, stabilizers, researchers, writers, promoters); 6) walk with a growing <u>awareness of a sense of destiny</u> and see some or all of it fulfilled.

From this study emerged a most important strategic concept—that of a focused life.

Definition  A <u>focused life</u>  is

- a life **dedicated** to exclusively carrying out God's effective purposes through it,

- by identifying the focal issues, that is, the **life purpose, effective methodology, major role**, or **ultimate contribution** which allows

- an **increasing prioritization** of life's activities around the focal issues, and

- results in a **satisfying life** of **being** and **doing**.

Note carefully the key words, which are boldfaced.

**Dedicated** usually indicates that there was some sort of second decision beyond just being a Christian.[5]  That decision places all that the leader is or has at God's disposal to be used by and for God.  From that moment on, the leader is on a pilgrimage to discover God's special purposes, that is, a personal destiny with God.  Sometimes this decision is called in some circles, a Lordship committal.  Other groups may give it the title of a special call or special time of anointing for something.  In any case it is a recognition that all of life is about serving the Lord.  What ever is done in life, it must revolve around work for the Lord.

**Life purpose, effective methodology, major role**, or **ultimate contribution** are called the focal issues.  That is, they are the major ways that God will reveal that for which we are designed.  In a nutshell **life purpose** is the driving force behind what we do.  **Major role** is the occupational position from which we accomplish that life purpose.[6]  **Effective methodologies** are means that are effective for us to deliver our ministry that flows from that life purpose.  And **ultimate contributions** are the lasting results of that ministry.  Each of these concepts will be defined in detail and explored fully in this manual.

---

[5]Of course in the case of adult conversions the decision to become a Christian and the decision to wholly follow and serve the Lord in some full time capacity can be concomitant.

[6]Major role is an illusive concept since it is often confused with formal titles or recognized full time Christian roles like pastor or missionary or parachurch worker.  But it is more than that.  In its essence there are basically three kinds:  1) those roles that flow from a Harvest Model or 2) those kind that flow from a Shepherd Model or 3) those roles which seek to facilitate one or the other of these dominant models. It is giftedness which inherently identifies a leader with either the Harvest Model or the Shepherd Model. Occasionally there are some gifted individuals who inherently operate out of both models.  See **Unlocking Your Giftedness**, pages 24-32, which correlate the notion of giftedness and New Testament philosophical leadership models.

It is the discovery of these focal issues, that is, their movement from implicit to explicit, which provides the possibility of **prioritization** or in other words, proactive decision making. The earlier we can discover these issues the earlier we can proactively act upon them. Many of the leaders in my case studies acted on implicit understandings of these focal issues for a good portion of their lives. However, many make breakthrough discoveries on one or more of these issues. Such breakthroughs, which allow an explicit understanding of something previously acted upon as implicit, seem to re-energize the leader toward a more effective ministry. The leader then makes strategic decisions, which take into account the discoveries. In short, they manifest aspects of a focused life. It is just such a phenomenon that has led us to hope that we can expose the concepts and see many more leaders desire, enter in, and enjoy focused lives.

Note the final boldfaced words in the focused life definition, a **satisfying life** of **being** and **doing**. Leaders who discover life purpose and any other focal issue, which synergizes with it, will see things happen in their lives. They will become people of character. They will accomplish. When all is said and done and life is drawing to a close they can look back and say, "Folks, you are looking at a fulfilled person. I am happy with the end product of God's shaping—who I am, what I have become. I am happy at what God has done through me—what I have done. Life was worth living. It has been a fulfilling pilgrimage. Praise God!"

What is the alternative? To come to the end of life and feel we have missed it! Life has not been worth living. We are not happy with our personality, character, and unique being. We are not happy with that which we spent our life doing. We do not have any lasting results that we shall leave behind. I don't personally like that alternative. So I am open to any thinking that will help me discover and use Covey's now well-known leadership value,

### Begin With The End In Mind.[7]

I think this manual will give some ideas that can help you do that. Hopefully you can,

1. earlier on, discover something more of what the **potential** is that God is developing you toward, that is, what the end can be for you,
2. along the way, **seize ideas for acting** on those discoveries, and
3. explore the opportunity to move toward **more** of a satisfied and fulfilled life.

I don't think we can guarantee you a focused life. I don't even think we want to. But we can help you see God's working in your life. And we can help you move more into a partnership with God in what He is doing in you and through you.

---

[7]Covey in his book, **7 Habits of Highly Effective People**, has exposed this idea, which is not original to him. It occurs widely in leadership literature. But he has probably done more to make it known and get its widespread acceptance. He has done much to get people to use it practically in their lives. All of us in leadership research are grateful for his efforts in these directions.

Our comparative study has unearthed a number of helpful ideas about these focal issues.

1. Life purpose is the linchpin[8] of a focused life.
2. Life purpose + any other focal issue can lead to a focused life.
3. Life purpose if synergized[9] by 2 or more focal issues will increase the effectiveness of the focused life.

So what is the bottom line? That is, what can we say definitively about the focused life? We have found that the focused life does not mature till in the late 40s and 50s. So we are in no hurry to get there. The process of getting there is just as important as getting there. It is the process that will bring about **maturity in character,** which is part of the satisfaction at the end of life. So then we can proactively work **with** the long-term process. Much can be done, developmentally, earlier on, which will increase the probability of a focused life. In fact, we actually list some very important steps that can be taken in each of the four important age groups:

1. **The Inklings of a Focused Life**, ages 30-40,
   We can make our first attempts at formulating a **Personal Life Mandate**.
2. **Adding the Synergizing Elements**, ages 40-50,
   We can revise the **Personal Life Mandate** to include other discoveries of focal issues. In particular, major role is the important discovery in this age group.
3. **Proactive Decision Making Using the Discoveries**, ages 50-60,
   We can use what we know in our tactical decision making—our everyday ministry decisions. Especially must we take advantage of effective methodologies.
4. **The Culminating Efforts of a Focused Life**, age 60+.
   We can conserve what we have done and proactively take advantage of our felt need to leave behind lasting legacies.

In short, each of the age groups will have steps, which will provide a tentative **Personal Life Mandate** or a modification of it. That mandate, in itself, will allow proactive decision making even as the focal issues are being worked out with more clarity. The **Personal Life Mandate** will become more firm as each of the focal issues are discovered and confirmed over time. But even in the meantime—a given younger leader will be developing as he/she moves toward focus. And there will be a sense of progress and hope as there is movement toward a focused life.

---

[8] A linchpin is the locking pin inserted crosswise (as through the end of an axle or shaft). Metaphorically speaking it is something that serves to hold together the elements of a situation. Life purpose winds its way throughout a whole life-time to integrate and hold together the various aspects of life that we experience.

[9] Synergy is the resulting action of two or more things combining to give an output greater than the sums of the individual things. In this case, effective methodology operates with life purpose to allow a way for the life purpose to be ministered to others through the leader's effective giftedness. Major role gives the authoritative backing and platform for the leader to act out his/her life purposes. Ultimate contributions are the increasing accumulation of results of the leader's ministry, which eventually become lasting legacies. The more elements that combine the greater the synergy.

So let me summarize.

1. A focused life is a legitimate and worthy developmental goal for a leader.
2. Understanding of what makes up a focused life is a major step forward in moving toward such a life.
3. Even preliminary understanding can issue in a **Personal Life Mandate**. This mandate forms the basis for decision-making leading to a focused life. It is a working document that can be used even though it is continually in need of modification.

This manual will give you the clarifying ideas about the focused life and some tools that will allow you to develop your own **Personal Life Mandate**.

Here is how the manual is structured so as to move you forward toward a focused life.

**Section I. Defining The Focused Life**, gives the overall context. Chapter 1 overviews the concept of ministry philosophy, the broader subject—out of which the focused life ideas come. Chapter 2 actually defines the essential concepts of the focused life—defining the focused life and describing each of its major elements. It is here that you will recognize the concepts of **life purpose, effective methodologies, major roles,** and **ultimate contributions.**

**Section II. Assessing The Focused Life**, helps you synthesize each of the issues of the focused life. Chapter 3 helps you understand your **life purpose**. Chapter 4 helps you see the importance of **effective methodologies** to your ministry. Chapter 5 suggests how you can begin to identify your **major role**. Chapter 6 helps you focus on the **legacies** you want to leave behind.

Then, **Section III. Proactively Moving Toward the Focused Life**, closes with Chapter 7, which helps you assess for your age bracket what you can do to arrive at steps toward the focused life. What should your **Personal Life Mandate** look like?

When all is said and done remember,

> **Leaders, must make decisions about life and ministry which flow from their understanding of who God has made them to be and for what God is shaping them. These decisions will lead them to full effective purposeful lives, which in retrospect will be seen to have been focused lives. But it is not a self-seeking individualistic choice of life but a seeking of what a SOVEREIGN GOD is doing—His purposes. All of the focused life thinking must be done in light of a strong understanding of the Sovereignty of God.**

And that is what we want you to do. I want to give you **Strategic CONCEPTS** that will inform your strategic decision-making about your ministry.

## Chapter 1 Overview: Ministry Philosophy and the Focused Life

This chapter gives the bigger context for the notion of the focused life. Ministry philosophy is the larger context into which the major concepts of the focused life fit. Ministry philosophy develops over a lifetime and includes values (its content) and the narrowing guidance of God toward realization of potential and contribution to His program, (its direction). In addition, a leader in maturity, living a focused life, will be able to give coherent written expression to both the content and the directional processes. It is this written expression that is the end product—a ministry philosophy. The study of God's shaping and impartation of values is categorized under an umbrella-like concept called the **Blend Variable**. The study of the guidance of God toward the narrow purposes for a leader is categorized under an umbrella-like concept called, the **Focus Variable**. The description of the written expression, the end product of a ministry philosophy, is described by an umbrella-like concept called, the **Articulation Variable**.

The drafting of the ministry philosophy, as described by the articulation variable is a time consuming process and is yet to be streamlined. But an intermediate process is very helpful—the identification of God's focusing activity—a study of the focus variable. That intermediate process resulting from a study of the focus variable can be expressed in a personal life mandate. This personal life mandate will change as the focus sharpens over time and with experience. But it is a good step forward toward a focused life. And it is the purpose of this manual to lead you to develop a personal life mandate. This mandate will change over time as you experience more of life and ministry and God's focusing activity becomes even clearer. But it can be a useful criterion for decision making in the meantime and will increase your development toward a focused life and eventually to a full blown explicit ministry philosophy.

This chapter defines the major ministry philosophy concepts so that you can see where the focused life concepts fit.

By the end of this chapter you will,

- recognize the definition and purpose of a ministry philosophy,
- recognize the three umbrella-like concepts used to categorize a ministry philosophy (Blend, Focus, Articulation),
- note generally that shaping incidents seen across a time-line accumulate in a set of values in a leader's life,
- recognize the useful concepts under the focus variable of critical incident, leadership values, focal values, and strategic definition, and
- have been introduced to the idealized notion of the focused life and see where it fits in relation to ministry philosophy in general.

This definition of the focused life, introduced in this chapter in the context of the bigger picture of ministry philosophy, will then be given detailed treatment in chapter 2.

### Ministry Philosophy/ Three Major Components

Introduction   Ministry philosophy refers to a related set of values that underlies a leader's perception and behavior in ministry. This set of leadership values influences decision making, the exercise of leadership influence, and serves as a means for evaluating ministry and deriving satisfaction from ministry.

Definition   A <u>ministry philosophy</u> is a set of implicit values
- which guides a leader's conduct and thinking in relationship to practice and understanding of his/ her ministry,
- which increasingly focuses the leader toward a more effective and unique God-directed contribution to the kingdom, and
- which gradually becomes explicit over a life time so as to be expressed in meaningful coherent categories understood by others.

Definition   Ministry philosophy can be described in terms of _three umbrella-like components_: the <u>Blend Variable</u>, the <u>Focus Variable</u>, and the <u>Articulation Variable.</u>

Stated as a formula Ministry Philosophy = $f(B, F, A)$; Where,

> f means,  is a function of or can be described by:
> $B$ = The Blend Variable, the shaping of critical values that affect life and ministry
>
> ----> $F$ = The Focus (sometimes called focal) Variable, the strategic guidance of the leader to be and do what God intended. Focused life concepts flow from study of this variable.
> $A$ = The Articulation variable, that is, the explicit identification of the blend and focal variable shaping in a coherent set of statements which express in written form the ministry philosophy.

Comment   This manual has as its primary thrust the explanation of the second of the umbrella concepts, the Focus Variable. It will touch on the Blend Variable somewhat since there is overlap between the two.

Comment   For the most part, the ministry philosophy of an individual usually remains implicit. The major purpose of this manual is to help a leader explicitly identify his/her ministry philosophy. It is an assumption that the identification of important values (from analysis of the Blend Variable) and recognition of strategic direction (from analysis of the Focus variable) will indeed allow the leader to proactively make decision which will move toward focused ministry in a more efficient manner.

Comment   The Articulation variable develops last in the normal progression of a ministry philosophy. Less research has been done on this variable. Much research has been done on the Blend and Focal Variables. This manual presents these findings. A future manual will develop fully the Articulation variable. Preliminary work has already been done.

## Normal Development Over A Leader's Time-Line

Introduction     A comparative study of many unique time-lines of leaders with respect to ministry philosophy variables has resulted in the following general time-line showing when the various variables develop.

**THE MINISTRY TIME-LINE AND MINISTRY PHILOSOPHY VARIABLES**

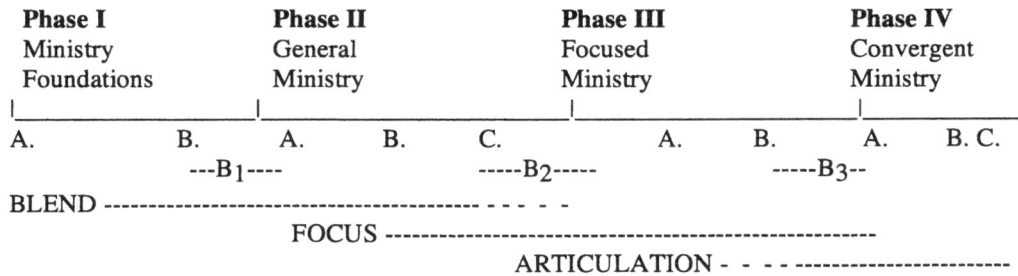

| **Phase I** | **Phase II** | **Phase III** | **Phase IV** |
|---|---|---|---|
| Ministry | General | Focused | Convergent |
| Foundations | Ministry | Ministry | Ministry |

```
 |_____|_____|_____|_____|_____|____|__|
 A.            B.   A.    B.    C.          A.    B.    A. B. C.
            ---B1----           -----B2-----      -----B3--

 BLEND ------------------------------------------- - - - -
               FOCUS ---------------------------------------------------
                        ARTICULATION - - - -------------------------
```

## Where the sub-phases are called:

### Phase I
A.  Sovereign Foundations -- (13-20 years)--early shaping of character/ personality
B.  Leadership Transition (3-6 years)--a time in which first steps in ministry are done

### Phase II
A.  Provisional Ministry  (2-6 years) --the first attempts at full time ministry assignments; it is provisional because it might not last, that is, the leader may not stay in ministry.
B.  Growth Ministry (6-8 years)--ministry utilizing known giftedness with efficiency; giftedness and role issues are learned; this sub-phase is more for developing the leader than the ministry which is accomplished.
C.  Competent Ministry<-- (2-6 years) -->operating out of giftedness in roles that fit that giftedness produces excellent results; still to be determined is the influence-mix profile, in other words, what is the potential level of influence.

### Phase III
A.  Role Transition--There is movement toward compatibility between role, giftedness and influence-mix profile. There is shaping of a role more ideally suited to giftedness and challenge toward influence-mix.
B.  Unique Ministry--ministering effectively as well as efficiently with giftedness. (Role plus unique may last 3-12 years)

### Phase IV
A.  Special Guidance--movement toward a role focusing on ultimate contribution
B.  Convergent Ministry--fulfilling a sense of destiny/ ultimate contribution
C.  Afterglow--fall out effects of a life well lived; spiritual authority dominant

And the boundaries are called: $B_1$ the logistics barrier,  $B_2$ the strategic barrier/ Doing to Being, $B_3$ The Convergence Springboard

Comment     Leadership emergence theory studies a leader's life using a time-line constructed uniquely for the leader. Of special interest is the shaping activity used by God to process the leader. Incidents in the life teach values.

**Feedback: Ministry Philosophy And Its Development**

1. Ministry philosophy was defined as a set of implicit values, which become gradually explicit over a lifetime.

   a. What is meant by implicit?

   b. What is meant by explicit?

2. The three umbrella-like concepts used to talk about ministry philosophy include (check the correct answer):
   _____ a. Blend, Focus, Realization
   _____ b. Direction, Focus, Realization
   _____ c. Blend, Focus, Articulation
   _____ d. Blend, Direction, Realization

3. The concept of the focused life relates most closely to which of the umbrella concepts:
   _____ a. The Blend Variable
   _____ b. The Direction Variable
   _____ c. The Realization Variable
   _____ d. The Articulation Variable
   _____ e. none of the above

4. According to the display of the ministry time-line which variable develops first?

5. According to the display of the ministry time-line which variable develops last?

**ANSWERS------------**

1. Implicit--capable of being understood from something else though unexpressed, synonym = implied. Many values a leader uses are in this category--hidden but operated on. These values are usually not expressed though they could be if reflection brought them to the surface.
   Explicit--characterized by full clear expression, fully developed or formulated, externally visible.
2. _c_
3. _e_
4. The Blend Variable develops first.
5. The Articulation Variable develops last.

## Blend Variable

| | |
|---|---|
| Introduction | The heart of a ministry philosophy lies in values learned in life, which affect how a leader operates. These values give meaning to leaders and their ministry. They shape how leaders feel about situations, how leaders define personal ethical conduct and how leaders evaluate ministry. Leaders learn these values in the various processes associated with life and ministry. These lessons accumulate into a growing set of values. It is this growing set of values which the blend variable addresses. |
| Definition | The <u>blend variable</u> of a ministry philosophy refers to the *process* and resulting *product* of accumulating values and relating these values to each other in a consistent and coherent fashion. |
| Comment | God uses certain incidents to shape leaders in various ways so as to give leadership values. God uses providential events, people, circumstances, special divine intervention, inner-life lessons and/ or other like items to develop a person. God shapes leadership character, leadership skills and leadership values. These values tell leaders what to do and what to avoid in relationships with people. Some tell about the leader's giftedness. Some tell leaders how authority is to be wielded. Some point leaders to what should be accomplished in ministry. Some help leaders understand what is happening to them and their ministry. Some help the leader to understand what God is doing and how he/she should relate to it. These values gradually accumulate to form a ministry philosophy. At first they are implicit. Leaders use them but hardly know they are there unless something forces serious reflection on them. |
| Comment | These lessons are *blended* into a leader's thinking as they happen. Leaders are hardly conscious of them as values which affect their thinking. But they do. Some are more important to the leader (core) and some are helpful but less important (preferential but not normative). But all affect further leadership. Leaders experience similar situations and the lesson or value learned previously begins to take hold and helps them in the new situation. As they continue to accumulate lessons and values they form a *blend* of ideas, which gives them standards to operate by, guidelines for applying influence, knowledge for making decisions, and the many other things that leadership influence entails. |
| Comment | Leadership emergence theory has helped us understand more explicitly the lessons and values learned. Careful observation of numerous leader's lives has resulted not only in many processes (including stages in them, kinds of lessons learned) but also patterns for integrating the processes over a life-time. Knowledge of these processes and patterns helps define the blend variable more explicitly. Explicit recognition fosters better consistency, coherency, and more proactive use and hence movement toward focus. |
| Comment | The essence of the blend variable is values and lessons learned from shaping processes in our lives. These processes take place throughout a lifetime but increasingly apply to ministry philosophy as we transition into leadership, have our early growth in leadership, become competent in leadership, and finally find our unique situation. The basic movement is from implicit understanding to explicit understanding of the values. |

## Leadership Value

Introduction    God shapes a leader over a lifetime with various kinds of interventions. These shaping incidents, called process items, teach important lessons which may affect character, leadership, and strategic guidance. These important lessons learned via shaping activities can be represented by statements called values.

Definition    A <u>leadership value</u> is an underlying assumption, which affects how a leader behaves in or perceives leadership situations or issues.

Comment    Values can occur in three categories: leadership character (called spiritual formation), leadership lessons about ministry (called ministerial formation) or leadership direction (called strategic formation).

Examples    Examples of all three categories taken from Samuel Brengle's life include:

*Spiritual Values* (those dealing more directly with leadership character):
1. Sensitivity to God in everyday life ought to be the natural outcome of one's following hard on God. This sensitivity can be broken by sin.
2. Obedience to anything God reveals must be the response if spiritual sensitivity is to be retained.
3. Using one's giftedness to help others ought to be the essential attitude of a leader (The Servant Leadership Model should dominate one's ministry.)
4. Ambition must be given over to God, and if He pleases, channeled for His glory. Particularly will this be tested in terms of financially attractive offers.

*Ministerial Values* (those dealing more directly with leadership skills or insights):
1. Commitment in response to preaching ought to be cultivated and should be the expected norm.
2. Services ought to be focused toward the commitment time with no detracting elements.
3. A Christian leader who wishes to communicate with power must discipline himself/herself to learn basic communication skills and be submitted to the notion that effective communication takes work. Some standards ought to be:
   a. Use simple language
   b. The flow of communication should use persuasive logic.
   c. Read your Bible so as to put life in it and gain attention.
   d. Use spontaneous dramatic vignettes from time-to-time.
   e. Have forceful pictorial illustrations, which fit the points being taught.
   f. Maintain powerful eye contact with the audience.
   g. Don't be afraid to use your knowledge of human personality.
   h. Identify sympathetically with the audience.
4. The Bible ought to be read publicly with clarity, proper enunciation, emphasis and attention getting power.

*Strategic Values* (those dealing with overall leadership guidance and achievement):
1. Submission to God through authority is necessary in an authoritarian organization. Faithfulness in assignments ought to be the essential attitude of a leader. Such an attitude will lead to more challenging assignments and eventually to a role for effective ministry.
2. A leader ought to expect that God will use contacts and friendships made all throughout ministry to open doors and link to further resources and opportunities down road. Serve and relate to folks to help them. Later God may use them to enhance your ministry. That is, a by-product of servant leadership will be expansion later on via important contacts that were served.
3. A leader ought to regard those who differ from himself/herself in doctrine or ministry emphases with as charitable an attitude as possible without compromising one's own core beliefs and values.
4. Honor, reward, status ought to be the by-products of servant leadership not the goals of life.
5. A leader should be aware of the potential dangers in a given type of ministry (like plateauing in itinerant ministries) and should take deliberate steps to offset these dangers.

**Feedback On Blend And Leadership Value**

1. The Blend Variable is associated most closely with:
    _____ a.   the shaping of a leader which leads to value(s)
    _____ b.   direction which will take the leader on to realization of potential
    _____ c.   the mixing of theoretical and practical ideas to integrate a ministry philosophy
    _____ d.   none of the above

2. Define in your own words the notion of a leadership value.

3. Leadership values can be organized into three categories.
    _____ a.   spiritual values, ministerial values, strategic values
    _____ b.   practical, theoretical, pragmatic
    _____ c.   inward, external, mystical
    _____ d.   none of the above

4. Identify one value that you hold in each of the categories which follow.

a. *Spiritual Values* (those dealing more directly with leadership character):

b. *Ministerial Values* (those dealing more directly with leadership skills or insights):

c. *Strategic Values* (those dealing with overall leadership guidance and achievement):

**ANSWERS-----------**
1. _a_
2. an underlying assumption which controls what a leader things about or does as a leader.
3. _a_
4. Your choice.

**Focus Variable**    syn. Focal Variable

Introduction    Whereas the blend variable concentrates on the *content* of the ministry philosophy, the focus variable relates more to the *development* of it. It is axiomatic in leadership emergence theory that over a life-time God shapes a leader toward maturity in leadership character, leadership skills, and leadership values. This movement toward maturity leads to achievement uniquely fitting the individual leader. The focus variable describes the movement toward unique achievement. We are back to the notion of productivity introduced earlier. The essence of the movement is a narrowing from general efforts in our leadership toward a more specific concentrated effort, which flows from who we are and what we were created for.

Definition    The <u>focus variable</u> refers to the narrowing process over a lifetime in which God *guides* a leader

- into understanding his/her *sense of destiny,*
- into an understanding of his/her *giftedness,*
- into *ministry compatible* with that giftedness, and
- into achieving lasting *contributions..*

Comment    This guidance process is best expressed in effective leaders by the concept of the focused life, which explicitly identifies the specific issues resulting from the narrowing process. Four have been identified and will be defined in chapter 2: life purpose, effective methodologies, major role, and ultimate contributions. More specifically the focused life describes the latter part of ministry resulting from the narrowing process.

Comment    It is not clear that all leaders will have an extremely focused life. But it is certainly an ideal that can guide decision-making.

Comment    Since the process is a narrowing process it follows that the older a person is and the more experience he/she has, the more clearly can the focal issues be seen. Earlier ministry can symptomatically point out focal issues, which then become clearer with affirmation over time.

Comment    Some important concepts that help us understand the focus variable include: critical incident (of which some are more related to focus—called prime critical incidents); focal value—a value which helps a leader narrow and prioritize on what is important; strategic direction—the shaping by God toward unique purposes.

Comment    Later we will give a definition of a focused life—a life, which has moved toward maturity in terms of the focus variable.

**Feedback On Focus Variable**

Preliminary     The focus variable was defined in terms of four major concepts. Each of the exercises below expands on one of those major concepts.

1.  A **sense of destiny** refers to a growing inner conviction in which a leaders senses in a special way that God's hand is on his/her life for special purposes. Usually it begins with some with retrospective reflection on earlier life that identifies that God has indeed prepared the leader for a destiny. It continues with on-going revelation or confirmation in numerous ways in which God opens the way toward ministry in general and specific aspects of it. It is usually in this process that the four focal issues begin to emerge. The sense of destiny becomes clearer, in fact, it becomes a driving force in the leader's life and ministry. The whole destiny process culminates, usually in latter life, with a time of seeing part or all of the destiny fulfilled. The focus variable then includes the tracing of destiny across a life. Destiny will be a strong factor in narrowing a leader toward God-given unique purposes in a life.

    With this brief introduction, see if you have grasped the whole notion of sense of destiny and the destiny process? List three Old Testament characters and two New Testament characters who clearly illustrate both a sense of destiny and the destiny process.

    Three Old Testament leaders with a sense of destiny:

    Two New Testament leaders with a sense of destiny:

2.  **Giftedness** refers to the innate resources a leader has to use in his/her ministry. Three elements make up the set: natural abilities, acquired skills, and spiritual gifts. Over a lifetime this giftedness set will firm up usually following a pattern of natural abilities recognized and used first, acquired skills added second, and emergence of spiritual gifts in the first ten or so years of ministry. One of these elements, either natural abilities, acquired skills, or spiritual gifts will dominate the giftedness set. By dominate, I mean that ministry efforts will centralize around the use of the element. The other two elements will then supplement or synergize with that dominant element. We call that dominant giftedness item the focal element of the set. The focus variable will trace the emergence of the giftedness set in a leader's life. The giftedness set will be a major factor in narrowing a leader toward a major role. Ideally a major role should freely enhance a leader's innate resources.

    With this brief introduction in mind answer the following question for yourself. What is the dominant element of your own giftedness set?

    ___ a. natural abilities ___ b. acquired skills     ___ c. spiritual gifts

3.  By definition a **major role** represents the ideal ministry in which the major efforts of a leader flow along gifted lines. The elements which make up a major role are: 1. ministry situation, 2. job description, 3. compatibility with giftedness, 4. freedom, 5. status. Ministry, which is compatible with giftedness, the third concept of the focus variable, means that there is a growing realization of these five role elements.

    With these five role elements in mind, can you think of an Old Testament character who had all of them in evidence and had a very focused ministry?

**Feedback On Focus Variable** continued

4.  The fourth notion of the focus variable is **achieving lasting contributions**.[10] That means, leaving behind a legacy. We have identified five major categories in which people achieve. They,

>   a.  live exemplary lives that set standards for others (personal or ministry-wise),
>   b.  have direct ministry focusing on development of individuals, or word ministries to the masses,
>   c.  have ministries that identify needs and find a way to meet them (this may involve bringing change to society in terms of justice, or starting a movement or organization or pioneer work),
>   d.  have ministries that focus on organizations and institutions (they give them new life, they stabilize them, they insure on-going effectiveness),
>   e.  ministries involved in finding, communicating, and promoting or using ideas.

With these notions in mind see if you can identify for which of these categories the Apostle Paul left legacies, that is, achieved fruitful ministry.


**ANSWERS-----------**

1.  In my opinion Abraham, Joseph, and Moses exemplify sense of destiny and the destiny process in the Old Testament. In the New Testament, Jesus and Paul both have much information which illustrates the concept of sense of destiny and the destiny process.

2. Your choice. For me it is  _√_ c. spiritual gifts.  About 30% of the leaders who study with me have natural abilities as the focal element. Another 15% have acquired skills. About 55% have spiritual gifts. Any combination of the giftedness set can support a focused life.

3.  Your opinion. For me, immediately Ezra came to mind. All of the role elements are in place. And he led a very focused life with powerful results. See Nehemiah 8-10 and Ezra 7-10 where the role elements and results of his focused life are given.

4.  I believe Paul left important results behind, that is, he achieved important things in all but d. And if you count the development of a local church model among Gentiles as an organization then he did that one too.

---

[10] For a detailed explanation of these categories see the Clinton leadership article, *The Ultimate Contribution—Living a Life that Counts*, in **The Leadership Emergence READER** available from the Fuller Seminary Bookstore.

## Prime Critical Incident

Introduction    When a leader's life is studied over time it is clear that God intervenes in special ways all through the leader's development. God's shaping activity forms leadership character (called technically, spiritual formation), builds leadership influence abilities (called technically, ministerial formation) and guides the leader to be and do that for which the leader was created and called (called technically, strategic formation). All of these shaping activities build values into the life—values that under gird and help determine the leader's guidelines for leading and evaluating leadership. There are many interventions by God over the lifetime, which shape the leader. Some of these are more formative. We call them critical incidents. A given leader will have from 15 to 30 critical incidents. From a list of critical incidents we can distinguish prime incidents, those, which are supercritical to the overall focus of the life—usually prime critical incidents are dominated by strategic direction interventions by God, though some are dominant values which pervade.

Definition    A prime critical incident is a special intervention (could be a series over time) in which God gives a *major value* that will flow through the life or will give *strategic direction* to narrow the leader's life work.

Comment    Prime critical incidents are more carefully distinguished in terms of their function:

1. some produce a dominant value which pervades the leader's ministry philosophy or
2. some pinpoint a key strategic directional factor
3. some do both.

This is diagrammed as follows.

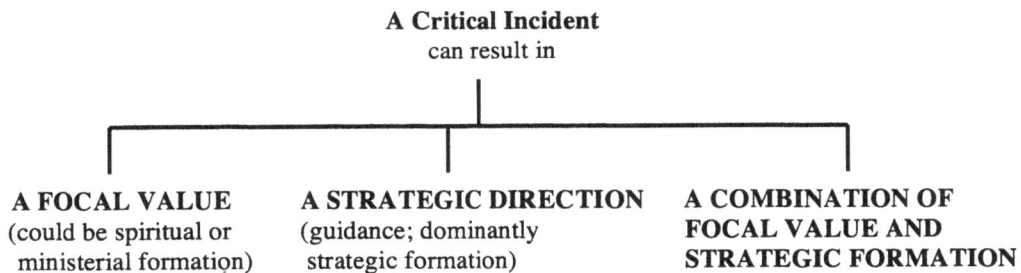

**A Critical Incident**
can result in

| A FOCAL VALUE<br>(could be spiritual or<br>ministerial formation) | A STRATEGIC DIRECTION<br>(guidance; dominantly<br>strategic formation) | A COMBINATION OF<br>FOCAL VALUE AND<br>STRATEGIC FORMATION |
| --- | --- | --- |

Example    G. Campbell Morgan at age 19 was suddenly unsure of his belief about the Bible. He isolated himself for two years with nothing but the Bible and studied it to ascertain its validity for him personally. At the end of that two years of special concentrated time he became convinced that the Bible was indeed God's powerful word. The value derived from this time was a focal value, which pervaded all the rest of his ministry. That value can be summarized in several sentences as follows. **The Bible Is The Word Of God. It Doesn't Have To Be Defended. It Can Convince People If It Is Clearly Taught In Terms Of Its Intent—On The Whole And Book By Book. People Have A Sense Of Need To Which Truth In The Bible Speaks.**

Example    In 1928 Henrietta Mears moved from Minnesota to California to assume a full time Christian ministry on staff with First Presbyterian Church of Hollywood. The decision to leave an educational vocation for full time work was done at age 38. The prime critical incident involved a challenging invitation from Pastor MacLennan, a divine contact. God used him over a space of several years to challenge Henrietta Mears into full time ministry. The culmination came after a sabbatical tour abroad, which allowed reflection. This accumulative series of incidents gave strategic direction.

**Feedback On Prime Critical Incident**

1. Examine the incident in Daniel 1, which was a major test for young Daniel. This prime critical incident probably was pivotal in the life of Daniel. See if you can word some value or values that were deeply impressed in Daniel through this incident. Explain how it may have affected other such incidents in the book.

2. Examine Acts 16:6-11. What kind of critical incident is this, primarily? Explain your reasoning.

___ a. focal value ___ b. a strategic direction ___ c. a combination of value and guidance

3. Examine comparatively the three renditions of Paul's Damascus road experience (Acts 9:1-19; 22:1-24; 26:1-32). Note especially 26:15-19. This is a prime critical incident, which is a combination of focal value and strategic guidance.

   a. List one or two values that you think may have come out of this incident for Paul.

   b. Describe the strategic direction that emerged.

**ANSWERS------------**

1. Your opinion is as good as mine. Daniel learned that he could stand on a conviction and not compromise his belief. If he did so God would provide a way for him to do so. Daniel learned that good relationships with those in power will be used fundamentally in many ways to enhance one's development. Daniel faced other integrity tests (Chapter 2, The Image Dream; Chapter 4 The Tree Vision; Chapter 5 The Handwriting on the wall; Chapter 6 The Lions Den), which increased in seriousness and possible resultant consequences. Each one strengthened his resolve further that God could be trusted to sovereignly work in his situation and that standing on his convictions (even revealing them fully) was for him a way of life.

2. _√_ b. a strategic direction

3. In terms of values, Paul learned that resurrection is a real fact (his drive to know more of and attain this permeate his life and ministry). Paul learned that Jesus was indeed the Messiah—the savior of the world and was worth following whole heartedly and serving whole heartedly all his life. In terms of strategic direction Paul switched from persecuting the sect called The Way to becoming a prime mover in expanding it. Verses 26:16-18 actually become Paul's life purpose. He will focus his life around this realization of this purpose. Notice in verse 19 he says, I have focused on this life purpose and moved toward accomplishing it (the **not** disobedient is a figure of speech, a litotes, an understatement in which an affirmative is expressed b the negative of the contrary—as in **not** a bad singer, meaning a very good singer). What Paul is emphasizing by the figure is, "I have really, really been obedient."

## Focal Value

| | |
|---|---|
| Introduction | A leader will accumulate many values due to God's shaping over a life time. These will affect character, ministry, and even guidance. Those, which dominate how ministry is done or its essence, are called focal values. Sometimes a focal value overlaps character and ministry. |
| Definition | A <u>focal value</u> is a dominant controlling perspective (a leadership value), which interweaves itself throughout a person's ministry and usually can be traced to a critical incident. |
| Example | Charles Simeon (1759-1836): Renewal must begin with genuine individual conversions, which reflect a personal relationship with God. If you have personally experienced something and it has radically altered you, you can recommend it to others with conviction and force. |
| Example | A. J. Gordon (1836-1895): A Christian leader must first of all please Jesus Christ in his/her ministry and recognize that Jesus is present in all ministry. |
| Example | Samuel Brengle (1860-1936): A leader ought to be that which he/she expects and demands of followers. |
| Example | G. Campbell Morgan (1863-1945): A Christian leader must maintain a personal vibrant relationship with God to enjoy real spiritual power. |
| Example | Robert Jaffray (1873-1945): On the value of research and guidance, Jaffray held that if we do not know anything about people without Christ, we are not likely to do anything about them. But if we know about people without Christ and we are engaged in a constant effort to learn more about them, the Holy Spirit will empower in conviction, guidance, and provision to reach them. |
| Example | R. C. McQuilkin (1886-1952): A Christian should have a relationship with the living Christ so as to walk above the controlling authority of sin in a life. Provision is available. A surrendered Christian who is willing to appropriate that provision by faith can have this kind of satisfying life— not a perfect life, but a life pleasing to God and demonstrating the power of Christ in a life. |
| Example | Henrietta Mears (1890-1963): If you place people in an atmosphere where they feel close to God and then challenge them with his Word, they will make decisions. |
| Example | L. E. Maxwell (1895-1984): On adventurous, risky faith, Maxwell believed that God can be trusted to intervene in His work. Prairie would be a place that would never survive unless "God came through." |

### Feedback On Focal Value

Each of the following are examples from the Scriptures of a focal value in the life of some important Bible leader. The more familiar you are with the leader and his life history the easier it will be for you to spot the focal value. In any case, there are many, many more illustrations from Scripture that I could refer to. I hope you will sense that the notion of a focal value is indeed a Biblical one.

1. Examine Joseph's statement to his brothers in Genesis 50:19,20. It captures a focal value that Joseph had learned over the years (see also Genesis 39:2,3,5,21,23; 42:52; 45:7,8 and Acts 7:9,10).

2. Look at Exodus 33:12-17 which occurs in a series of 4 prime critical incidents. It reveals a major value that permeated Moses' leadership. Can you spot it?

3. Examine the prime critical incident of Joshua 9:1-27. It shows how Joshua learned an important value through a negative incident. What value, hinted at in verse 14, was learned by Joshua?

4. Jephthah, the ninth judge, had a difficult family background. After being rejected by his family, he became a para-military leader. He was called upon by the elders of Gilead to help defend Israel against the Ammonites. The details of this crisis are given in Judges 11. Note verses 1-10, which give the details of the appeal to Jephthah. Then ponder over verse 11, which reveals a wise value that Jephthah used in his leadership.

5. Examine Samuel's final public leadership act given in 1 Samuel 12:1-25. Note especially verse 23, which identifies a focal value in Samuel's leadership. Give your wording of this value.

6. The following verses indicate an underlying value in David's ministry. Scan these quickly (you may need to read the whole vignette for each to refresh your memory) 1 Samuel 23:1,2,4  30:7,8 2 Samuel 2:1. Can you spot a value that was important for David?

**Feedback On Focal Value** continued

7.  There are many, many incidents in Jesus' life, which illustrate the notion of focal value. But see Matthew 16:21-27 and note especially Matthew 16:23. Can you write a value, which describes what Jesus saw in this verbal opposition given by Peter?

8.  The first mention of Barnabas in Scripture reveals a critical incident from which flowed a major value that permeated his life. Read Acts 4:32-37. See if you can spot it? This value is reflected in Paul's own ministry (2 Corinthians 8,9) giving evidence that Barnabas, as a mentor, did impact Paul in other ways besides sponsoring him (Acts 9:27; 11:25).

9.  Read carefully Luke 1:1-4 to see a focal value that Luke held. See if you can put it in words.

10. Read 2 Timothy 3:10-17 in which Paul is giving some important advice to Timothy. This passage contains several values. But focus on that value indicated in verses 16,17. Can you word a value that describes this important focal value for the Apostle Paul?

**ANSWERS------------**

In all of the answers which follow I recognize that we are dealing with highly subjective interpretation. So I don't expect you to necessarily agree with mine. Nor do I feel mine are absolutes. But they are at least a good start at attempting to understand values.

1.  Joseph believe that God sovereignly overruled and guided him in his life even through very negative events. God blessed him in every situation he found himself in because he responded as positively as he could and believed that God would work through it to His purposes.

2.  Moses believed that the powerful presence of God in his life and ministry was the essential ingredient of his leadership. Without it he could not lead.

3.  Even everyday incidents may not be what they seem. A leader must always be asking God's discernment on issues that face him/her daily.

4.  Jephthah did not trust political leadership. He knew they might promise something in the midst of the crisis and later renege on it. Therefore, he made them make a public stand on their promises. He got them to admit publicly before many witnessed what they had told him privately. Today's equivalent— get it in writing!

### Feedback On Focal Value continued

**ANSWERS-----------**

5. Samuel saw, as inherently part of his leadership ministry, the burden of praying for those in his ministry. To generalize it, If God calls you to a ministry, then He calls you to pray for that ministry.

6. David believed that in major decisions in his leadership he needed clear guidance from God on what to do. To say it in other words or generalize it, a leader needs clear guidance from God when facing crucial decisions.

7. Jesus was able to discern spirit caused activity in normal incidents around him. The value could be stated as, "A leader must be able to discern the causes of happening around him/her—that is, if the happenings are spirit induced or not. It is clear from the relatively few times that Jesus illustrates this value comparatively that there was balance. He did not see everything as spirit directed. Nor did he see all things as having natural causation.

8. Barnabas was a generous man. He believed that what he had came from God and belonged to God. He, therefore gave generously to meet needs knowing that God would meet his own needs in turn. Barnabas was generous in more than monetary things. His time. His attitudes toward others (e.g. John Mark in the dispute with Paul).

9. Luke believed that careful analytical research should underlie his work. Such careful work was not incompatible with Spirit directed activity. For Luke it was all part of the same package. Note his use of Pauline phraseology about the Spirit throughout the Gospel of Luke.

10. Paul believed that God's revealed truth given in Scripture (probably thinking of Old Testament at the time—but by extension certainly the New as well) contained insights that would equip a leader to lead as God wanted. See also Romans 15:4 and 1 Corinthians 10:6,11, which contain this same kind of thought. Hence, broadly speaking the value would be, A leader must constantly study the Scriptures in order to be prepared to lead as God would have that leader lead.

## Strategic Direction

Introduction   Over a lifetime decisions are made by a leader which affect how the leader will serve, where the leader will serve, what kind of ministry will be involved, etc. God actively shapes these decisions in ways that upon reflection clearly show sovereign guidance. This guidance is crucial to the leader realizing leadership potential and fulfilling God's purposes for that leader. The label describing this process is called strategic direction.

Definition   <u>Strategic direction</u> refers to God's intervention which helps move a leader along toward the focal issues: role, life purpose, effective methodology, or ultimate contribution of the leader. That is, it is God's guidance directing toward life work and accomplishment.

Example   In response to a letter for help from Three Hills, Alberta, Canada, Daddy Stevens, the head of a small Bible School, Midland Bible Institute, recommended L. E. Maxwell, one of his senior students as the potential leader of a Bible study group for youth. This teaching ministry eventually evolved into Prairie Bible Institute. The recommendation came after Daddy Stevens saw Maxwell's response to strong correction dealing with his character. This link to Canada was a sterling example of strategic guidance in a life. Maxwell was tailor made for the position.

Example   In a series of sovereign blocks, the McQuilkin family was deterred from serving on the foreign mission field and instead were directed to training and sending many in their place. A prime critical incident that strongly indicated this sovereign action was the sinking in the harbor of the City of Lahore, the ship they were to sail on just two days before departure. This was one in a series of such blocks that led them strategically on to a training ministry.

Example   At age 55 after 31 years of mission experience in South China, Robert Jaffray was led by God, via special sovereign guidance including a mystical dream and incidents on several exploratory research trips, to move to Indonesia and begin a new field there. The next 11 years culminated Jaffray's missionary career with the most important contribution of his whole life—the planting of a national church in Indonesia with 139 centers of operation and 141 national workers and a church membership of 13,093. This was strategic direction that resulted in accomplishment of God's purposes in Indonesia.

Example   In December 1887, G. Campbell Morgan, who was to become one of the great pulpiteer ministers of his generation, failed the portion of his ordination exam that dealt with preaching. In an unusual incident his trial sermon went flat. This disappointing reversal led him on eventually to the Congregational church. It also insured his self-study and development rather than training via the Methodist seminary. This allowed his creative Bible study methods and exposition to develop. This unusual time can clearly be seen in retrospect as divinely guided, a beautiful example of strategic direction.

Example   In 1890, at age 30, Samuel Brengle was floored when a drunk hit him in the head with a brick. He was near death. Two years of recuperation were involved. During this time he could do very little. He wrote a series of talks on holiness summing up what he had learned in his ministry to date. This series was gathered into a booklet, **Hints To Holiness**, which sold more than 100,000. The whole notion of writing simple books that captured what he was learning became a hallmark of Brengle's ministry. This brick incident, seemingly so negative, was used by God in strategic direction, leading Brengle to a facet of ministry that otherwise might have been missed.

Example   At age 33 Charles Simeon, who had already been in the ministry as a pastor for 10 years, came upon a copy of Jean Claude's **Essays** on preaching. This forever changed his approach in the pulpit. What he continued to learn about public ministry he used in his mentoring. This 100 year old work was part of God's strategic direction for Simeon's ministry.

## Feedback On Strategic Direction

1. Exodus 3:1-4:18 indicates a major intervention by God, which affected all of history. Strategic direction was given to a great leader. Who was it? What was the means whereby the strategic direction came? And what was the strategic direction?

2. See 1 Samuel 16:1-13 which indicates strategic direction for one great Old Testament leader. Who was he? What was the means whereby the strategic direction came? What was the strategic direction indicated?

3. Read Isaiah 6:1-13 which indicates strategic direction for a great intellectual? Who was he? What was the means whereby the strategic direction came? What was the strategic direction indicated?

4. Read John 1:44-51 which shows a powerful recruiting technique, which was a strategic direction intervention in the life of a disciple. Who was he? What was the means whereby the strategic direction came? What was the strategic direction indicated?

5. Scan quickly Acts 10, 11, which show a major leader being taken through a paradigm shift which was a strategic direction intervention in his life. Who was he? What was the means whereby the strategic direction came? What was the strategic direction indicated?

**ANSWERS------------**

1. Moses. The means was a supernatural sense of destiny experience, the burning bush, which would not burn up, in which Moses experienced the awesome presence of the Lord who revealed to Moses his marching orders. He ceased being a shepherd under Jethro's authority and became a deliverer of God's people—the greatest of Old Testament leaders.
2. David. The means God used was a respected leader anointing the one of God's choice revealed to Samuel inwardly by conviction. Such an unusual occurrence would carry powerful influence with David and Jesse. David was informed that he would be a great leader some day.
3. The prophet Isaiah. He received an unusual supernatural vision from God. In it he received a major prophetic call with indication of what he must say and how long.
4. Nathaniel. He was recruited by Jesus using a word of knowledge describing Nathaniel's character and revealing where and what he had been meditating on. Nathaniel became a disciple and was part of the core which began the Christian movement.
5. Peter. He receives a vision which is explained somewhat by the visitors who come and the events surrounding Cornelius' conversion when God gives an outward sign of His approval. This changed Peter's view of the church. It was to be a church composed of all those who would believe in and follow God regardless of race.

## Articulation Variable

Introduction     At this point I have made initial attempts to describe the articulation variable.[11] It is not clear at this point how a person can give written expression to a ministry philosophy. This will be the central part of my research over the next five years. At this point I have identified and defined the concept of values and the notion of core and peripheral. Probably more helpful at this point is the notion of the personal life mandate, a shorthand description of the focus variable. But I anticipate a breakthrough on the articulation variable with further research.

description     The articulation variable refers to the *process* and resulting *product* of integrating the values of the blend variable, the content, and the direction provided by the focus variable, the narrowing purpose, into an explicit statement of the ministry philosophy.

Comment     Many leaders never develop this variable but simply operate intuitively on implicit values. This is not necessarily a bad thing. It is the use of the philosophy, after all, which is extremely important. However, the raising awareness of an implicit value allows both for acceptance or dismissal of it or for modification of it and most importantly for proactive and deliberate steps to employ it. And certain types of leaders, those who are establishing major paradigm changes in organizations—we call them cultural pioneers— do need to operate very explicitly in terms of values.

Comment     A helpful start toward the integration and organization of this variable and thus bringing an integrating closure to ministry philosophy is to use an organizing framework, which includes four components.

Comment     Normal order of development. The blend variable develops throughout a life time but decreases in the latter stages. The focus variable has increasing weight from competent ministry onward. The articulation variable develops last, in the convergence phase of unique ministry.

Comment     A well integrated ministry philosophy that is expressed in written format is an excellent legacy to pass on to those who will carry on your work into the next several generations. A ministry philosophy will be unique to an individual so that it cannot be passed on in a deterministic fashion. But much can be learned by seeing the process of its development. And many values, not all, will be transferable.

---

[11] See my position paper (1992), *A Personal Ministry Philosophy--One Key to Effective Leadership*, in **The Focused Life READER** available at the Fuller Seminary bookstore. In that paper, I explore the notion of core and periphery with respect to values. I also outline my initial attempts to formulate a written ministry philosophy.

**Focused Life**

Introduction    Having seen the background of ministry philosophy and where the focus variable fits in, it is time to derive the major concept flowing from a study of the focus variable. Studies of effective leaders who have finished well show that, in general, they became increasingly more deliberate in what they did and how they accomplished it. There was a process whereby God led them to prioritize their lives and ministries around fundamental issues. This process is described by the term, a focused life.

Definition    A <u>focused life</u> is
- a life **dedicated** to exclusively carrying out God's unique purposes through it,
- by identifying the focal issues, that is, the **life purpose**, **effective methodology**, **major role**, or **ultimate contribution** which allows
- an **increasing prioritization** of life's activities around the focal issues, and
- results in a **satisfying** life of being and doing.

Example    Henrietta Mears' life[12] (1890-1963) focused around her **life purpose** of initial recruitment, training, and motivational release of emerging leaders into ministry both at home and abroad. Her **major role** involved several thrusts: Christian education director at a flagship church, prime mover in a National Sunday School Movement, founder and director of a publishing ministry, and director of a retreat center. She had many **effective methodologies** for motivating and recruiting—especially the concept of varied fishing pools. She left behind **legacies** including major results from the following types: Mentor, Promoter, Founder, Public Rhetorician and writer.[13]

Comment    My comparative study of many effective lives including in-depth work in eight resulted in the above definition of a focused life.

Comment    I have arrived at initial definitions for each of the focal issues: life purpose, major role, effective methodologies, and ultimate contributions. I am at present continuing research by using these concepts with numerous mentorees in helping them enter in to a focused life. This interaction is helping me modify and clarify these definitions. It is the working out of these definitions in real life that makes them valuable. At present I am further along in the life purpose and ultimate contribution definitions. My grounded theory research methodology is one of observation and comparison and reflection. I continue to gather data and compare. I intend in about three years to write another manual, which will incorporate not only the findings of this manual but add an in-depth account of the articulation variable.

---

[12] See Clinton (1995) **Focused Lives** for detailed explanation of Mears and others.

[13] See Clinton (1989) position paper, *The Ultimate Contribution--Living a Life that Counts* in **The Leadership Emergence Theory—READER** available at the Fuller Seminary bookstore.

**Final Commentary On Overview Material of Chapter 1**

Introduction   The development of a ministry philosophy over a lifetime involves three major steps:

1. The accumulation of important values which determine how a leader thinks and acts (represented by the Blend variable),
2. The directive activity of God, which leads the leader toward that destiny for which he/she was created and has been uniquely crafted (represented by the Focus Variable),
3. The explicit recognition of values and direction of life as given in a well written coherent statement (represented by the Articulation variable) .

Order   The accumulation of important values affecting leadership occurs from the first attempts of leadership right on to very effective focused ministry with the majority of values accumulated during growth and competent ministry. There is a tapering off of new values. This step is described by the Blend variable. The directive activity occurs in a somewhat hidden fashion in the early portion of a leader's life, then picks up momentum during growth ministry and competent ministry (at the height of the Blend variable) and peaks in focused ministry (when the Blend variable has slackened). Finally, the articulation variable matures in the latter stages of focused ministry and convergence.

Focus Variable   It is the study of the focus variable which is the intent of this manual. The focused life, which we have defined finally in this chapter represents the ideal goal of the focus variable.

Full Blown   A full-blown ministry philosophy is a complex composition involving an ordering of values—Biblical beliefs, personal spiritual, ministerial, and strategic. It includes a tracing of the focus variable and a well-articulated coherent presentation. Few leaders will be able to develop such a comprehensive statement. Probably more helpful are intermediate stages which include:

1. **A Mini-Value Draft**: which is a summary of identification of most important ministry values.
2. **A Personal Life Mandate**: A draft statement, which captures an up-to-the-moment analysis of the focus variable and gives the basis for current proactive decision making.

And of these two it is the second of the two intermediate stages, **A Personal Life Mandate,** which this manual attempts to enable a leader to complete. It is probably the more useful of the two.

(This page deliberately blank.)

# Chapter 2 The Essential Concepts of the Focused Life

This chapter defines the focused life in terms of four focal issues. Focal issues are those items that God clarifies over a ministry lifetime as He narrows a leader toward fulfillment of His purposes for the leader. These four include: life purpose, effective methodologies, major role, ultimate contributions. One of these, life purpose, is seen to be obligatory if one is to achieve any kind of focus. The other focal issues serve to supplement and synergize with life purpose to increase the focus of the life.

There is no normal order for discovery of these four focal issues though ultimate contribution is usually discovered last. Any one of life purpose, effective methodologies, or major role can be discovered first though life purpose or effective methodologies in seed form are usually seen first. The basic pattern is that life purpose, effective methodologies and major role are discovered in an unfolding manner. Each of these is seen in embryonic form first. Usually it is a general idea. Later discoveries clarify and make more specific. For example, an early challenge by God to a leader might be to serve God in some full time capacity. Later the challenge might be clarified—it will be in cross-cultural ministry. Later it may be cross-cultural ministry among Chinese of the Diaspora. Later it may be more specific—straits Chinese among the Diaspora. Later it may be leadership training among straits Chinese among the Diaspora in Singapore, Malaysia, and Indonesia. And so it goes. The life purpose clarifies. Along with it will be needed the major role which will allow it to be accomplished. And along the way the leader will pick up effective methodologies to carry out that life purpose within the major role.

By the end of this chapter you will:
* grasp the essential notions of the focused life including:
  1) dedicated exclusively,
  2) unique purposes,
  3) life purpose,
  4) effective methodology,
  5) major role,
  6) ultimate contributions,
  7) increasing prioritization, and
  8) satisfying life.
  so that you can explain them in your own words,
* identify any of the essential notions for which you have recognized in your own life some progress or understanding,
* recognize the 4 parameters used for grouping activities that lead to the focused life, by listing under them any of the activities that fit, and
* have a foundational framework from which you can explore the focused life for yourself.

Throughout this chapter I will be using examples drawn from my extended research of eight effective leaders who finished well.[14]

---

[14] See Clinton (1995) **Focused Lives** for detailed analysis of each of the eight in terms of focused life concepts: Charles Simeon (1759-1836), A. J. Gordon (1836-1895), Samuel Brengle (1860-1936), G.

## 2 Warnings About The Focused Life

Introduction        I have received mixed reception to focused life concepts. First, always, there is an intense longing for this kind of life. Second, recipients are either greatly encouraged or greatly discouraged. Now, I don't want to discourage anyone. So I ask myself, "Who are the ones who are generally discouraged? Why so? Can I alter my teaching to alleviate the discouragement?" As a result I have tabulated the following warnings. I now adjust my teaching so as to offset the discouragement. In fact, my identification of the 4 age groupings and approaches to use with each, were prompted by these warnings.[15]

| Warning | Label | Explanation |
|---------|-------|-------------|
| 1 | HURRY UP | In our western world, especially America, everybody wants everything very quickly. If you talk about the focused life you will **frustrate** young people. Leaders in our culture are conditioned for quick and easy fixes and to get anything they want immediately. But, in fact, in this development process they **are going to take a long time to find and move into focus**. Especially is this frustration so with younger leaders and those who are facing long periods of apparent inactivity, at least from their perspective, toward focus. All of these types want the focused life, and they want it now. |
| 2 | NO CHOICE | There are people whose lives, for the moment, seem determined and over which they have little or no control. To talk about focused life concepts to them seems almost cruel. It is beyond their reach. They will never have it. You simply frustrate them. They want it but their situation seemingly does not allow for that kind of thinking. They feel they have no choices. Their situations are fixed and they don't feel, at least for the foreseeable future, anything they can do about it. They have no hope. They do not feel as if the focused life is a possible reality for them. |

Comment **Antidote 1**        I have found that the best antidote to the warning about **Hurry Up** is to carefully teach that focus takes a long time. For each age grouping (30-40, 40-50, 50-60, 60+) I define what being on target for focus is. I give the symptoms and the goals of development toward focus for each age grouping. I show which of the focal issues most likely comes into focus for each of the age groupings. I try to help the HURRY UP people relax. By knowing that focus takes a long time the pressure should be off. They don't have to be completely focused yet. Just making progress!!!

Comment **Antidote 2**        As to warning 2, **No Choice**, I have found that even in tough situations which seem almost determined there is hope. Recognition of focal issues in embryonic form at least brings hope. I try to help these folks look at even this determined time period in their lives with a developmental focus. Is their anything they can do that will be developmental in terms of any of the symptoms of focal issues? Most of the time I can identify some things. And too, I point out that this time will pass. Many historical case studies show this to be true. Knowing that the time will pass and that something, even if it is small, can be done to develop toward focus, relieves despair.

---

Campbell Morgan (1863-1945), Robert Jaffray (1873-1945), R. C. McQuilkin (1886-1952), Henrietta Mears (1890-1963) , L. E. Maxwell (1895-1984).

[15] See Chapter 7 for the fourfold approach in terms of the 4 age groupings (30-40, 40-50, 50-60, 60+).

**Feedback On Warnings**

1. Which of the age groups is most likely to need the **Hurry Up** Warning?

___a. 20-30    ___b. 30-40    ___c. 40-50    ___d. 50-60    ___e. 60+

2. Which of the age groups is most likely to need the **No Choice** Warning?

___a. 20-30    ___b. 30-40    ___c. 40-50    ___d. 50-60    ___e. 60+

3. Why do you think I have inserted these warnings here in this chapter, before I even talk about the focused life?

4. Check which age group you are in:

___a. 20-30    ___b. 30-40    ___c. 40-50    ___d. 50-60    ___e. 60+

Now read the antidote comments. Which of the antidote comments fits you the most?

___a. Antidote 1    ___b. Antidote 2    ___c. both    ___d. Neither

**ANSWERS------------**

1. √a. 20-30 √b. 30-40  2. √b. 30-40 √c. 40-50
3. **Forewarned Is Forearmed**. You will most likely respond like many others to these teachings. You should recognize the symptoms of HURRY UP or NO CHOICE for what they are even as you study. You should know if you are a HURRY UP person that the focused life matures over much time. But there are things you can be doing to move toward it. If you are a NO CHOICE person you should know that there are things you can be doing now to develop yourself even in an apparent no win situation, which eventually will find its place as you break out of your situation and begin to move toward focus.
4. Your choice. For me √d. 50-60. √d. Neither But if you would have asked me earlier in life I could have given either answer at some point in my life.

**Focused Life**

Introduction  Studies of effective leaders[16] who have finished well show that, in general, they became increasingly more deliberate in what they did and how they accomplished it. There was a process whereby God led them to prioritize their lives and ministries around fundamental issues. This process is described by the term, a focused life.

Definition  A <u>focused life</u> is
- a life **dedicated** to exclusively carrying out God's unique purposes through it,
- by identifying the focal issues, that is, the **life purpose, effective methodology, major role**, or **ultimate contribution** which allows
- an **increasing prioritization** of life's activities around the focal issues, and
- results in a **satisfying** life of being and doing.

Example  Henrietta Mears' life[17] (1890-1963) focused around her **life purpose** of initial recruitment, training, and motivational release of emerging leaders into ministry both at home and abroad. Her **major role** involved several thrusts: Christian education director at a flagship church, prime mover in a National Sunday School Movement, founder and director of a publishing ministry, and director of a retreat center. She had many **effective methodologies** for motivating and recruiting—especially the concept of varied fishing pools. She left behind **legacies** including major results from the following types: Mentor, Promoter, Founder, Public Rhetorician and Writer.[18]

---

[16] Effective leaders are those who manifest several of the major leadership lessons (usually 4 or more), leave behind a legacy (usually 3 or more ultimate contributions) and who finish well (strong manifestations of most of the six finishing well characteristics). The major leadership lessons include, Effective leaders: (1) view present ministry in terms of a life time perspective; (2) view leadership selection and development as a priority function; (3) maintain a learning posture throughout life; (4) see relational empowerment as both a means and a goal of ministry; (5) value spiritual authority as a primary power base; (6) have a dynamic ministry philosophy; (7) evince a growing awareness of their sense of destiny. Legacies are described in terms of 13 prime types of ultimate contributions including: 3 Character types (Saint, Stylist Practitioner, Family); 2 Ministry types (Mentor, Public Practitioner); 3 Catalytic types (Pioneer, Change Person, Artist); 2 Organizational types (Founder, Stabilizer); 3 Ideation types (Researcher, Writer, Promoter). Six finishing well characteristics include: (1) They maintain a <u>personal vibrant relationship</u> with God right up to the end. (2) They maintain a <u>learning posture</u> and can learn from various kinds of sources--life especially. (3) They portray <u>Christ likeness in character</u> as evidenced by the fruit of the Spirit in their lives. (4) Truth is lived out in their lives so that <u>convictions</u> and promises of God are seen to be real. (5) They leave behind one or more <u>ultimate contributions</u> (saint, stylistic practitioners, mentors, public rhetoricians, pioneers, crusaders, artists, founder, stabilizers, researchers, writers, promoters). (6) They walk with a growing awareness of a sense of destiny and see some or all of it fulfilled.

[17] See Clinton (1995) **Focused Lives** for detailed explanation of Mears and others.

[18] See Clinton **The Leadership Emergence Theory READER** for the article, *The Ultimate Contribution—Living a Life that Counts.*

**Focused Life** continued

| | |
|---|---|
| Comment | My comparative study of many effective lives including in-depth work in eight resulted in the above definition of a focused life. This definition will continue to be tested with further comparative studies.[19] |

| | |
|---|---|
| Comment | I have arrived at initial definitions for each of the focal issues: life purpose, major role, effective methodologies, and ultimate contributions. I am at present continuing research by using these concepts with numerous mentorees in helping them enter in to a focused life. This interaction is helping me modify and clarify these definitions. It is the working out of these definitions in real life that makes them valuable. At present I am further along in the life purpose and ultimate contribution definitions. My grounded theory research methodology is one of observation and comparison and reflection. I continue to gather data and compare. I intend in about three years to write another manual, which will incorporate not only the findings of this manual but add an in-depth account of the articulation variable. |

| | |
|---|---|
| Comment | Wherever we teach these concepts, to missionaries, to pastors, or to those preparing to go into ministry there is a sense of great challenge. Leaders want to move on to accomplish, to know that their lives count, and to leave behind something when it is all said and done. They want to be satisfied at the end of life. There is such disillusionment with leaders and leadership in our world that many are challenged to want this kind of life. Many are challenged to finish well. |

| | |
|---|---|
| Comment | Two verses from Psalm 90, attributed to Moses, really challenge us to think about the focused life. I paraphrase them both. |

**Psalm 90:12 Teach us to use our time well so that our lives count.**

**Psalm 90:17 Establish what we have done so that it lives on.**

We need to heed Moses advice. We need to think about the focused life.

---

[19]I have challenged a number of groups (missionary organizations and denominations) to take the heroes and heroines of their movement and to do comparative studies from a focused life viewpoint. Such studies will most likely help us tighten up definitions we have arrived at in this initial research.

**Feedback On The Focused Life**

1. Read again the definition, then my example of Henrietta Mears. What questions come to your mind as you read this example?

2. Examine the definition again. What is the final result of the focused life?

3. Give here an a name of a leader that you know of who you feel is leading a focused life or has led a focused life and is finishing well.

**ANSWERS------------**

1. What ever questions you surmised are as good as mine I'm sure. But here are some that I would propose were I reading this definition for the first time. Doesn't every person dedicate his/her life to exclusively carry out God's purposes? What is life purpose? Effective methodologies? Major role? Ultimate contributions? How do you discover them? Have I unknowingly already begun to discover them? What does increasingly prioritize mean? How did Henrietta Mears discover her life purpose of initial recruitment, training, and motivational release of emerging leaders into ministry both at home and abroad? How successful was she at this? Do all leaders, like Mears, have multi-roles? This sounds scattered to me, not focused. What is a fishing pool? How did she motivate? You probably had even more questions than I did. But at least your curiosity is aroused. Read on in this manual to get some answers.[20]
2. A sense of satisfaction with a life well lived—both in development of personhood and achievement
3. One of my contemporary heroes of the faith, Howard Hendricks, a long time Dallas Theological Seminary professor, fits the definition of a leader who has led a focused life and who is finishing well. In fact, I heard him voice the notion of having lived a satisfied and fulfilled life in a plenary session at Estes Park, Colorado just last year. It is good that we have such heroes and heroines to challenge and inspire us and to show us that it can be done.

---

[20]And of course you may well want to read Chapter 8 Henrietta Mears (1890-1963) Teacher, A Destiny for Challenging Emerging Leaders in my book, **Focused Lives, Inspirational Life Changing Lessons From Eight Effective Christian Leaders Who Finished Well**.

## Life Purpose

| | |
|---|---|
| Introduction | When a leader surrenders to God, in terms of an all-out commitment to be the leader God wants, a whole process begins in which that leader begins to discover for what purposes he/she was uniquely created. Life purpose represents the descriptive label that characterizes the underlying motivational thrust(s) that energizes a given leader to be and do and around which life begins to center. It becomes that overall centralizing ideal or accomplishment or task to which all of a leader's life is committed. |
| Definition | A <u>life purpose</u> is a burden-like calling, a task or driving force or achievement, which motivates a leader to fulfill something or to see something done. |
| Example: | My purpose is to challenge, motivate, and enable—via teaching, modeling, and available resources and materials—high level leaders to finish well. |
| Example: | My life purpose is basically two-fold, to lead many non-believers to a personal saving knowledge of Christ and many believers to a holiness experience that will let them live lives well pleasing to the Lord. God has gifted me to speak publicly with effectiveness before all kinds of audiences.  I want to live a consistent holy life so that my message, backed by my life, will carry great power. I will serve the whole body of Christ by promoting this salvation and holiness message in a wide itinerant public pulpit ministry all over the United States and abroad. |
| Example | My purpose will involve a transient cross-cultural ministry, which will focus on high level influence in the equipping of leadership both at individual and at organizational levels. My ministry will involve stepping out in faith many times, the use of modeling from my own life and will be marked by unusual blessing of God. I know that I am to model leadership as a woman to encourage others to freely operate out of who they are. |
| Comment | It usually starts with a general burden and becomes more specific over the years. It may come very early in life in terms of some value personally experienced. How to get that value into the lives of others becomes a driving force that eventually results in a more definitive life purpose as the leader grows. |
| Comment | Frequently leaders will have one to three dominant life purposes or some combination of one or more or at least an umbrella one, which is clarified by more detailed sub-purposes. |
| Comment | Life purpose, of all of the four focal issues, is the only **obligatory item** for a focused life. A leader cannot have a focused life apart from some life purpose which lies at the core of his/her being. However, life purpose alone, is not enough to generate a focused life. There must be life purpose plus at least one other focal issue to generate a focused life. |
| Comment | In general, the more focal issues that supplement life purpose, the more focused and effective will be the life. |

**Feedback On Life Purpose**

1.  Read again the introduction to life purpose. What is the starting point of a focused life? What part of the definition of a focused life is in view in this starting point?

2.  Examine the three examples of life purpose again. Underline the words, which are motivational in nature or which indicate a driving force for the leader or are the central thrusts of what they are about.

3.  So far we have named four focal issues: life purpose, effective methodologies, major role, and ultimate contributions. We have said that of the four, only one is obligatory? What do you think is meant by that statement?

ANSWERS------------

1.  An all-out commitment to God to serve God; sometimes this is called a Lordship committal; sometimes it comes in response to some perceived call by God; sometimes it comes accompanied by some manifestation of God's approval like an anointing. But it must come. It is the notion of *a life dedicated to exclusively carrying out God's unique purposes* that is being emphasized here. That is the starting point of the focused life. And that kind of commitment almost certainly insures that God will begin to reveal symptoms of life purpose with increasing clarity in shaping events as each event is responded to by the leader.

2.  Here are the words which indicate motivation or challenge or life-giving reason or central integrating point of the life.

Example:     My purpose is to **challenge, motivate**, and **enable** — via teaching, modeling, and available resources and materials — high level leaders **to finish well.**

Example:     My life purpose is basically two-fold, to **lead many non-believers** to a personal **saving knowledge of Christ** and many believers to **a holiness experience** that will let them live lives **well pleasing to the Lord**. God has gifted me to speak publicly with effectiveness before all kinds of audiences. I want to live a **consistent holy life** so that my message, backed by my life, will carry great power. I will **serve the whole body** of Christ by promoting this salvation and holiness message in a wide itinerant public pulpit ministry all over the United States and abroad.

Example      My purpose will involve a transient cross-cultural ministry, which will focus on **high level influence** in the equipping of leadership both at individual and at organizational levels. My ministry will involve **stepping out in faith** many times, the use of **modeling from my own life** and will be marked by **unusual blessing** of God. I know that I am to **model leadership as a woman** to encourage others to freely operate out of who they are.

3.  Obligatory means absolutely necessary. That is, there can be no focused life over the life-time of ministry without a life purpose. The other focal issues are helpful and will add to life purpose but are not necessary. Life purpose with any other single focal issue will lead to a focused life. Of course, the more focal issues there are to harmonize with life purpose the more effective will be the focused life.

## Major Role

| | |
|---|---|
| Introduction | All full time Christian leaders will have some job description (maybe implicit) for their basic work. Someone may be a youth worker on a staff of a large church or may be a visitation pastor on a large church staff. Another may be a Christian education director or a missionary church planter. Whatever the job title, there are usually several major roles under that title which describe the major functions that a leader does. As a leader moves toward focus, the job description will usually have to be adapted so that the major functions will line up with the leader's life purpose or effective methodologies. Such a role, which enhance focus, is called the major role. The adapted role breaks down into two components — a *Base Component* and a *Functional Component.* |

Definition

A <u>major role</u> is the official or unofficial position, or status/ platform, or leadership functions, or job description, which basically describes what a leader does and which allows recognition by others and which uniquely fits who a leader is and lets that leader effectively accomplish life purpose(s). It breaks down into a *base component* and a *functional component.*

| | |
|---|---|
| Example: | An itinerant public Bible teacher at national level who teaches different large groups of 1000 or more in face-to-face ministry on a repetitive basis. |
| Example: | A seminary professor who has contacts with leaders from all over the world with freedom to minister (via workshops, seminars, conferences) outside the seminary as well as inside it both in classes and via mentoring. |
| Example: | A senior pastor of a flagship church who ministers 50% in the church and 50% outside the church in conferences as a public rhetorician and who has a sodality on the side for producing radio ministry and written materials. |
| Components | Five components combine to make up an effective major role: 1. a suitable ministry base, 2. a job description which covers the major thrusts needed, 3. ministry compatible with giftedness, 4. Freedom to proactively choose ministry, which enhances focus and to refuse that which does not, 5. a respected status, which enables effective entrance to ministry situation, bespeaks of spiritual authority, and gives a good hearing. Ministry, which is compatible with giftedness, the third component, describes a process, which includes a growing realization of these role components. |
| Comment | A major role is characterized in that it enhances giftedness and allows use of effective methodology. It will also enable the leader to leave behind special contributions or ultimate contributions. And finally, it will also screen out ministry functions, which detract from a focused life. It will also screen out ministry functions, which detract from a focused life. |
| Comment | A major role will usually have to be adapted. See Chapter 5 for a detailed explanation of how this role is adapted in terms of a base component plus a functional component. Organizations rarely define such a role to fit a person. They hire to positions or qualification rather than hiring people and defining the position in terms of the people. That is, they have a tendency to use people rather than enhance their development. The major role may be a combination of formally recognized issues and informal ones done implicitly. |
| Comment | Major role does not emerge strategically till mid-40s, after 10-15 years of varied kinds of ministry experiences with a variety of roles. Experience helps force the need for focus and prioritizing of ministry functions. |

**Feedback On Major Role**

1.  The terminology is significant—**Major role**. All Christian workers have a role. But when I use **Major role**, I am indicating,
    ___ a.  an important well paid position recognized as such in the Christian world,
    ___ b.  a starring position that has tremendous visibility,
    ___ c.  a descriptive label of the functions that a leader has come to prioritize as most important and which reflects life purpose and effective methodologies; Oh, by the way, it may be the name of some recognized Christian full-time role; it may not. MAJOR means it is a focal role that is being emphasized and not just some ordinary role.
    ___ d.  none of the above.

2.  The single most important determinant of major role and that which must be well known by the leader, if that leader is to move to focus in the life is,
    ___ a.  giftedness ___ b.  destiny processing ___ c.  successful experience
    ___ d.  none of the above.

3.  In your opinion, what do you think might be the major factors that keep a leader from realizing a major role?



4.  One major drawback to teaching a concept like major role to a younger leader is,
    ___ a.  they may be tempted too early to refuse job descriptions or functions they don't like under the excuse of saying no in order to become focused. Young leaders all the way up to the 40s should get varied experience in order to better identify major role. Early extensive exploration will lead to later pinpointing.
    ___ b.  they may become frustrated and give up if they think they can not reach a major role due to circumstances or factors seemingly prohibiting them.
    ___ c.  the inability to recognize the difference between the notion of a formal ministry role with its recognized name, like Pastor, and the concept itself which describes functions of a non-existent formal role.
    ___ d.  all of the above.

**ANSWERS-----------**

1.  _√_ c. 2. _√_ a.
3.  The question called for your opinion. Your answers may well be as right as my own. (1) A leader may identify too prominently with a formal role and its expectations by the constituency being served and providing finances for the role; (2) can not economically fund the optimum role, hence must do other things not in focus for financial reasons; (3) a lack of knowledge, of both the major role concept or even that roles should be adapted to fit ministry flowing out of one's being. (4) It is often easier to flow and react to things that happen rather than trying to proactively make them happen. Such a habit will usually preclude someone from adapting toward a major role.
4.  _√_ d. At least I think all of them are possible.

## Effective Methodology Defined

| | |
|---|---|
| Introduction | A leader usually discovers personal insights on how to do ministry well. Some of these ministry insights become polished and reused frequently so that the leader effectively delivers his/her ministry. Such a concept when exploited over a life-time becomes an effective methodology. Most focused leaders will have several ministry insights or even a cluster of them, which form a main means for delivering ministry. |
| Definition | An <u>effective methodology</u> is some ministry insight around which the leader can pass on to others the essentials of doing something or using something or being something, that is, a means of effectively delivering some important ministry of that leader which enhances life purpose or moves toward ultimate contribution. |
| Example: | I will use personal counseling, one-on-one, with a framework derived from Larry Crabb to help people move to wholeness. |
| Example: | The basic methodology for moving people in literacy is captured in the phrase, each-one-teach-one. This will be the major force of my efforts. If I can motivate those who have just learned to read and are excited about it to teach others I will have a mechanism, which can expand exponentially. And I have found some important techniques for doing this. |
| Example: | A workshop format, which includes pre-workshop introduction to concepts, intensive application of them at the workshop in a small group interactive setting, and post-workshop application in-depth of some concept will be the main methodology for delivering off campus ministry. |
| Example: | Development of self-study materials for use in supplementing classes and workshops. |
| Example: | A framework for the development of materials along a continuum all the way from definitions of concepts all the way up to classical texts. |
| Example: | Abilities to lead a small group into discovering their uniqueness in spirituality and taking steps to develop it. |
| Example: | Abilities to organize a ministry so that it runs efficiently. |
| Comment | Leaders discover ministry insights, breakthroughs in how to deliver ministry effectively. This will happen as they get varied experience in ministry and learn to use giftedness effectively. Some of these ministry insights will be used for a period of time while a given role is in place and may not come into play again. Others will find repeated use in varied ministry settings. Such repeated use of ministry insights in all kinds of ministry efforts are candidates for effective methodologies. |
| Comment | This methodology becomes a major means, which moves people toward results in line with life purposes or ultimate contributions. |

**Feedback On Effective Methodology**

1. Review again the generalized ministry time-line that was given in chapter 1, and is reproduced below. In your opinion when do you think the most ministry insights are recognized. Order the three most important time periods for getting ministry insights. Use 1 for most, 2 for next most, and 3 for the next. Put 0 beside the time period which is least likely to produce new ministry insights.

____A.   Sovereign Foundations—(13-20 years)—early shaping of character/ personality
____B.   Leadership Transition (3-6 years)—a time in which first steps in ministry are done
**Phase II**
____A.   Provisional Ministry  (2-6 years)—the first attempts at full time ministry assignments; it is provisional because it might not last, that is, the leader may not stay in ministry.
____B.   Growth Ministry (6-8 years)—ministry utilizing known giftedness with efficiency; giftedness and role issues are learned; this sub-phase is more for developing the leader than the ministry which is accomplished.
____C.   Competent Ministry<-- (2-6 years) -->operating out of giftedness in roles that fit that giftedness produces excellent results; still to be determined is the influence-mix profile, i.e. level of influence.
**Phase III**
____A.   Role Transition--There is movement toward compatibility between role, giftedness and influence-mix profile. There is shaping of a role more ideally suited to giftedness and challenge toward influence-mix.
____B.   Effective Ministry—ministering effectively as well as efficiently with giftedness. (Role plus effective may last 3-12 years)

**Phase IV**
____A.   Special Guidance—movement toward a role focusing on ultimate contribution
____B.   Convergent Ministry—fulfilling a sense of destiny/ ultimate contribution
____C.   Afterglow--fall out effects of a life well lived; spiritual authority dominant

2. When do effective methodologies most likely show up? Go back to the answers of question 1 and place a UM in the blank beside the time period when you feel that effective methodologies begin to appear.

**ANSWERS------------**

1.  _1_B. Growth Ministry (6-8 years)
    _2_A. Provisional Ministry (2-6 years)
    _3_B. Leadership Transition (3-6 years)
    _0_C. Afterglow

2.  _UM_ C. Competent Ministry<-- (2-6 years)
    _UM_ B. Effective Ministry

## Ultimate Contribution Defined

| | |
|---|---|
| Introduction | An **ultimate contribution** is a legacy that a leader will leave behind after life is over. Leaders usually have several of these. As a leader ages he/she recognizes the shortness of time left in ministry, especially when compared with the time already gone by. This usually brings on a reflection as to what to do that will really count in the remaining years. The concept of ultimate contribution is very useful in channeling that kind of thinking productively. In fact, even younger leaders who reflect this way can begin to proactively move toward these legacies much earlier in their ministries. |
| Definition: | An <u>ultimate contribution</u> is a lasting legacy of a Christian worker for which he or she is remembered and which furthers the cause of Christianity by one or more of the following:<br>• setting standards for life and ministry,<br>• impacting lives by enfolding them in God's kingdom or developing them once in the kingdom,<br>• serving as a stimulus for change which betters the world,<br>• leaving behind an organization, institution, or movement that will further channel God's work,<br>• the discovery of ideas, communication of them, or promotion of them so that they further God's work. |

**Categories include the following**:

| Type | Basic Notion |
|---|---|
| **CHARACTER**: | |
| SAINT | A Model life, not a perfect one, but a life others want to emulate. |
| STYLISTIC PRACTITIONER | A Model ministry style which sets the pace for others and which other ministries seek to emulate. |
| FAMILY | Promote a God-fearing family, leaving behind children who walk with God carrying on that Godly-heritage. |
| **MINISTRY**: | |
| MENTOR | A productive ministry with individuals, small groups, etc. |
| PUBLIC RHETORICIAN | A productive public ministry with large groups. |
| **CATALYTIC**: | |
| PIONEER | A person who starts apostolic ministries. |
| CHANGE PERSON | A person who rights wrongs and injustices in society and in church and mission organizations. |
| ARTIST | A person who has creative breakthroughs in life and ministry and introduces innovation. |
| **ORGANIZATIONAL**: | |
| FOUNDER | A person who starts a new organization to meet a need or capture the essence of some movement or the like. |
| STABILIZER | A person who can help a fledgling organization develop or can help an older organization move toward efficiency and effectiveness. In other words, help solidify an organization. |
| **IDEATION**: | |
| RESEARCHER | Develops new ideation by studying various things. |
| WRITER | Captures ideas and reproduces them in written format to help and inform others. |
| PROMOTER | Effectively distributes new ideas and/or other ministry related things. |

## Historical Examples Of Ultimate Contributions

Introduction          Below are given several examples taken from my comparative study of eight effective leaders as detailed in **Focused Lives**.

| Prime Type | Major Thrust of the Type | Historical Example |
|---|---|---|
| 1. Saint | A Model life, not a perfect one, but a life others want to emulate. | Samuel Brengle, R. C. McQuilkin |
| 2. Stylistic Practitioner | A model ministry style; a flagship church or ministry organization which effectively delivers the ministry output of a leader. | A. J. Gordon, G. Campbell Morgan |
| 3. Family | Children who walk with God | A. J. Gordon, Henrietta Mears' Mom |
| 4. Mentor | A productive ministry with individuals. | Henrietta Mears, Charles Simeon |
| 5. Public Rhetorician | A productive ministry with large public groups. | G. Campbell Morgan, Samuel Brengle |
| 6. Pioneer | Founds apostolic type works. | Henrietta Mears, Robert Jaffray |
| 7. Change Person | Rights wrongs and injustices in society | A. J. Gordon |
| 8. Artist | Creative breakthroughs. | Henrietta Mears, A. J. Gordon |
| 9. Founder | Starts new organizations. | R. C. McQuilkin, L. E. Maxwell |
| 10. Stabilizer | Solidifies organizations. | G. Campbell Morgan, R. C. McQuilkin |
| 11. Researcher | Develops new ideation. | G. Campbell Morgan, A. J. Gordon |
| 12. Writer | Captures new ideation for use of others. | G. Campbell Morgan, Henrietta Mears |
| 13. Promoter | Distributes effectively new ideation. | L. E. Maxwell, Samuel Brengle |

## Feedback On Ultimate Contribution

1.  Note the groupings of the major categories of ultimate contributions.
    ___ a.   **Character contributions** (saint and stylistic practitioner)—the essential nature of this grouping is modeling which impacts others.
    ___ b.   **Ministry Output** (mentor influencing by relationships with many; influencing by strong public preaching or teaching)
    ___ c.   **Catalytic Work** (recognizing needs and bringing about change to meet those needs by pioneering something, by correcting things, by introducing new and different ways of seeing and doing things)
    ___ d.   **Organizational Work** (by starting new organizations, by making organizations more effective)
    ___ e.   **Ideation—Analytical Work** (by discovering new helpful ideas, by writing about ideas so as to influence, by promoting ideas so that they can be used)

    Which of these groupings is most or least appealing to you? Place a M (for most) in space beside the most important category and an L (for least).

2.  Glance at the table given below. Supply from your own experience the name of someone who fits at least three of the categories.

| Prime Type | Major Thrust of the Type | Historical Example |
|---|---|---|
| 1. Saint | A Model life, not a perfect one, but a life others want to emulate. | |
| 2. Stylistic Practitioner | A model ministry style; a flagship church or ministry organization which effectively delivers the ministry output of a leader. | |
| 3. Family | Promote a God-fearing family, leaving behind children who walk with God carrying on that Godly-heritage. | |
| 4. Mentor | A productive ministry with individuals. | |
| 5. Public Rhetorician | A productive ministry with large public groups. | |
| 6. Pioneer | Founds apostolic type works. | |
| 7. Change Person | Rights wrongs in society | |
| 8. Artist | Creative breakthroughs. | |
| 9. Founder | Starts new organizations. | |
| 10. Stabilizer | Solidifies organizations. | |
| 11. Researcher | Develops new ideation. | |
| 12. Writer | Captures new ideation for use of others. | |
| 13. Promoter | Distributes effectively new ideation. | |

ANSWERS-----------
1.  Your choice. For me it is a toss-up between two for most. _M_ e. **Ideation— Analytical Work** (by discovering new helpful ideas, by writing about ideas so as to influence, _M_ b. **Ministry Output** (mentor influencing by relationships with many). For least, again it is a toss-up between two; _L_ c. **Catalytic Work** _L_ d. **Organizational Work**
2.  Your choice. But notice carefully what categories you noted people in. For there is a basic principle that like-attracts-like. The ones you note intuitively without thinking are probably those you are most attracted to and may give a hint at your own categories.

**Order Of Discovery In The Lives Of 8 Effective Leaders**

Introduction    The following table shows the eight leaders who were studied comparatively and the first instance in which one of the focal issues was discovered, usually in some seed form (embryonic fashion). For each of these, there were further discoveries later on which added to or modified or clarified or changed in some fashion.

**8 Leaders—Ordering of Focal Issues and Age When First Discovered**

|  | Life Purpose | Effective Methodology | Major Role | Ultimate Contributions |
|---|---|---|---|---|
| Leaders |  |  |  |  |
| Simeon | 1 (age 19) | 3 (age about 30) | 2 (age 22) | 5 (age 54+) 4 (age 54) |
| Gordon | 2 (age 36) 4 (age late 30s) | 3(age 36) | 1 (age 16) | 5(age 50+) |
| Brengle | 1 (age 22) 2 (age 25) | 3 (late 20s) | 4 (age 37) | 5 (age 50+) |
| Morgan | 1 (age 21) | 3 (age 29) | 2 (age 25) 4 (age 41) 7 (age 51) | 6(age 42) |
| Jaffray | 1(age 22) | 2 (age 24) | 3 (age 38) | 4 (age 40s) 5 (age 55) |
| McQuilkin | 1 (age 25) 2 (age 29) | 4 (age 40s) | 3 (age 34) | 5 (late 40s) |
| Mears | 1 (age 27) | 2 (age mid 30s) | 3 (age 38) | 4 (age late 40s) |
| Maxwell | 1 (age 24) | 2 (age 27) | 3 (age early 30s) | 4 (mid 60s) |

Observations    One can see that life purpose is generally discovered early on, at least in embryonic form by mid-thirties; major role is usually fashioned between 35 and 50. Effective methodologies may be discovered anywhere during the early years but start taking on powerful effect from 50 on or sometimes after the major role is in place; ultimate contribution usually flows out of the other three being in place and hence occurs later on in life though it can be seen in embryonic form as early as mid-thirties.

**Feedback On Order Of Discovery**

1. According to the table of the eight leaders which one leader did not discover life purpose as his/her first focal issue? What was discovered first? At what age was it discovered?

2. Brengle, Jaffray, Mears, and Maxwell all have a similar pattern of discovery of focal issues which is typical of many leaders. What is the order of discovery?

3. What is unusual about Morgan's discovery pattern?

4. While there are differences in the order of discovery for three of the focal issues, one focal issue has the same order for everyone—it occurs last. Which one? Who discovered this last focal issue the earliest? At what age? Who discovered it later than the rest? At what age?

**ANSWERS-----------**

1. Gordon. Major Role. He knew he was called to the pastorate at age 16. He knew that all that he did would be centered in some pastoral role. At first he thought it would be rural. In fact, it evolved into a senior pastoral role in a large city flagship church.
2. Each of them discovered life purpose first, effective methodology second, major role third, and ultimate contributions fourth.
3. Note the 3 discoveries of major role. Morgan vacillated on two major roles swinging between 1. small church and quasi-parachurch simultaneously first, parachurch only briefly—(I don't actually show this on the chart) next, 1a. large church and quasi-parachurch again, 2. parachurch only for a lengthy time, 3. then return to church and quasi-parachurch again which tailed off to church only as age limited travel.
4. Ultimate contributions. The average age in which this began to be a central issue, a target for the eight, was about 52.

**4 Focusing Parameters Streaming Toward Focal Issues**

Introduction    In doing my original comparative studies I was using some individual factors to help me see focal issues (the focal issues were not that clear when I began the research). After I identified the focal issues more clearly, toward the end of the research, I then came back to these screening factors, and categorized them in terms of 4 overall headings, which in fact were actually pointing toward the 4 focal issues. The tree diagram below helps sort out the organizational process I went through. Now, having this tree diagram, I can use any of the 12 screening factors directly when I am working with leaders individually and know what it is contributing for me in terms of focal issues.

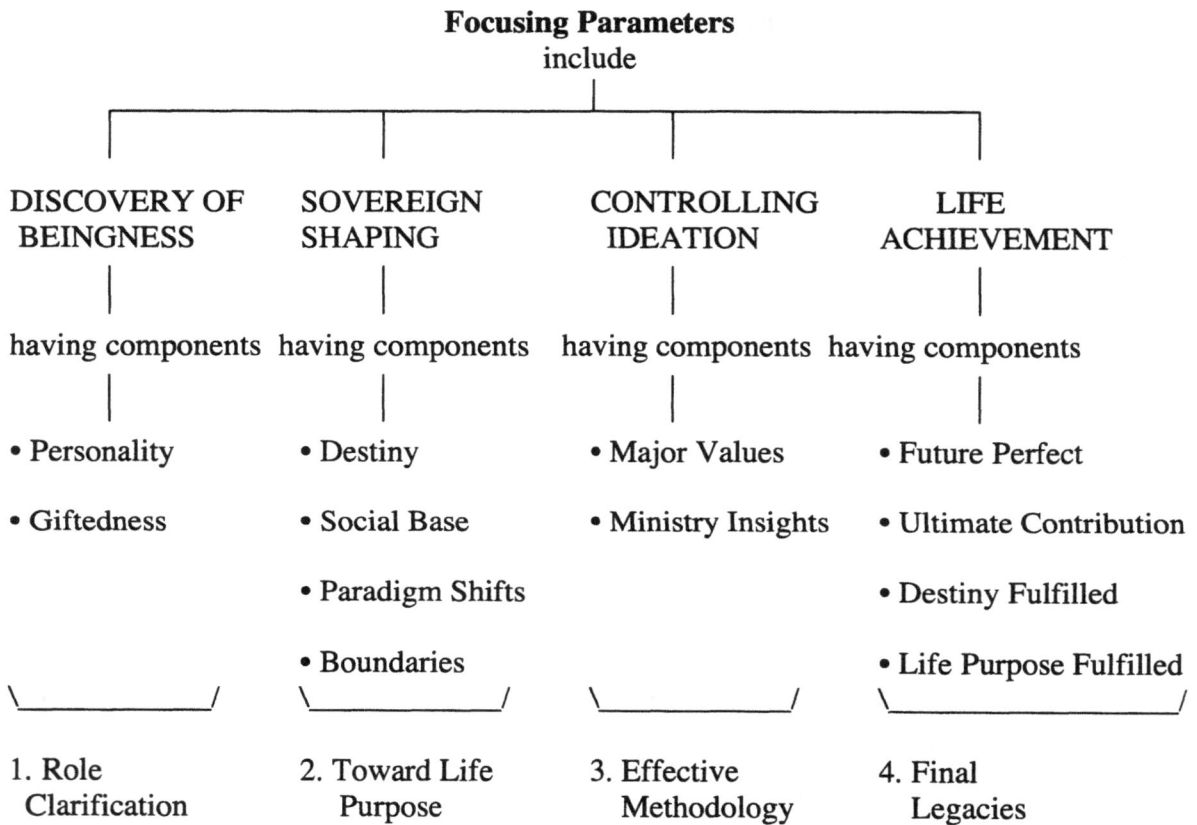

**Focusing Parameters**
include

| DISCOVERY OF BEINGNESS | SOVEREIGN SHAPING | CONTROLLING IDEATION | LIFE ACHIEVEMENT |
|---|---|---|---|
| having components | having components | having components | having components |
| • Personality | • Destiny | • Major Values | • Future Perfect |
| • Giftedness | • Social Base | • Ministry Insights | • Ultimate Contribution |
|  | • Paradigm Shifts |  | • Destiny Fulfilled |
|  | • Boundaries |  | • Life Purpose Fulfilled |
| 1. Role Clarification | 2. Toward Life Purpose | 3. Effective Methodology | 4. Final Legacies |

Comment    The factors (personality, giftedness, destiny, social base, paradigm shifts, boundaries, major values, ministry insights, future perfect, ultimate contribution, destiny fulfilled, life purpose fulfilled) are called screens because they help one filter information through to some specifics, which can be helpful. That is, you obtain information and pour it through each of these colanders which allows a focus on results that tell you something about the screening factors and hopefully the focal issues.

Comment    When working with individuals it is helpful to get information that reflects some of the above screens

## 2 Beingness Factors

Introduction    The 4 focusing parameters—DISCOVERY OF BEINGNESS, SOVEREIGN SHAPING, CONTROLLING IDEATION, AND LIFE ACHIEVEMENT—help us understand more of the implications of Ephesians 2:10 for each of us. God has made us and is shaping us for His unique purposes through us. He has developed within us key ideas that help us perceive and act. And all of this is unique for each of us. And it is another way we see God's love for us. The first of these focusing parameters has to do with essential beingness: personality and giftedness.

### 2 Beingness Factors

| Factor | Explanation |
|---|---|
| Personality | Each of us are shaped uniquely in how we express ourselves, how we relate to others, how we perceive things, how we are affirmed, etc. I use several kinds of tests that are available to help me understand these kinds of things. I don't rely totally on them as all tests have their strengths and weaknesses. I try not to stereotype as I use these tests. But I do find them helpful. I use Myers-Briggs and the DISC. If a person has already done a SIMA test I will use that too. I have found that certain types of people react differently to Focused Life concepts. It helps me to anticipate this and recognize that not all personality types need cognitive information about focused life concepts. But all can experience focused life symptoms in their life. And I can help them to better experience it—no matter what the personality type. I am still experimenting with this so I won't go on record as to profiles and what they tell me about focused life concepts. But I do find this helpful as I evaluate the focal issues for people. |
| Giftedness | People experience natural abilities very early on. They begin to pick up acquired skills from ages 3 on upwards. And as they begin to transition into leadership, sometimes ages 17-21, they begin to see symptoms of spiritual gifts. As they move through the first several years of ministry their spiritual gifts will begin to unfold. By mid-30s they have a good initial grasp of their giftedness set (some spiritual gifts may yet unfold) and particularly their focal element.[21] By the 40s most leaders will understand giftedness with good accuracy. Such an understanding allows proactive movement toward role adaptation. |

Comment    I go for personality information for anyone no matter what age. I use the simplified Myers-Briggs given in Keirsey/ Bates book, **Please Understand Me**, if they have not DONE the professional expanded version.

Comment    I have people, no matter what age, do a Venn diagram (a pictorial display of their giftedness set). But I recognize that until mid to late 30s there is probably still more to come with giftedness. Never-the-less the information gives tentative help in affirming life purpose which is being indicated by destiny processing and much help in pinpointing potential roles that will eventually move toward major role.

---

[21] In the giftedness set made up of three elements (natural abilities, acquired skills, spiritual gifts) one dominates a life and is central to who a person is and what they do. That element is called the focal element. Apparently it does not change over a life-time. At least it is infrequently that it changes.

## Feedback On 2 Beingness Factors

1.  If you know your Myers-Briggs profile, check below the one fitting you. If you do not know, then you may want to read the Kiersey/ Bates book, **Please Understand Me** and do their simple analysis to identify your type. There are many available web sites for also getting Myers-Briggs information.

    | | | | | | | | |
    |---|---|---|---|---|---|---|---|
    | ___ | a. ESTJ | ___ | e. ENTJ | ___ | i. ISTJ | ___ | m. INTJ |
    | ___ | b. ESTP | ___ | f. ENTP | ___ | j. ISTP | ___ | n. INTP |
    | ___ | c. ESFJ | ___ | g. ENFJ | ___ | k. ISFJ | ___ | o. INFJ |
    | ___ | d. ESFP | ___ | h. ENFP | ___ | l. ISFP | ___ | p. INFP |

2.  Which of the elements of the giftedness set is most dominant for you.[22] That is, the element is now strongly affecting what you do, what you want to do, how you minister, etc.?
    ___ a. natural abilities ___ b. acquired skills ___ c. spiritual gifts ___ d. not sure

## Do whichever question, 3 or 4 or 5, which best fits you.

3.  If natural abilities dominate who you are. Describe them. Then suggest what implications this might have for your understanding of focal issues.
    a.  Describe them:
    b.  Implications for Life Purpose:
    c.  Implications for Effective Methodology:
    d.  Implications for Major Role:
    e.  Implications for Ultimate Contribution:

4.  If acquired skills dominate who you are. Describe them. Then suggest what implications this might have for your understanding of focal issues.
    a.  Describe them:
    b.  Implications for Life Purpose:
    c.  Implications for Effective Methodology:
    d.  Implications for Major Role:
    e.  Implications for Ultimate Contribution:

5.  If spiritual gifts dominate who you are. Describe them. Then suggest what implications this might have for your understanding of focal issues.
    a.  Describe them:
    b.  Implications for Life Purpose:
    c.  Implications for Effective Methodology:
    d.  Implications for Major Role:
    e.  Implications for Ultimate Contribution:

**ANSWERS------------**

1.  My profile is INTJ but I am close on the I (E) and N (S) so that the entire first row (ESTJ, ENTJ, ISTJ, INTJ) have characteristics describing me.
2.  Spiritual Gifts are most dominant for me.
5.  Teaching, exhortation, word of wisdom. I need a role, which allows me to get out my ideas and to see those ideas impact people. The actual dominating ideas have helped me form my life purpose—that is, I want to enable high-level leaders to finish well. So I want to communicate with clarity as many perspectives that will challenge, motivate and enable leaders to finish well.

---

[22]You may well want to study (1994) Clinton and Clinton, **Unlocking Your Giftedness**, Barnabas Publishers.

## 4 Sovereign Shaping Factors

| | |
|---|---|
| Introduction | The 4 focusing parameters, DISCOVERY OF BEINGNESS, SOVEREIGN SHAPING, CONTROLLING IDEATION, AND LIFE ACHIEVEMENT, help us understand more of the implications of Ephesians 2:10 for each of us. God has made us and is shaping us for His unique purposes through us. He has developed within us key ideas that help us perceive and act. And all of this is unique for each of us. And it is another way we see God's love for us. The second of these focusing parameters has to do with God's purposes for us; we can be assured that He is directing us strategically to that for which He has created us. Among many things, four factors help us assess this movement: destiny, social base, paradigm shifts, boundaries. These vary in importance from person to person. It is these sovereign shaping factors, which will contribute most to life purpose, the driving force behind a focused life. |

### 4 Sovereign Shaping Factors

| Factor | Explanation |
|---|---|
| destiny | A sense of destiny is an awareness of God's touch on the life to use it for His purposes. Normally the awareness grows as the leader recognizes preparation for a destiny, a revelation of what the destiny is about, and eventually a fulfillment of a destiny. |
| social base | The home base that a leader operates out of will enhance or put limitations on ministry. The home base that a leader grew up in will have strong influence on his/her present home base. The social base factors of emotional needs, economic needs, strategic needs and physical needs must be met if there is to be freedom to focus. The stronger the social base the more effective will be the focus and ministry output. Weak social base factors will be reflected in limitations of focus. |
| paradigm shifts | One way God gets the attention of the leader is through paradigm shifts, that is, major changes in how the leader sees and does things. These paradigm shifts are frequently used to strategically guide the leader into life purpose, understanding of giftedness, and discovery of ministry insights which become effective methodologies. |
| boundaries | As a leader grows he/she will move through major time periods in their lives. The movement from one major boundary to another is frequently a time of retrospective reflection as well as forward thinking. The results of this kind of thinking is usually to move the leader more toward focus. Each succeeding major time period will see development toward focus. Boundaries are especially reflective times which may signal focal issues. |

| | |
|---|---|
| Comment | Each of the factors above is explored in depth in other literature—See **Leadership Emergence Theory** for a general treatment of all of the factors. See *Social Base Processing*: a position paper dealing with those issues. See *Paradigm Shifts*, a position paper dealing with major change in thinking and its implications for ministry. See *Boundary Processing*, a position paper for treatment of how God uses boundaries to shape a life. See **The Leadership Emergence Theory READER** for these papers. |

## Feedback On Sovereign Shaping Screens

1. Indicate your understanding of and familiarity with the 4 shaping factors by checking the appropriate column.

One √ means some
Two √√ means a definite yes
Three √√√ means very much so
0 means don't know enough to be sure

| | Have experienced destiny preparation | Have experienced destiny revelation | Have seen some destiny fulfillment | No Real Experience |
|---|---|---|---|---|
| destiny shaping | | | | |

| | Not so important for my focal issues | Somewhat important for my focal issues | very important for my focal issues | will deeply affect my focal issues | don't know |
|---|---|---|---|---|---|
| Social base processing | | | | | |

| | | Have not experienced any that affect focal issues | Have experienced one or more that I think have implications for my focal issues | don't know |
|---|---|---|---|---|
| paradigm shifts | | | | |

| | | I have no real boundary experience yet. | I have gone through one or more boundaries but no implications for focal issues. | I have gone through one or more boundaries with some strong implications for focal issues. | don't know |
|---|---|---|---|---|---|
| boundaries | | | | | |

2. For any of the issues in question 1 for which you thought you had strong implications, jot down what the implications is for what focal issue.

Implications for Life Purpose:

Implications for Effective Methodologies:

Implications for Major Role:

Implications for Ultimate Contributions:

**ANSWERS-----------**

Your choices on both of these answers.

## 2 Controlling Ideation Factors

Introduction    The 4 focusing parameters, DISCOVERY OF BEINGNESS, SOVEREIGN SHAPING, CONTROLLING IDEATION, AND LIFE ACHIEVEMENT, help us understand more of the implications of Ephesians 2:10 for each of us. God has made us and is shaping us for His unique purposes through us. He has developed within us **key ideas** that help us perceive and act. It is these key ideas, whether what is important or how to do it, that contributes the most toward our understanding of the focal issue—effective methodologies.

### 2 Controlling Ideation Factors

| Factor | Explanation |
|---|---|
| Major Values | Frequently, God will challenge us to accept some important perspective about who we are, about what is important to us in general, and/or what is important to us about ministry. If it is about ministry, it may challenge us about what we pass on or how we do it. But it is frequently a value which shapes our very being which will lead us to want to get this value in the lives of others. This will often drive us to learn a way to do that—eventually leading to a effective methodology. |
| Ministry Insights | Once we have something we want to pass on or once we begin to discover our giftedness, we want to pass it on effectively or use our giftedness effectively. Frequently, God will give ministry breakthroughs, insights that help us to minister effectively. Many times this will necessitate a paradigm shift with regard to our ministry means. In any case, a number of these ministry insights well be seen repeated throughout our life time as we become more focused about our life purpose. |

Example    A most illustrative case of the two above screening factors is seen in the life of G. Campbell Morgan. At age 19, after two years of isolation in which he searched the Scriptures themselves solely to know if the Bible was really the Word of God, Morgan became convinced that the Bible was the Word of God. And if taught properly, that is, exposing it for what it intended to say, it could radically change lives. This value, which was a paradigm shift for Morgan, led him to commit his whole life to the study of and effective communication of the teaching of the Bible so that it could change lives. He was forced to discover personal study techniques and unique means that fit him for communicating his findings to others. His ministry insights for both of these (studying and teaching) became means that were finely honed over his life time and repeated with great effectiveness.

Example    A second good illustrative factor is seen in the life of L. E. Maxwell. Between the ages of 24 and 27, Maxwell studied at a small Bible institute. There he went through a life transforming experience, entering into the Union Life paradigm, an engaging experiential experience, which led him to desire to walk effectively as a Christian. It was the Bible School, which as a whole provided the ambiance and teaching for him to go through this experience. He immediately saw it as an important means to achieve this transformation in the lives of many. He thus started such a school, which became the platform for him to introduce many to victorious living.

## Feedback On Ideation Screens

1. Jot down here one or two values that you have learned in ministry which you think may have some significance for you as you move toward focus in your life.

    a. Value 1:


    b. Value 2:



2. Jot down here one or two ministry insights which you think may have implications for effective methodologies as you move toward focus in your life.

    a. Ministry Insight 1:


    b. Ministry Insight 2:



**ANSWERS------------**

Your choices on both of these answers. Here is how I would answer these.

| | |
|---|---|
| 1. a. Value 1: | I will give as much of myself as I can to help a leader learn what I can teach them about life and leadership as long as they continue to be responsive to me and are continuing to learn. |
| Implications: | This has definite implications for my life purpose and ultimate contribution. In terms of life purpose I intend to develop leaders so that they can finish well. I will use mentoring as a major means. This value affects both of these ideas. |
| b. Value 2: | People learn what they respond to and use. |
| Implications: | When I mentor and teach I must give follow-up exercises which forces the leaders I am working with to use what I am teaching. My intent is to help leaders finish well. I must get them to use what I teach. |

2. a.   Ministry Insight 1: **1970-1989 Materials Preparation—the materials continuum**
Parables materials for H.S. class; then educational technology training; programmed materials; information mapping. Various kinds of writing; actual development of the continuum. Continuous movement along the continuum; getting partnerships in writing to further proliferate the concepts. **Effective Methodology**: Constantly be aware of where some item is along continuum; update; set out new projects along the continuum; will lead eventually to high fulfillment of writing ultimate contribution.

   b.   Ministry Insight 2: **1990-1994 Power of Mentoring**
Experimented with various forms of individual mentoring as well as groups; very powerful means of training. **Effective Methodology**: Deliberately mentor—use all three forms of connecting; select life time mentorees and proactively assess and challenge to growth through letters of intent; use Simeon's circles of intimacy as a guideline. This will lead to fulfillment of mentor ultimate contribution.

**4 Life Achievement Factors**

Introduction    The 4 focusing parameters, **Discovery Of Beingness**, **Sovereign Shaping**, **Controlling Ideation**, and **Life Achievement**, help us understand more of the implications of Ephesians 2:10 for each of us. God has made us and is shaping us for His unique purposes through us. God often challenges us with a look into the future, a faith vision, of what He wants to accomplish through us. This challenging look may come through a vision (mystical or simply analytical), a strong desire to achieve something, a driving sense to complete a previous destiny that was revealed, or the notion, in general, of fulfilling our life purpose.

**4 Life Achievement Factors**

| Factor | Explanation |
|---|---|
| Future Perfect | Future Perfect refers to a paradigm. It is a way of seeing something in the future as though it were real. Such a view dominates what one does and perceives. All activity moves toward the actual realization of the already felt reality. A leader with a future perfect vision of something—usually a life purpose achieved or an ultimate contribution to be done—approaches everything in ministry with a positive attitude that will lead to the realization. |
| Ultimate Contribution | Most focused leaders will have from four to eight of the prime types of ultimate contributions already introduced: saint, stylistic practitioner, mentor, public rhetorician, pioneer, change person, artist, founder, stabilizer, researcher, writer, promoter. These usually correlate strongly to giftedness. One or more of these can be part of the driving force of future perfect thinking. This particularly happens in the 50-60 age period as a leader begins to think about leaving behind something worthwhile from a lifetime of ministry. |
| Destiny Fulfilled | Some leaders, more than others, have a strong sense of destiny. The stronger, the more likely it is that the fulfillment of it will dominate the life as the leader moves into the 40s, 50s, and 60s. Frequently, the sense of destiny, if it has sufficiently been clarified through revelation, will actually dominate the life purpose more and more. It will pinpoint the ultimate contribution. It will become a driving force that needs to be realized if the leader is to see life as satisfying and fulfilling. |
| Life Purpose Fulfilled | As life purpose clarifies and becomes uniquely specific for a leader, which happens over time, it will become a driving force which issues in ultimate contributions. The ultimate contributions may both illustrate the life purpose, and/or provide the means for accomplishing it. In short, the life purpose fulfilled gives the sense of a satisfied life, a fulfilled life which is the culminating concept of a focused life. |

**Feedback On 4 Life Achievement Factors**

1.  Think of some leader you know whom you intuitively feel is very focused. List the name of that leader. Tell why you think that leader is focused.

2.  For the leader you named in exercise 1 which of the 4 Life Achievement Factors do you think has most affected his/her focus? Check your answer (s).

    One √ means some
    Two √√ means a definite yes
    Three √√√ means very much so
    0 means don't know enough to be sure

    ___ a. Future Perfect thinking

    ___ b. Moving toward Ultimate Contribution

    ___ c. Moving toward Destiny Fulfillment

    ___ d. Concentrating on Fulfilling Life Purpose

**ANSWERS------------**

The answers called for your choices. Here is how I would have answered them.
1.  I feel Peter Wagner is strongly focused. I have watched and studied his development over the past 16 years. He is strongly focused on making church growth happen around the world. Everything he does hinges on that issue. For about the past ten years he has been researching and promoting spiritual causes for church growth. Prior to that it was social and other factors dealing with church growth.
2.  _√_ a. Future Perfect thinking
    _√√_ b. Moving toward Ultimate Contribution
    _√√√_ c. Moving toward Destiny Fulfillment
    _√√√_ d. Concentrating on Fulfilling Life Purpose

### Focusing Parameters And Prime Critical Incidents

Introduction    In chapter 1, I introduced the notion of a prime critical incident. I said that along a leader's time-line, one could identify 15 to 30 incidents, which help a leader to understand more of what his/her focused life is to be. To illustrate this I give a table below, which looks at the eight leaders and identifies the most important prime critical incidents that affected their understanding of focus. I boldface the most crucial of the prime critical incidents.

### Table 2-1. Prime Incidents in terms of Focusing Parameters

| | Categories | | | |
|---|---|---|---|---|
| **Leaders** | Discovery of Beingness 1. Role Clarification | Sovereign Shaping 2. Toward Life Purpose | Controlling Ideation 3. Effective Methodology/ Viewpoint | Life Achievement 4. Final Legacies |
| Simeon | **C3(SD)** | **C1(V)** | C4(V); C12(SD) | C7(SD); |
| Gordon | **C1(SD)** | C12(V) | C6(V); C7(V) | **C8(V/SD)** |
| Brengle | **C3(SD/V)** | **C12(SD)** | C6(V) | C7(V) |
| Morgan | **C4(SD)**; C6(SD) | **C3(V)** | C11(V) | C15(SD); C17(SD) |
| Jaffray | | **C4(SD/V)** | C3(V); C10(V) | **C11(SD)** |
| McQuilkin | C7(SD) C11(SD) | **C6(V)** | C9(V) | **C13(SD)** |
| Mears | **C13(SD)** | C6(V/SD) C12(V) | | C11(V/SD) C20(V/SD) |
| Maxwell | **C7(SD)** | **C5(V)** | **C5(V)** | C16(V/SD) |

Legend  (SD) means was a major intervention that gave *strategic direction* for the life.
  (V) means was a major intervention that imparted a controlling *value* in the life.
  (V/SD) means was a major intervention that imparted a controlling *value* and gave *strategic direction.*
**boldfaced** means a prime critical incident

Comment     It may be helpful to note the total number of prime critical incidents I identified for each: Simeon (12), Gordon (14), Brengle (12), Morgan (18), Jaffray (12), McQuilkin (12), Mears (15), Maxwell (20).

Observations    Notice that it is **Discovery of Beingness** and **Sovereign Shaping** that dominate the movement toward focus.

**Feedback**: **Focusing Parameters/ Prime Critical Incidents**

1. Which leader discovered (received strategic direction about) **major role** the latest of all? How can you tell?

2. Which leader received a value very early on which moved him/her strongly toward **life purpose**? How can you tell?

3. Examine Brengle. What was the order of his discovery of focal issues? Which of these was a prime critical incident?

4. How many of the eight leaders experienced a prime critical incident, which was both a value and an indicator of strategic direction?

5. Which leader drifted into a major role? How can you tell?

6. Which leader has no indication for effective methodology? What does that mean?

**ANSWERS------------**

1. Mears. The prime critical incident for major role discovery was 13. That probably means it took place later in life. In fact it did—at age 38.
2. Simeon. Under life purpose, the prime critical incident was 1.
3. Brengle discovered his role clarification first, then his effective methodology second, his final legacy third, and his life purpose fourth. Though this is slightly misleading because some of these prime critical incidents also carried other implications in seed form. His Role Clarification and his Life Purpose were both signaled by prime critical incidents.
4. Five of the eight did. Only Simeon, Morgan and McQuilkin did not.
5. Jaffray did. There was no critical incident which led to its discovery. This probably meant that he moved into the major role without any special discovery or processing.
6. Mears. It could mean she had no effective methodology. But in fact that is not true. She had many, many. In fact, many of them dealt with ministry insights for recruiting and motivating people to move into ministry. She had so many of them that none were given in some special intervention. Her discovery of them happened as she ministered on a very regular basis without special intervention calling attention to them.

## 6 Observations About The Focused Life

Introduction    At this point, I have introduced the focused life. Chapters hereafter will simply go into more details on it and suggest ways of discovering it. I think we do well to stop for the moment and reflect on six observations that I have started to emphasize when I teach on the focused life. Some serve as warnings. Some simply provide information. But all are probably important if you are thinking of pursuing the focused life.

### 6 Observations About The Focused Life

| Observation | Statement/ Implication |
|---|---|
| 1 | LIFE PURPOSE WITHOUT ANY OTHER FOCAL ISSUE WILL DIE ON THE VINE. <br> / **Implication**: A leader who desires to be focused must not only have a life purpose but also must identify a supporting focal issue of either effective methodology, major role, or ultimate contribution. |
| 2 | LIFE PURPOSE + ANY ONE OF THE OTHER THREE (Effective Methodology , Major Role, Ultimate Contribution) CAN LEAD TO A FOCUSED LIFE. <br> / **Implication**: A leader who desires to be focused and has a life purpose can do so if any other focal issue is there to supplement it. |
| 3 | EFFECTIVE METHODOLOGY WITHOUT A LIFE PURPOSE BECOMES FADDISH AND WILL FADE OR LEAD TO A SENSE OF SO WHAT. <br> / **Implication**: Knowing how to do something very well, in and of itself is not significant. There must be a driving force to which it can attach if there is to be long lasting significance flowing from that ability. |
| 4 | MAJOR ROLE WITHOUT A LIFE PURPOSE SIMPLY BECOMES SELF-SERVING. <br> / **Implication**: A leader who has found an important role but no life purpose to flow through it will simply amass plaudits to himself/herself and will simply build a reputation but not a significant eternal contribution. There will be glory, no doubt, but whose? Such a case becomes a means for building one's ego not the Kingdom. |
| 5 | ULTIMATE CONTRIBUTION WITHOUT A LIFE PURPOSE BECOMES SELF-GLORIFYING. <br> / **Implication**: For whom and what are we working? Ambition without partnership with God becomes or leads to a monument to self. Ultimate contribution in partnership with God, that is, Holy Ambition, will lead to a lasting contribution for the Kingdom. |
| 6 | THE MORE FOCAL ISSUES THERE ARE TO SUPPLEMENT A LIFE PURPOSE THE MORE FOCUSED IS THE LIFE. <br> / **Implication**: Life purpose with a effective methodology for carrying it out, that is, a means for effective ministry, is good. Life purpose with an effective methodology for carrying it out and a platform from which to launch it, that is a recognized major role is even better. But life purpose with a recognized role to operate effective methodology from and some lasting God-given goals, ultimate contributions, to motivate is best. |

## 7 Secrets Of The Focused Life

Introduction    At this point, you have an overall introduction to the focused life. Chapters hereafter will simply go into more details on it and suggest ways of discovering it. I think we do well to stop for the moment and reflect on six observations and seven important concepts I have started to emphasize when I teach on the focused life. Some serve as warnings. Some simply provide information. But all are probably important if you are thinking of pursuing the focused life.

| Secret | Statement/ Explanation |
|--------|------------------------|
| 1 | Within **destiny processing** lies the seedbed of life purpose. Hence keep a personal log of destiny processing. Then seek to integrate life purpose across your time-line. Later I will explain how you can do this. For now it is good for you to recognize that a sense of destiny is important for a focused life. |
| 2 | Within **ministry insights** lies the seedbed of effective methodologies. Hence, integrate ministry insights across your time-line. Again, I will tell you more about how to do this. For now, you should recognize that God has and will teach you breakthrough insights on how to deliver your ministry effectively. |
| 3 | **Effective methodology** — when you find something **that really works, use it** to death! Over time, a leader sometimes forgets some things that worked will earlier on. Rejuvenate some of those useful things from the past. |
| 4 | **Giftedness** is a major factor in all focal issues but **dominantly so with major role**. If you have not done a solid analysis of your giftedness, you should do so. See **Unlocking Your Giftedness** (1994) by Clinton and Clinton--Barnabas Publishers. |
| 5 | **Future perfect thinking feeds** the focused life. Let this paradigm permeate your vision, your actual planning, and your ministry effort. |
| 6 | Yes! **Say yes** proactively. Choose to embrace the things God has focused you on and make it happen! During the years 40-50 and 50-60 you must learn to proactively more toward the focal life. Deliberate decisions must be made which harmonize with focal issues. |
| 7 | No! **Say no** to those things which will scatter you, i.e. not focus you. During the 20-30 and 30-40 you must discover things, so say yes to many things even things you don't want to do. It is in a varied experience that focal issues will come clearer. But from 40-50 and especially 50-60 you must say no to those things that will detract from focus. From 60+ you will have less physical energy so that a more deliberate focus requires many more **NOs** than ever before in life. |

Comment    Be sure you understand the last two secrets, **SAY YES** and **SAY NO**. These really only apply in the 40s, 50s, and 60s. Younger leaders still have a lot of discovering to do. Take advantage of many different ministry assignments, those you want and even those you don't want.

**Final Commentary On Focal Issues**

Introduction     Read again the definition of the focused life. I promised at the beginning
                 of the chapter you would be able to comment on almost every part of the
                 definition. So I want to give my explanation for the important ideas by
                 way of review for you.

> A <u>focused life</u> is
>
> - a life **dedicated** to exclusively carrying out God's unique purposes
>   through it,
>
> - by identifying the focal issues, that is, the **life purpose, effective
>   methodology, major role**, or **ultimate contribution** which allows
>
> - an **increasing prioritization** of life's activities around the focal
>   issues, and
>
> - results in a **satisfying** life of **being** and **doing**.

Note carefully the key words, which are boldfaced.

Comment     **Dedicated** usually indicates that there was some sort of second decision beyond just
            being a Christian.[23] That decision places all that the leader is or has at God's disposal to
            be used by and for God. From that moment on, the leader is on a pilgrimage to discover
            God's special purposes, that is, a personal destiny with God. Sometimes this decision is
            called in some circles, a Lordship committal. Other groups may give it the title of a
            special call or special time of anointing for something. In any case it is a recognition that
            all of life is about serving the Lord. What ever is done in life, it must revolve around
            work for the Lord.

Comment     **Life purpose, effective methodology, major role**, or **ultimate contribution** are called
            the focal issues. That is, they are the major ways that God will reveal that for which we
            are designed. In a nutshell **life purpose** is the driving force behind what we do. **Major
            role** is the occupational position from which we accomplish that life purpose. **Effective
            methodologies** are means that are effective for us to deliver our ministry that flows from
            that life purpose. And **ultimate contributions** are the lasting results of that ministry.
            Each of these concepts will be defined in detail and explored fully in this manual.

Comment     It is the discovery of these focal issues, that is, their movement from implicit to explicit,
            which provides the possibility of **prioritization** or in other words, proactive decision
            making. The earlier we can discover these issues the earlier we can proactively act upon
            them. Many of the leaders in my case studies acted on implicit understandings of these
            focal issues for a good portion of their lives. However, many make breakthrough
            discoveries on one or more of these issues. Such breakthroughs, which allow an explicit
            understanding of something previously acted upon as

---

[23]Of course, in the case of adult conversions, the decision to become a Christian and the decision to wholly
follow and serve the Lord in some full time capacity can be concomitant.

## Final Commentary On Focal Issues continued

implicit, seem to re-energize the leader toward a more effective ministry. The leader then makes strategic decisions, which take into account the discoveries. In short, they manifest aspects of a focused life. It is just such a phenomenon that has led us to hope that we can expose the concepts and see many more leaders desire, enter in, and enjoy focused lives.

Comment          Note the final boldfaced words in the focused life definition, a **satisfying life** of **being** and **doing**. Leaders who discover life purpose and any other focal issue which synergizes with it will see things happen in their lives. They will become. They will accomplish. When all is said and done and life is drawing to a close they can look back and say, "Folks, you are looking at a fulfilled person. I am happy with the end product of God's shaping—who I am, what I have become. I am happy at what God has done through me—what I have done. Life was worth living. It has been a fulfilling pilgrimage. Praise God!"

Comment          Look one final time again at the focused life definition and note what I have added to it.

A <u>focused life</u> is

Age 20-30          • a life **dedicated** to exclusively carrying out God's unique purposes through it,

Age 30-40          • by identifying the focal issues, that is, the **life purpose, effective**
Age 40-50          **methodology, major role**, or **ultimate contribution** which allows

Age 50-60          • an **increasing prioritization** of life's activities around the focal issues, and

Age 60+          • results in a **satisfying** life of **being** and **doing**.

Note how each of the major concepts of the definition comes into play dominantly for given age group. The 20-30 year olds should make sure that they have really **dedicated** themselves to exclusive service for God (by a specific calling, an anointing, a Lordship committal, a willful committal to leadership, etc.). Age 30-40 should **clarify life purpose** and then seek to see any other one of the focal issues identified. Age 40-50 should clarify **major role** and tie down any remaining focal issue previously unidentified. Age 50-60 must SAY YES and SAY NO, that is, they must **prioritize** to make the most of what they have already learned about focal issues. Age 60+ should finish well, confirming and accomplishing ultimate contributions that will lead to a satisfying life.

Challenge          You now have a good overview of the focused life. This framework should allow you to go on to work on assessing your own progress toward focus, which is the goal of Section II. You should have some tentative ideas as to whether you have indications of one or more of the focal issues. Go on and work in detail to see if you are on target toward focus in your life.

# Chapter 3 Moving Toward Life Purpose

Introduction     Life purpose forms the prime integrating factor around which a focused life operates. The seeds of life purpose are contained in a leader's unusual experiences with God. We call these experiences sense of destiny experiences. We label this shaping effect on the leader toward his/her destiny as destiny processing.

All leaders have a sense of destiny. For some this destiny is more explicit than others. Our studies have led us to identify a general 3 stage pattern and to categorize 4 basic types of destiny experiences, which may occur in these 3 stages. Generally, as a leader experiences God's direction toward a destiny it involves movement from a committal about something general to a much more specific involvement as on-going destiny processing clarifies, specifies, and enlarges the original understanding of destiny. Obviously, an understanding of sense of destiny forms a basis for recognizing and moving from implicit to explicit life purpose.

Overview     In this chapter you will be introduced to:

- the overall flowchart leading to assessment of a focused life,
- where this chapter fits in that assessment,
- the time-line—the approach for integrating life purpose,
- the notion of critical incidents that indicate crucial shaping activities of God and point out destiny processing,
- several sample time-lines with critical incidents pointing to life purpose,
- Sense of Destiny,
- the destiny pattern—destiny preparation, destiny revelation, destiny fulfillment,
- four types of destiny processing categories,
- the personal destiny log,
- step 1 in writing your personal life mandate—using your personal destiny log to write the introductory paragraph on life purpose.

End Result     By the conclusion of this chapter you will have a tentative introductory paragraph for your personal life mandate.

**Flowchart — Overview Of Assessment**

# Basic Flow Chart
# For Moving Toward A Focused Life

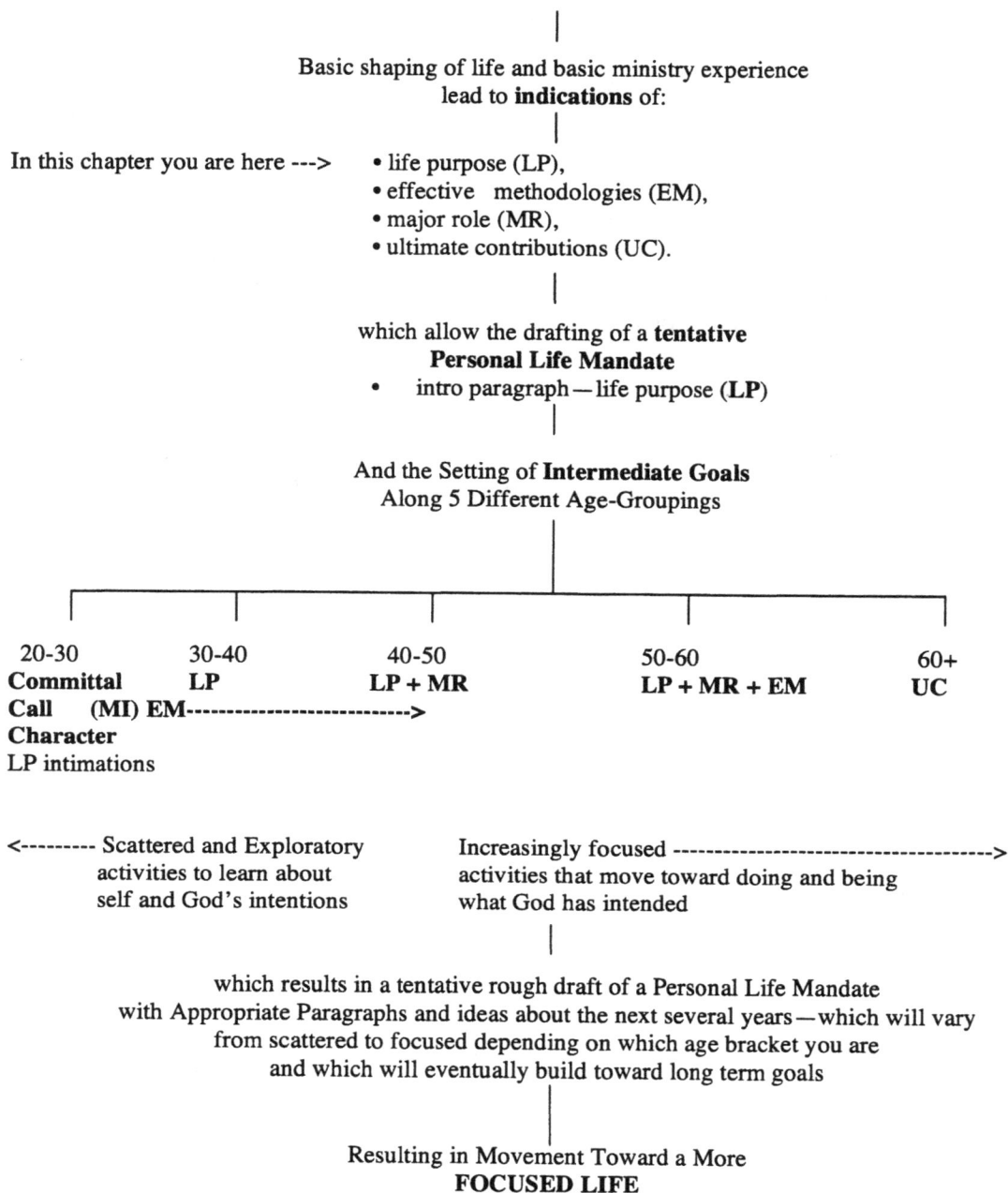

Basic shaping of life and basic ministry experience
lead to **indications** of:

In this chapter you are here --->
- life purpose (LP),
- effective  methodologies (EM),
- major role (MR),
- ultimate contributions (UC).

which allow the drafting of a **tentative**
**Personal Life Mandate**
- intro paragraph — life purpose (**LP**)

And the Setting of **Intermediate Goals**
Along 5 Different Age-Groupings

| 20-30 | 30-40 | 40-50 | 50-60 | 60+ |
|---|---|---|---|---|
| **Committal** | **LP** | **LP + MR** | **LP + MR + EM** | **UC** |
| **Call** (MI) EM----------------------> | | | | |
| **Character** | | | | |
| LP intimations | | | | |

<--------- Scattered and Exploratory     Increasingly focused ------------------------------------>
activities to learn about              activities that move toward doing and being
self and God's intentions           what God has intended

which results in a tentative rough draft of a Personal Life Mandate
with Appropriate Paragraphs and ideas about the next several years — which will vary
from scattered to focused depending on which age bracket you are
and which will eventually build toward long term goals

Resulting in Movement Toward a More
**FOCUSED LIFE**

## Time-Line

Introduction    This chapter will suggest that recognition of special experiences with God, called destiny processing, will be the seedbed of life purpose. The best way to do this is by use of a time-line. We identify critical incidents along a time-line. Then we choose those critical incidents, which give us information about destiny processing. Ideally, each leader should construct his/her own unique time-line. However, even using the general time-line for full time Christian workers and indicating critical incidents is a good first step. Below is the general time-line with brief explanation. You should read through it and determine where you are.

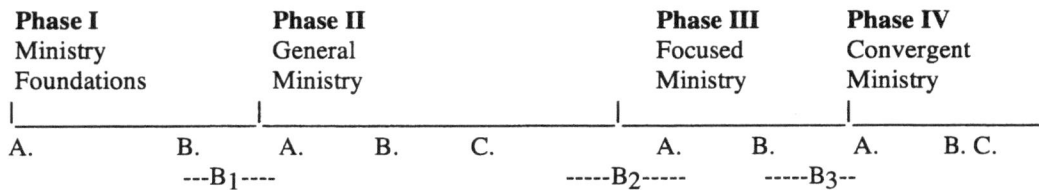

| **Phase I** | | **Phase II** | | | **Phase III** | | **Phase IV** | | |
|---|---|---|---|---|---|---|---|---|---|
| Ministry | | General | | | Focused | | Convergent | | |
| Foundations | | Ministry | | | Ministry | | Ministry | | |
| A. | B. | A. | B. | C. | A. | B. | A. | B. | C. |
| | ---$B_1$---- | | | | -----$B_2$----- | | -----$B_3$-- | | |

Where the sub-phases are called:

### Phase I
A.   Sovereign Foundations — (13-20 years)—early shaping of character/ personality
B.   Leadership Transition (3-6 years)—a time in which first steps in ministry are done
### Phase II
A.   Provisional Ministry (2-6 years) —the first attempts at full time ministry assignments; it is provisional because it might not last, that is, the leader may not stay in ministry.
B.   Growth Ministry (6-8 years)—ministry utilizing known giftedness with efficiency; giftedness and role issues are learned; this sub-phase is more for developing the leader than the ministry which is accomplished.
C.   Competent Ministry<— (2-6 years) —>operating out of giftedness in roles that fit that giftedness produces excellent results; still to be determined is the potential level of influence.
### Phase III
A.   Role Transition—There is movement toward compatibility between role, giftedness and influence-mix profile. There is shaping of a role more ideally suited to giftedness and challenge toward influence-mix.
B.   Unique Ministry—ministering effectively as well as efficiently with giftedness. (Role plus unique may last 3-12 years)

### Phase IV
A.   Special Guidance—movement toward a role focusing on ultimate contribution
B.   Convergent Ministry—fulfilling a sense of destiny/ ultimate contribution
C.   Afterglow—fall out effects of a life well lived; spiritual authority dominant

And the boundaries are called: $B_1$ the logistics barrier–moving from non-full-time Christian role to a full time paid Christian role; $B_2$ the strategic barrier/ Doing to Being–recognizing that fulfillment does not come from achievement alone but from ministry which flows out of being; $B_3$ The Convergence Springboard–moving into a focused life role that brings about very effective ministry.

### Figure 1. THE MINISTRY TIME-LINE

## Feedback On Time-Line

1. Identify where you are on the time-line below with an X. Remember this is a linear approach and in real life you can be at more than one point on this time-line simultaneously. For most purposes you can identify the point which is generally most true of your development to this point.

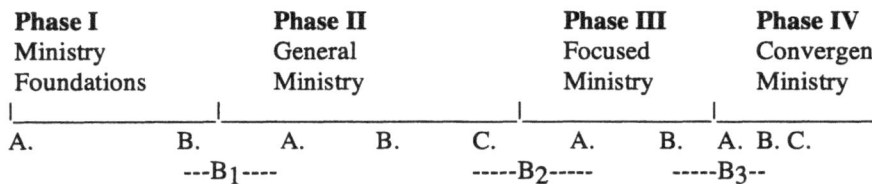

| **Phase I** | **Phase II** | **Phase III** | **Phase IV** |
|---|---|---|---|
| Ministry Foundations | General Ministry | Focused Ministry | Convergent Ministry |

```
|_____|_____|_____|_____|
A.         B.   A.        B.        C.   A.      B.   A. B. C.
      ---B1----                  -----B2-----   -----B3--
```

2. Now review the table below which was drawn from the **Basic Flow Chart For Assessing Movement Toward a Focused Life** given earlier in this chapter. Note your category of age grouping. Reflect back on the general time-line redrawn in exercise 1. Knowing where you are on the time-line and your basic age grouping, what kind of critical incidents can you expect? How much destiny processing?

| Age Groupings ---> | 20-30 | 30-40 | 40-50 | 50-60 | 60+ |
|---|---|---|---|---|---|
| Focused Life Issues ---> | Committal Call Character Life Purpose Intimations | Basic Life Purpose forms up; this may be added to later or take on other major thrusts | One or more additional life purposes may be added or old ones clarified, modified and expanded. Major Role is the dominant focal issue in this period. | Here life purpose is very firm. Major Role is clear. Effective methodologies are used with great power. This is a key time for a focused life | Here the major focus is on pressing on to the fulfillment of ultimate contributions. A further focus is on conserving the fruit of a lifetime. |
| critical incidents ---> | dealing with character some early ones dealing with strategic direction and crucial ministry values | numerous dealing with ministry values; few but very important ones dealing with strategic direction | fewer dealing with ministry values; several dealing with strategic guidance– especially shaping of a role | many dealing with strategic direction in terms of productive ministry | few in general |
| destiny processing ----> | destiny preparation | destiny revelation | destiny revelation | fewer destiny revelation; more destiny fulfillment start- to occur | destiny fulfillment occurs with many closures to past destiny items |
| number of destiny items normally occurring | Including up to age 20: 1-15; usually on the low side–maybe 2 or 3 | By this time could accum- ulate 10-15 | By this time probably 15-25 | By this time over 30 | Numerous though some leaders will not explicitly identify them |

a. For your situation what kind of critical incidents would you expect to be seeing?

b. For your situation what kind and how many destiny processing items would you expect to be seeing?

**ANSWERS------------**

1. Your choice. I am simultaneously in two places: Phase III, sub-phase B and Phase IV, sub-phases A and B for different functions of my ministry. 2. a. few in general (50-60); b. destiny fulfillment beginning to increase.

## Example Time-Line—Critical Incidents And Life Purpose Samuel Brengle

**Samuel Brengle (1860-1936) Discovery of Life Purpose**

| I. RUGGED PRAIRIE FOUNDATIONS | II. DESTINED FOR THE SALVATION ARMY | III. NATIONAL SPIRITUAL SPECIAL |
|---|---|---|

|------------------------|------------------------|------------------|

1860  1868 1872 1874 1877     1883                          1897                    1936
Age     8    12   14    17     23  24      27          32

                                                              37        44    51   60s    76

**C1 Early Destiny Items**
1. Parent's Covenant
2. Abraham's Promise, Stars in the Sky
**LP**—Serve God; God is going to use him to reach many.

**C2 Harnessing Ambition**
**LP**—Will be Public Rhetorician for God; God puts a spiritual touch on natural oratorical drive.

**C6 Personal Pentecost**—Brengle will always preach out of his experience.
**LP**—God is going to use him as the Apostle of Holiness.

**C7 Attractive Offer**—The Faith Challenge; here Brengle gets other major thrust—evangelism
**LP**—God will use him to lead many to the Lord.

**C8 Shiny Black Books**—
**LP**—it is to the Salvation Army he will have major Holiness thrust—fellow Soldiers

**C12 National Spiritual Special**
**LP**—His Major Role will enhance his life purpose of Holiness and Evangelistic Ministry to the Masses. His ministry will be itinerant and national and international.

Age=8 Hint, Reach Many
      Age=22 Public Rhetorician

Age 25                Age 27 Ministry To
Holiness Thrust    Soldiers
Age 25
Evangelism Thrust

Age 37 Life Purpose Firmed; wide spread public ministry leading many to personal holiness and many to Christ in national and international ministry

1868          1882          1885          1887
                             1885

1897 Life Purpose Firmed, Age = 37

## Example Time-Line—Critical Incidents And Life Purpose—CRJ

| I. NAÏVE NATURAL LEADER | II. NATURAL TO SPIRITUAL LEADER | III. DESTINY LEADERSHIP |
|---|---|---|

|------------------|------------------------|-----------------|

| 1936 | 1964 | 1970 | 1974 | 1978-1981 Geographical Convergence | 1987-1988 | Present |
|---|---|---|---|---|---|---|
| | | 34 | 38 | | | |
| Age | 28 | 34 | 38 | 43-45 | 51, 52 | |

A. (1936-57)
Great Depression Values,
Sovereign Foundations

A. (1971-74)
The Minors—Educational Technology
Perspectives

A. (1981-87)
The Majors—Developing Content &
Effective Methodology for Teaching;
Researching Leadership and
Developmental Framework

B. (1957-64)
Marriage, Early Career

B. (1974-79)
Authority Lessons, Learning to
Produce Materials

B. (1988-1993)
Influence-Mix Challenge; Expansion
by Taking Concepts Out; Writing via
Barnabus

C. (1964-70)
Transition to Ministry, Home
Bible Study Experience

C. (1979-81)
Broadening—Getting Missiological
Perspective

C. (1994—present)
Reflection and Intentionality Toward
Destiny Fulfillment; Developing
Others To Carry Out My Legacy

### Life Purpose Indications ▸

1952 Graham Crusade; serve
　　God
　1964 Lordship
　　　Committal; Missions
　1965 Bible Teaching;
　　　Observing Leaders

1971 Cross-cultural Training
　　First Hand Missionary
　　Experience

1982 Life Long Development
Perspective; Helping Leaders
From All Over the World
　1987 Influence Expands Via
　　Teaching and Writing
　　and Distributing
　　Materials
　1990 Non-Formal
　　Training Experience
　　1992 Bible Leadership;
　　　Legacy Mentoring

## Example Time-Line—Critical Incidents And Life Purpose—TGS

| I. DISCOVERING HERITAGE | II. DISCOVERING MINISTRY | III. DISCOVERING THE FUTURE |
|---|---|---|

|------------------|---------------------------|----------------|

| 1963 | 1983   1986 | 1991           Present |
| | 34     38 | |

| Age | 34     38     43-45 | 51, 52 |

A. (1963-1980))
Farm/Ranch Heritage; Freedom
To Discover; Foundations For
Adventurous Spirit; Life Is About
Discovering Things

A. (1983-1986)
Discovering Christ as Lord;
Leadership Committal; 1$^{st}$ Steps in
Ministry

A. (1991-1994)
Discovering Self; Self-chosen
Isolation; Future Perfect Thinking

B. (1994-Present)
Back into Ministry; Discovering
Teaching as a Means to Develop
People; Asia the Base for a World
Wide Ministry of Teaching/
Developing people;

B. (1986-1991)
Discovering Drivenness in Ministry—
Intervarsity; Isolation

B. (1980-1983)
Discovering Influence; Secular
Leadership Experiences

### Critical Incidents—Destiny Experiences   ·······························▶

C1 Influencer of People;
    **LP—Basic Thrust**

C2 1984 Global Christian; Urbana 84
**LP—World wide Ministry**
    C3 1985 Live Dangerously For
      Jesus
**LP-Value; EP-Natural Ability**
    C4 1986 Seeds of Future
       Thinking; Organizational
       Intuition
**LP, MR Parachurch Ministry**
    C5 1988 CC Relationships
**LP, Missions Influencer**
    C6 1989 Little Flower/
      Mighty Warrior
**LP, Value; Developer & Healer Via
Perspective**
    C7 1989 Wisdom
      Beyond Years
**EM—Perspectives can change lives**

C8 1991 Blessing of Life
**LP-Value; Impart Blessings Because
of God's Blessings on Own Life**

    C9 1991 Throne Room Vision
**LP-Value; Intimacy With God a Key
to Developing Others**

    C10 1993 Wonderlust
      Affirmation
**MR—strategic direction; ministry
will continue to be an adventure;
discovering influence world wide**

    C11 1993 Word Blessing/
      Teach With Spiritual
      Power
**EM—Spiritual Authority to be a
major means of teaching with power.**

    C12 1994 Malaysia/
      Singapore; Seeds of
      Asian Ministry To
      Come
**LP—Strategic Direction intimated**

| Age   17 | 21  22  23  25 26  26 | 28  28   30  30  31 |

## Prime Critical Incident

Introduction     We previously introduced the notion of prime critical incident. A given leader will have from 15 to 30 or even more of such critical incidents. For purposes of this chapter we are looking specifically at those prime critical incidents in life in which we can sense that God has intervened in a special way to give strategic direction to our life. That is, those critical incidents which are tinged heavily with destiny processing. This will become clearer after the definitions of this chapter about sense of destiny concepts.

Definition     A <u>prime critical incident</u> is a special intervention (could be a series over time) in which God gives a *major value* that will flow through the life or will give *strategic direction* to narrow the leader's life work.

Comment     Prime critical incidents were more carefully distinguished in terms of their function:

--->
1.   some produce a dominant value[24] which pervades the leader's ministry philosophy or
2.   some pinpoint a key strategic directional factor
3.   some do both.

This is diagrammed as follows.

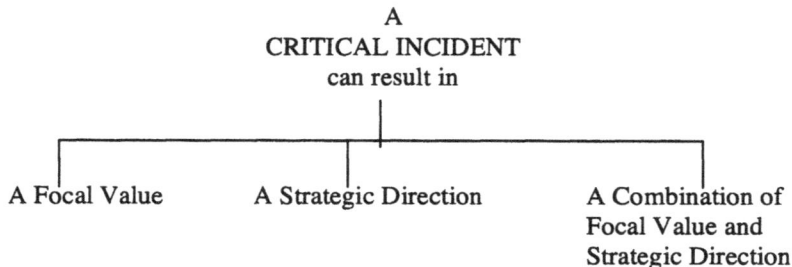

A
CRITICAL INCIDENT
can result in

A Focal Value          A Strategic Direction          A Combination of
Focal Value and
Strategic Direction

Example     See the unique time-lines, which follow which identify shaping incidents in which God indicated life purposes clarification.

---

[24]Sometimes this kind of prime critical incident can be a destiny experience, which does in fact contribute to life purpose.

**Feedback On Critical Incidents**

1.  Usually the things you remember, those things that standout as you reflect back on what has happened to shape you as a person of God and as a leader for God, will be at the root, a critical incident. See if you can list some critical incidents. Think back over your own personal time-line. See if you can identify some people, activities, events, crises, conflicts, character shaping issues, etc. Give each a label and date it so you could put it along your time-line.

    a.  early critical incidents—during your sovereign foundations:

    b.  critical incidents—during your leadership transition time:

    c.  critical incidents—during your provisional ministry time:

    d.  critical incidents—during your growth ministry time:

    e.  critical incidents—during your competent ministry time:

    f.  critical incidents—during your focused ministry time:

2.  For each critical incident you listed above with a date and a label now go back to it and categorize it as a focal value (put FV beside it), strategic direction (put SD beside it), or combination (put COMB beside it).

**ANSWERS------------**

Your choice on all answers.

**Sense Of Destiny/ Destiny Processing/ The Destiny Continuum**

Introduction    Destiny experiences refer to those experiences, which lead a person to sense and believe that God has intervened in a personal and special way. Encouraging experiences which affirm the emergence of leadership toward some purpose of God during that leader's lifetime fit this category of processing. A leader does not learn all at once about sense of destiny or destiny experiences. Fortunately God prepares the leader by preliminary experiences. After a time of growing sensitivity to this kind of processing God usually clarifies the sense of destiny with revelation experiences. Finally toward the end of life God culminates these destiny experiences by bringing many of them to fulfillment.

Definition    <u>Sense of destiny</u> is an inner conviction in a leader arising from an experience or a series of experiences in which there is a growing sense of awareness in that God has His hand on that leader in a special way for special purposes.

Definition    The shaping incidents or means God uses to instill this growing sense of awareness of a destiny is called <u>destiny processing</u>.

Comment    Sometimes the experience is awe inspiring and there is no doubt that God is in it and that the leader or emerging leader is going to be used by God. Such are the destiny revelation experiences of Moses in Exodus 3 and Paul in Acts 9. But at other times it is not so clear to the individual. Over a period of time various experiences come to take on new light and an awareness of that sense of destiny dawns. For example, Moses' birth and deliverance into Pharaoh's palace was an indicator of God's hand on his life and in retrospect can be seen that way. Bertelsen's study of sense of destiny in the scriptures pointed out that sense of destiny may be a process as much as a unique awe inspiring experience. The idea of the destiny continuum comes out of Bertelsen's thinking.

**The Destiny Continuum–Three Stage Pattern**

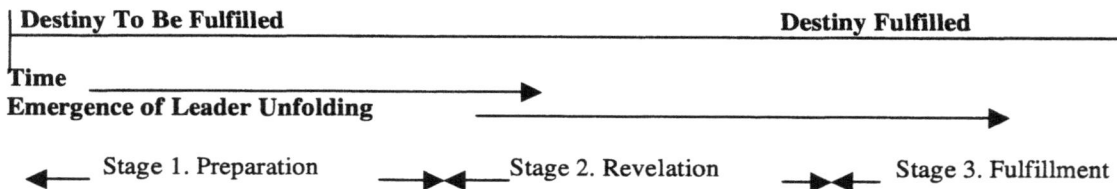

| **Destiny To Be Fulfilled** | **Destiny Fulfilled** |
|---|---|

Time _____→
**Emergence of Leader Unfolding** _____→

←— Stage 1. Preparation    →►←— Stage 2. Revelation    →►←— Stage 3. Fulfillment

Comment    This continuum describes a spiritual leadership pattern in which there is a growing awareness of a sense of destiny, progress seen in that destiny, and finally, culmination as the destiny is fulfilled.

**Feedback On Sense Of Destiny/ Destiny Processing**

1.  Think of Moses. Can you think of any destiny processing incidents in each of the three stages?

    a.  Preparation:

    b.  Revelation:

    c.  Fulfillment:

2.  Think of Paul. Can you think of any destiny processing incidents in each of the three stages?

    a.  Preparation:

    b.  Revelation:

    c.  Fulfillment:

3.  What dangers are there in teaching about sense of destiny?

**ANSWERS------------**

1.  a.  preparation: Saved in the Ark, Raised in the Palace, educated as an Egyptian, Slays the Egyptian
    b.  revelation: the burning bush
    c.  fulfillment: the Exodus, Red Sea
2.  a.  preparation: educated in Tarsus, educated by Gamaliel
    b.  revelation: the Damascus Road experience, Come over and help us dream
    c.  fulfillment: See Acts 26:19
3.  A concept like sense of destiny can be taken by ambitious leaders and abused.

**Commentary On Destiny Concepts And The Focused Life**

Introduction    Not all leaders respond to the notion of sense of destiny. Some see it as a pride thing—
something to be avoided. If God is going to do something let Him do it. They are afraid
of what they see of leaders who abuse the notion. Some leaders under the cover of a sense
of destiny do things for their own self-interest. But remember this principle, "Never avoid
a truth simply because it is abused!" Sense of Destiny is a valid Biblical concept that can
encourage a leader and can bring that leader to focus on what God wants to accomplish.

Comment    I have found it helpful to suggest three guidelines for those wanting a
sense of destiny.

1. **Become sensitized to the notion of sense of destiny.**
   Joseph, one of the Old Testament leaders with a clear sense of destiny, provides a
   model for becoming sensitized to a sense of destiny.
   a.  He sensed he was part of a Godly heritage (following the God of Abraham,
       Isaac, and Jacob and not the gods of Laban, for example),
   b.  He was familiar with ways in which sense of destiny experiences occurred in the
       lives of Abraham, Isaac, and Jacob. He would have heard the stories about
       Abraham's call, Isaac's birth and near sacrifice, and Jacob's ladder, etc. He was
       thus conditioned by a sense of Godly heritage and knowing how God had
       intervened with his great grandfather, grandfather, and father. He would be
       sensitive to such a destiny himself. (But why were not his brothers just as
       sensitive?)
   c.  He was there when his father had major sense of destiny experiences (Peniel and
       Bethel).
   d.  He saw evidence of sovereign protection of his family (Laban crisis).
   e.  He knew he, himself, was an answer to prayer (Genesis 30:24).
   f.  He had personal experience with God (prophetic word given in dreams).
   g.  He knew his own life had been preserved (the slavery crisis).
   h.  His daily life, working at whatever tasks he was given, reflected the presence
       and blessing of God so as to be recognized by others (Genesis 39;2,3; 21-23).

2. **Reflect back in light of this knowledge and begin now to identify
   sense of destiny experiences.** You will find that there are many more
   incidents that upon retrospective reflection begin to take on new meaning for you.
   This will be particularly true of Types II, III, and IV destiny experiences.

3. **Expect God to give you destiny experiences.** If you have never had a
   Type I destiny experience, then pray and trust God to give you one. Learn to
   recognize the hand of God in your affairs. By faith recognize that incidents are
   destiny incidents.

**4 Types Of Destiny Processing Categories**

Introduction    Various kinds of means are used by God to intervene in a leader's life so as to create a sense of destiny. In terms of easiest to distinguish God's hand in them they can be ranked from very high indication of God's touch to not so sure of God's involvement according to the four types below. The following tree diagram describes this continuum notion of a varied range of incidents, which reveal God's destiny for a leader.

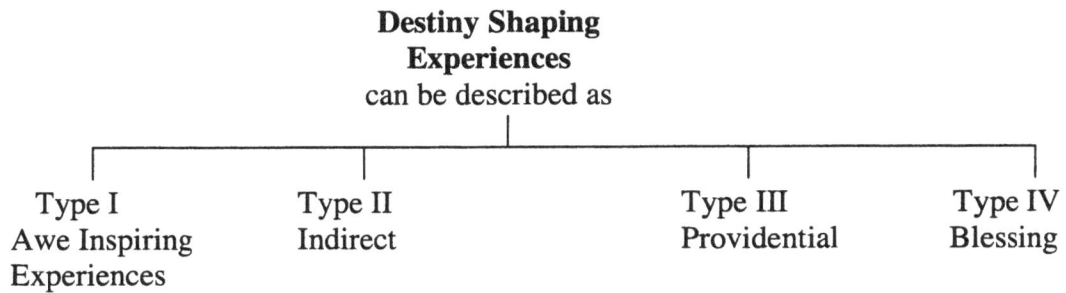

**Destiny Shaping
Experiences**
can be described as

| Type I | Type II | Type III | Type IV |
|---|---|---|---|
| Awe Inspiring Experiences | Indirect | Providential | Blessing |

Comment    Usually most people identify sense of destiny concepts only with Type I experiences. But each of these kind of experiences when accumulated over a lifetime will add to and clarify and assure that the leader is indeed walking toward a destiny in partnership with God.

Comment    God imparts and develops a person's *sense of destiny* in many different ways. Familiarity with the four types above and retrospective reflection will usually allow a leader to see much more of God's destiny processing than would be suspected. We shall describe each of the four in the next several pages. All of these types have numerous Biblical examples of them. In fact, they also have numerous contemporary examples as well. Our study of 3000+ case studies includes more than 2500 contemporary leaders. These cases have validated each of the four primary types of sense of destiny experiences listed above.

## Type I. Sense of Destiny—Awe Inspiring Experiences With God

**Introduction**      Scriptures provide us with a number of incidents in Scriptures in which God intervened in a special awe inspiring way in the life of leaders. For some, it was an overpowering presence. For others, it was not only an overwhelming presence but also a revelation from God—sometimes an audible voice, sometimes a speaking through an Angelic being, sometimes a shaking dream, etc. But always Type I experiences are those that are never forgotten over a lifetime.

| Type | Label | Explanation/ Examples |
|------|-------|----------------------|
| I | Awe Inspiring—dominantly presence. | Joshua and the Captain of the Lord's Army. |
| I | Awe Inspiring—dominantly presence. | Jacob wrestling with the Angel. |
| I | Awe Inspiring—both presence and revelation. | Moses experience at the burning bush in Exodus 3 shows both an awe inspiring presence and a revelation about his future. |
| I | Awe Inspiring—both presence and revelation. | Abraham's Dream in Genesis 15 |
| I | Awe Inspiring—both presence and revelation. | Mary's experience with Gabriel. |
| I | Awe Inspiring—both presence and revelation. | Paul on the Damascus Road. |
| I | Awe Inspiring—both presence and revelation. | Isaiah's call in Isaiah 6. |
| I | Awe Inspiring—dominantly revelation. | Joseph's two dreams |
| I | Awe Inspiring—dominantly revelation. | Revelation to Ananias about Paul's experience on the Damascus road and his future ministry. See Acts 9, 22, 26. |

**Comment**      In this kind of incident, the person experiences an overwhelming presence of God. God reveals Himself to the person in some kind of clear and unmistakable way and the person knows that God is involved in his/her life and has a special purpose for it. In addition to just the overwhelming presence of God as an awe inspiring experience, frequently in conjunction with this presence God reveals something about the person's future purpose. Joseph's dreams in Genesis 37 are an example. Joshua's encounter with the Captain of the Host in Joshua 5 is another example.

**Comment**      The results of such an encounter usually are:
1. An indelible experience that lasts for a lifetime. You know God is real and that you are serving an awesome God. You can always come back to this experience and it encourages you on through life.
2. Usually God affirms who you are or what you are to do for Him.
3. You are left with a sense of destiny—that is, you know that your life is moving with God; you are involved in something bigger than yourself.

## The Call—A Special Sense of Destiny—Type I Experience

Introduction | Sometimes, usually in the leadership transition time, a potential leader opts to go into ministry. Usually this choice is spurred by a call of some kind. In Scripture this call is frequently a Type I destiny experience. Though a call does not have to be a Type I destiny experience, it is usually the case that the more a call moves toward a Type I experience, the more sure is the leader and the more likely is the leader to stick it out when the complexities and pressures of leadership overwhelm that leader.

Definition | The <u>call</u> is a response to God's invitation to serve Him, frequently a Type I Experience, and can occur in a moment–in–time in which a leader chooses to serve God whole heartedly, unreservedly as a leader, willing to go anyplace, anytime, to do anything God wants or it can be a step-by-step leading over time until that same decision has been accomplished.

Example | Isaiah's experience in Isaiah 6.

Example | Moses' experience in Exodus 3.

Example | Jeremiah's experience in Jeremiah 1.

Example | Paul's Damascus Road experience told in Acts 9, 22, and 26.

Example | Abraham's call in Genesis 12.

Comment | Recognize that not all calls are awe inspiring Type I experiences. Sometimes there is the gradual awakening to responsibility as the light of the Word breaks through. A person chooses. Later in looking back on that choice a person can see God's hand all along the way leading up to that choice although at the time it seemed a human choice. Notice that in this definition I have merged two very important issues—call and committal. Frequently, they occur simultaneously but they can also occur apart.

Comment | For awe inspiring calls the pattern is usually:
1. An occasion, which sets up the potential leader to be ready for the experience.
2. The experience in which suddenly the emerging leader is aware of something beyond the natural.
3. An interaction with God.
4. A response to what God has done or said.
5. An identification of this as the rock, the stable anchor point to which the leader will look back time and time again over his/her leadership.

Comment | In terms of life purpose, the **call**, will usually be the first step in initiating **life purpose**. Many times it will contain in simplified form the actual life purpose. In terms of the various age groupings the call usually occurs between the ages of 20 and 30. These young leaders get an intimation of a life purpose—it will be clarified down road. The young leader then learns to experience God in terms of processing which shapes character—for ministry flows out of being. God works on that foundational beingness. During the 30s and 40s the life purpose will be clarified and added to.

**Feedback On Type I. Awe Inspiring Experiences With God**

1. Which of the following are Type I destiny experiences? Check (√) any which are.

___a.  Zechariah's experience in Luke 1.
___b.  Timothy's call in Acts 16.
___c.  The warning about the shipwreck in Acts 27:10 and 27:25.
___d.  John's experience as he saw the 7 Golden candlesticks in Revelation 1
___e.  Peter, James, and John's experience on the Mount of Transfiguration.
___f.  The experience of the church leaders in Antioch in Acts 13:1-3.
___g.  The sending of Barnabas to Antioch on the Apostolic mission in Acts 11:22

2. List here any Type I destiny experiences that you have experienced:

3. For any such experiences you listed in exercise 2, make an effort to describe what they indicated about life purpose for you.

**ANSWERS------------**

1. _√_ a.  _√_ d.  _√_ e.  _√_ f.      2. Your choice.          3. Your choice.

## Type II. Sense of Destiny—Indirect Destiny Experiences

| | |
|---|---|
| Introduction | God often moves in ways that are mysterious. That is, He does not always break into our lives with awe-inspiring experiences. Sometimes our destinies hinge on other people's actions on our behalf. We may not even have had a choice in them. For example, in this kind of incident, the person can experience a sense of destiny, which comes through another person. It could be a prophetic word or prayer. It is an experience that is mediated from God to you through another person. Saul and David were anointed by Samuel to be kings over Israel. This experience was a sense of destiny experience that came from another person. Hannah's covenant with God concerning a son is another example. |
| Description | A <u>Type II Indirect destiny experience</u> is an experience in which some aspect of destiny is linked to some person other than the leader and is done indirectly for the leader who simply must receive its implications. |

| Type | Label | Explanation/ Examples |
|---|---|---|
| II | Indirect—name with meaning; timing of birth. | Rachel's naming of Joseph. His was a long awaited birth. The timing was clearly of God and controlled by God. See Genesis 30:22-24. |
| II | Indirect—Moses saved by parents in the Ark. | Moses parents recognized that Moses was a special child. They defiantly acted against the Egyptian edict and saved Moses. See Exodus 1. This unusual experience led to his destiny in the Egyptian court and eventually to his experience in freeing Israel in the exodus. |
| II | Indirect—Hannah's contract with God. | Samuel had little or no choice in his committal to serve God. The decision was essentially made for him by his mother in her moment with God in 1 Samuel 1. |
| II | Indirect—Zechariah's experience with the Angel concerning the son to be born, John the Baptist, and his destiny with God. | John the Baptist was given over and dedicated to the Lord by his parents following the unusual revelation by the angel about his birth. He grew up primed for his role. |

| | |
|---|---|
| Comment | Of course, even when some prophetic utterance or some heritage decision is made, the emerging leader will have some moment in time in which that prior decision is endorsed and accepted personally. But the power of the knowledge of that previous indirect sense of destiny is often a major decision making factor in itself. |
| Comment | Sometimes a parent dedicates a child to the Lord prior to birth or even after birth and does not reveal that to the child. Later the child as an adult ratifies that earlier indirect destiny experience by a personal decision. Then revelation of such an event occurs. Such a revelation gives added affirmation and assurance to the decision. I have seen many of these kind of indirect experiences. |

**Feedback On Type II. Indirect Destiny Experiences**

1.  Which of the following are Type II destiny experiences? Check (√) any which are.

___a.  Timothy's early indoctrination into the Scriptures.
___b.  Samson's parents experience in Judges 13.
___c.  The incident between Paul and Barnabas which led to John Mark's training with Barnabas.
___d.  Peter's prophetic call by Jesus in John 1.

2.  List here any Type II destiny experiences that you have experienced:

3.  For any such experiences you listed in exercise 2, make an effort to describe what they indicated about life purpose for you.

**ANSWERS**------------

1.  _√?_ a.  _√_ b.  _√?_ d.          2. Your choice.          3. Your choice.

## Type III. Sense of Destiny—Providential Circumstances

Introduction | In this kind of incident, the person realizes that in the providence of God, he/she senses the Lord has a special purpose for him/her. It is not something that is done by others but is usually recognized through the contextual factors. In retrospect, one can see the hand of God in using birth circumstances, location of birth, timing of birth, contextual factors that press, etc. as lining up toward God's purposes. An accumulation of these when viewed at a later point in time will give confirmation that God is indeed in the life time direction. Sometimes this kind of activity by God is called the left hand of God. It is probably most clearly seen in the life of Joseph.

Description | Destiny can be sensed and affirmed when in retrospect a leader sees an accumulation of past experiences or providential circumstances used to indicate that the leader has been led and must or should be doing something for God because of this evidence.

Example | Joseph's jealous brothers sold him into slavery. He was taken by a Mideanite caravan to Egypt and sold to Potiphar, an important military leader. Eventually, via a discouraging experience in prison, he was providentially put in touch with a palace official for whom he did a favor—interpreting a dream. This contact at a crucial moment in Egypt's history brought Joseph to the attention of Pharaoh. His ability to interpret the Pharaoh's dream and his wise counsel gave the Pharaoh grounds for appointing Joseph to a high position in the court. That position allowed Joseph to carry out his destiny—preserving Israel during the famine which came.

Example | Barnabas was born on the island of Cyprus. (Acts 4) He grew up in a bi-cultural situation. Isn't it interesting that when the apostles needed someone to go to Antioch that Barnabas was chosen? The church in Antioch was started by men from Cyprus. Who was better prepared to relate to them than Barnabas? This is the kind of experience through which a sense of destiny is imparted through a providential circumstance. Another common providential experience in which people gain this sense of destiny is in near death situation in which the person has the feeling that his/her life was spared for a reason.

Example | Paul was reared in Tarsus, the 3rd University city in its time. It was a multi-cultural city. Paul knew several languages. He was a Roman citizen. Gamaliel was Paul's mentor. Gamaliel exposed Paul to Greek thought as well as Hebraic thought. He was well prepared to contextualize the movement of the Way from a Hebrew focused religious movement to a Gentile universal institution.

**Feedback On Type III. Sovereign Circumstances**

1.  Which of the following are at least partially Type III destiny experiences or could contribute to them? Check (√) any which are.

    ___a.  The fact that Timothy was half Jew and half Gentile.
    ___b.  The fact that Paul was born a Roman citizen.
    ___c.  The fact that Barnabas grew up in Cyprus.
    ___d.  The fact that Lydia was a successful business woman.

2.  List here any Type III destiny experiences that you have experienced:

3.  For any such experiences you listed in exercise 2, make an effort to describe what they indicated about life purpose for you.

**ANSWERS-----------**

1. All of these are contributing factors to reasons why God used these people in special ways. 2. Your choice. 3. Your choice.

## Type IV. Sense of Destiny Experience—The Blessing Of God

Introduction    An unusual statement is made about Joseph in Stephen's historical narration in Acts 7. It is said of Joseph, "God was with him." And in the Genesis account of Joseph's life beginning with Genesis 39 there is the repeated phrase in whatever thing he turned his hand to—God gave him success or God blessed him. This kind of affirmation imparts a tremendous sense of destiny.

Description     When a leader enjoys the powerful presence of God in life and ministry and has repeated experiences, which show that God is <u>blessing the life and ministry,</u> this accumulated evidence sustains a strong sense of destiny.

Example         Genesis 39 and following give a number of vignettes on Joseph. He was prosperous because of God's blessing. There was a sense of God's presence upon his life. Note:

Genesis 39:1 Now Joseph had been taken down to Egypt. Potiphar, an Egyptian who was one of Pharaoh's officials, the captain of the guard, bought him from the Ishmaelites who had taken him there. 2 The **LORD was with Joseph and he prospered**, and he lived in the house of his Egyptian master. 3 When his **master saw that the LORD was with him** and that the **LORD gave him success in everything he did**, 4 Joseph found favor in his eyes and became his attendant. Potiphar put him in charge of his household, and he entrusted to his care everything he owned. 5 From the time he put him in charge of his household and of all that he owned, the LORD **blessed the household of the Egyptian** because of Joseph. The **blessing of the LORD was on everything Potiphar had**, both in the house and in the field. 6 So he left in Joseph's care everything he had; with Joseph in charge, he did not concern himself with anything except the food he ate. ... 20 Joseph's master took him and put him in prison, the place where the king's prisoners were confined. But while Joseph was there in the prison, 21 the **LORD was with him**; he showed him kindness and granted him favor in the eyes of the prison warden. 22 So the warden put Joseph in charge of all those held in the prison, and he was made responsible for all that was done there. 23 The warden paid no attention to anything under Joseph's care, **because the LORD was with Joseph and gave him success in whatever he did.**

Genesis 41:39 Then Pharaoh said to Joseph, "Since God has made all this known to you, there is no one so discerning and wise as you. 40 You shall be in charge of my palace, and all my people are to submit to your orders. Only with respect to the throne will I be greater than you."

Acts 7:9 "Because this brothers were jealous of Joseph, they sold him as a slave into Egypt. **But God was with him.**

Comment         This kind of destiny experience comes through reflection. The sense of destiny comes as a result of realizing that God's blessing has been on you in your situations. Most often, other people recognize this before you do. Joseph and Daniel are two key examples of this kind of destiny experience. Other people recognized that God was with them and that God was blessing them. This kind of affirmation imparted a sense of destiny to them.

**Feedback On Type IV. Blessing Of God**

1. Besides Joseph what other Bible character(s) can you think of who saw blessing repeatedly in their lives and were regarded as people of destiny?

2. List here any Type IV destiny experiences that you have experienced:

3. For any such experiences you listed in exercise 2, make an effort to describe what they indicated about life purpose for you.

**ANSWERS-----------**

1. David, Elijah, Elisha, Daniel (probably others)  2. Your choice. 3. Your choice.

## Personal Destiny Log

| | |
|---|---|
| Introduction | The human mind does not always remember things—even things that were positive experiences with God. We do well to learn to record our experiences with God. The value of a **Personal Destiny Log** is that it forces us to discipline ourselves to remember God's working in our lives. The value of studying others **Personal Destiny Log** is that we become sensitized to destiny experiences. Seeing what others have experienced and logged as destiny experiences can stimulate us to remember similar or spin-off kinds of destiny experiences in our own lives, which we might not otherwise have seen as such. Two actual examples of destiny logs follow. |
| Description | A <u>personal destiny log</u> is a written record of God's dealing with a leader in terms of destiny experiences, of all types, which can enforce a growing awareness of a sense of destiny. |
| Format | Number the entry, date it, identify it as to type, then give it a descriptive label; finally describe it and interpret its relevance toward your understanding of life purpose or any other of the focal elements: major role, effective methodologies and ultimate contributions. |
| Example | From TGS<br>2. 1984 Type I Global Christian<br>Challenged to make all decisions of life with the people of the world and world evangelization in mind. Partly logical/ partly mystical. Eric Alexander's strong exhortation heeded.<br>**Life Purpose**—I must operate so as to be involved in and affect missions. |
| Example | From CRJ<br>19. 1994 Type IV **Unusual Blessing of God on Ministry**<br>Workshops over past 4 years; hands laid on Richard and I. Fulfillment of a sense of destiny for Richard with me. Increased anointing in our workshops; much broader impact; yet penetrative. Malaysia/ Singapore—fulfillment of destiny longings of 30 years ago; indications of things to come—thoughts of Canada, all over U.S., India, repeated influence in Asia, desire to write, intentional mentoring (Simeon concentric circles).<br>**Life Purpose**—God has given great affirmation of my purpose to enable high level leaders to finish well by providing training. |
| Comment | After you have been introduced to the definitions of three types of destiny process items (destiny preparation, destiny revelation, and destiny fulfillment) you will be better prepared to see your own destiny experiences. |
| Comment | One of the major leadership lessons that we have learned about from comparative study expresses the importance of sense of destiny. |

**Effective leaders evince a growing awareness of their sense of destiny and a proactive move toward seeing some or all of it fulfilled.**

| | |
|---|---|
| Comment | Remember that destiny experiences are the seedbed of life purpose. Find out as much as you can about your own destiny processing and its implications for life purpose. Seek God about revealing more destiny experiences to you. |

## Example 1. Personal Destiny Log—TGS

Introduction        The following log uses the standard format: date, type, label, then explanatory
                    description, followed by analysis toward life purpose issues.

1.  **Early Years Type IV Made to Influence**
    From early on I saw that I had abilities and desire to influence people. This was seen in many ways.
    **Life Purpose**—I will be involved in leadership.

2.  **1984 Type I Global Christian**
    Challenged to make all decisions of life with the people of the world and world evangelization in
    mind. Partly logical/ partly mystical. Eric Alexander's strong exhortation heeded.
    **Life Purpose**—I must operate so as to be involved in missions and affect missions.

3.  **Fall 1985 Type I Live Dangerously for Jesus**
    Strong message from Word challenged me to give myself for ministry; a leadership committal;
    posture toward ministry.
    **Life Purpose/ Major Role**—I will serve full time for Christ; my leadership abilities and drive and my
    desire for missions will find a full time outlet somehow. Implication—If I sense something is true I
    can go for it.

4.  **Fall 1986 Type IV Organizational Strategy**
    As I prepared to go into ministry I found I had the ability to get a future perfect vision of what should
    happen and how it should look; a sort of blueprint for action.
    **Effective   Methodology**—I have an innate ability to sense what needs to be done and how to do it.

5.  **Summer 1989 Type IV Cross-cultural Relationships**
    I knew I was to be involved in cross-cultural ministry as I was drawn to establish such relationships.
    **Life Purpose**—I knew cross-cultural ministry, perhaps travel would be involved in my ministry.

6.  **January 1989 Type II Little Flower/ Mighty Warrior**
    Inklings of ministering out of beingness. A prophetic heavenly name given describing who I am as I
    minister. Painful experiences over my lifetime will be used for others as I am honest and share my
    vulnerability.
    **Life Purpose**—Part of my influence will come through modeling and transparent sharing of what
    God has done in me in my weakness. Seeds of spiritual authority.

7.  **Spring 1989 Type II Wisdom Beyond Her Years**
    A prophetic word was given to me directly at a Vineyard conference. Nyla prayed, "Lord, give her
    wisdom beyond her years." A confirming manifestation backed her word. I accepted it as valid.
    **Life Purpose**—My ministry will involve influence and wisdom speaking into situations beyond that
    which should be expected of me.

## Example 1. Personal Destiny Log—STG continued

8.  **Fall 1991 Type II Blessing of Life**
    At a Renovare conference Richard Foster prayed individually for me, "I bless these hands that they would call forth life in others." The thrust to me was that I would help people see what they were meant to be and help move them toward that. I received the blessing.
    **Life Purpose**—My ministry will involve helping people develop to who they were meant to be. In seed form I knew I would be involved in a training ministry involving developmental things.

9.  **Fall 1991 Type I Throne Room Vision**
    In a mystical vision I saw myself before a throne. I was presented to God on the throne in full womanhood by Jesus. I was fully accepted for what I was a, woman. I was affirmed that I could lead out of who I was. Freely I could do this. It would affect other women. Again I was impressed with ministering out of being.
    **Life Purpose**—Part of my leadership ministry would involve modeling leadership fully as a woman and freeing up other women to lead.

10. **February 1993 Type IV Wanderlust**
    My adventurous spirit is part of who I am. It is all right. Ministering out of being means I should be free to go for it when I have stirrings of an adventurous nature concerning ministry.
    **Life Purpose**—I will be involved in discovering and trying out things and going places. Travel will be an exciting part of it.

11. **5 May 1993 Type II Blessing/ Teaching/ Spiritual Authority**
    Bobby Clinton at the end of several months of mentoring in the Psalms wrote out a blessing for me which involved motivation toward life long development in the Word and using it with power.
    **Life Purpose**—I am going to be involved in using the Word as I train and develop people. And I need to use it with great power.

12. **Summer 1994 Type IV Malaysia/ Singapore Destiny Awaits**
    Trip to Malaysia and Singapore on Barnabas Resource team with Bobby, Richard and Lora was anticipated as a destiny experience. Powerful prayer before and during by intercessors was answered. This was a major step forward in my training ministry. I found myself speaking with spiritual authority to Type C, D, and E leaders. Personal ministry with many was also powerfully blessed.
    **Life Purpose/ Effective  Methodology**—Leadership training/ equipping internationally is part of what I am about. Saw workshop format, personal interviews, team teaching as a major delivery means.

### Example 2—Personal Destiny Log—CRJ

**abbreviations:**     p(dp) = destiny preparation process item; p(dr) = destiny revelation process item
p(df) = destiny fulfilled process item

### 1. 1936 TYPE II Dedication to Lord as Baby
Mom's Hannah-like dedication to God; prayers that I would be a full time Christian worker (25 years). p(dp)
**Life Purpose/ Major Role**—given over to God for His purposes

### 2. 1953 TYPE III Crusade—Surrender to Be Used By God
Billy Graham crusade; leadership committal on youth night. God apparently took that more seriously than I did; I forgot it quickly. p(lco), p(dp)
**Life Purpose**—willing to be used by God

### 3. 1958 TYPE I—Taste of Teaching
Antenna Theory class — 5 minute presentation; knew someday that I would have a formal teaching role. p(dp)
**Major Role**—I knew inwardly that I would do this in life.

### 4. 1965 TYPE I—Historical Mentor, Receiving God's Challenge
China — reading all of CIM books; surrender to go to China; intent accepted, destination different. p(dp)
**Life Purpose**—call not only to serve God but in terms of a mission's call.

### 5. 1965 TYPE I—Ultimate Contribution, Mentor
At Bell Labs, I was walking down the hall and saw Roy Deming draped over a drawing board working on a circuit design. He was near the end of his career. Is that what I wanted? No, I wanted at the end of my life to look back and see my path strewn with people whom I had decisively influenced towards God. This was an inward leadership committal. p(dr)
**Life Purpose/ Ultimate Contribution**—I would leave behind me many people whom I had changed personally with my ministry.

### 6. 1966 TYPE I—Sometime in Future, A Doctorate
Bible study with a young couple (Revelation). There was a prophetic utterance after I taught the class. They said, "Someday when you've got your doctorate I'll say I knew you when you were just a Bible teacher." p(dp), p(dr)
**Major Role**—I would need and have a doctorate for carrying out my life purpose.

### 7. 1967 TYPE III—My Role, Missions not Pastorate
Integrity check (alternative attractive offer) Pastor L. Thompson woke up in the middle of the night. He wanted us to take over the church. Marilyn and I had battled through on rural pastorate, staying in Reynoldsburg, going to CBC to open the way for missions. David's costly principle (1 Chronicles. 21:24) p(dr)
**Major Role**—God clearly led to a missions alternative even though we did not fit current profile for missionary types (already had four kids, our age, etc.)

### Example 2—Personal Destiny Log—CRJ continued

**8. 1967 TYPE IV—God Will Supply if We Are Generous**

Overtime at Bell Labs; 2 Corinthians 8:13,14,15. Extra giving in time of plenty—be sustained in time of need. Man (Joe Jack Hurst) in Jackson heard we were going to CBC and would give up our electrical engineering job. Sent cash gift. We gave it to couple at Applachian Bible Institute. God supplied for three years at CBC. p(fchk), p(dr).

**Effective Methodology**—Generosity is to be a part of my ministry. I must learn to give of myself, my knowledge, and what I have materially to meet others needs. God will take care of us.

**9. 1967 TYPE III—Free To Move**

Muller influence. Stay out of debt. Marilyn's $1000 saved. Two in need first week at CBC. Gave it away. God provided. p(ic), p(dr)

**Life Purpose/ Effective Methodology**—Affirmed God's supply experience but added to it; stay out of debt in order to be mobile. I must be free to carry out life purpose.

**10. 1968 TYPE I—Future Will Involve Overseas Ministry**

Giving for CLTC - Gil McArthur's drive for chapel-GI bill-late; gave entire check; promise to someday preach in that chapel; fulfilled in 1983 during my summer in PNG. p(oc), p(dr).

**Life Purpose—My ministry will involve overseas travel. I will go to PNG someday.**

**11. 1968 TYPE I—Large Sphere of Influence/ Worldwide**

CBC chapel—Gil McArthur—eschatological potential (500 students to be used around the world)— God's clear inner voice, "I am going to use you greatly around the world." p(dr) Pivotal destiny item.

**Life Purpose/ Major Role**—My ministry will involve not only an overseas emphasis in the area of missions but will have wide impact.

**12. 1969 TYPE III—Divine Contact, Pat Arnold**

CBC—L.O. Heiden—boyhood prearranged circumstances—real step of guidance. Contact with Pat Arnold—his challenge. p(dc), p(np), p(dr)

**Life Purpose/ Major Role**—The next step is opened; it will be with the West Indies Mission.

**13. 1969 TYPE I—Quiet Presence**

CBC—day of prayer in Wally Ip's room. Knew I needed to be able in the future to meet God—sense of God's presence—knew I would be able to do so in the future. Importance of a day of prayer. p(dr)

**Life Purpose**—Renewed sense of destiny; need for God's presence and affirmation of me in my life purpose.

**14. 1970 TYPE I—Leadership Selection and Development**

Reynoldsburg — Titus 1:5 I'll give you leaders to train: Robbie Levy, Maxwell Providence, Hobson Nicholson, Joachim Immanual, Sampson Osimba Obwa, 15 women p(mc), p(dr).

**Life Purpose**—further clarified; not only missions, not only large sphere of influence, not only affecting people around world but also focusing on leaders.

## Example 2—Personal Destiny Log—CRJ continued

### 15. 1977 TYPE I/III—Prophetic Release

WIM — conflict with director; Don Bjorkman made the comment, "the WIM is too small for you; you need room to expand." p(c), p(dr)

**Major Role**—I am going to need further study to expand me for my major role—It took negative preparation to move me out. The role I was in would limit my potential. One man saw it.

### 16. 1980 TYPE I—Teaching/ Wide Sphere of Influence

Prayer day - seeking God's direction - 3 unsolicited calls: Fuller Evangelistic Association (Carl George was the head), WorldVision (David on my MA Thesis at CBC advised), CBC McQuilkin (letters going astray) principle - move to greater sphere of influence. p(da), p(dr).

**Life Purpose/ Major Role**—God opens door to next role by pointing out a principle for decision making at crucial boundary time and closing doors to those roles that are not it.

### 17. 1984 TYPE I—Selection and Development Must Be Deliberate

October - on jumbo jet returning from New Zealand; God's renewal of challenge to pray for high level leaders to train with a particular emphasis on upward development pattern (and union life). p(dr), p(fchg).

**Life Purpose/ Ultimate Contribution**—I must focus on developing high level leaders and must always ask and trust God to give them to me.

### 18. 1987 TYPE IV—God Affirms

CLTC - last day; Acts 20 deja vu; knew I would never see some of these again; knew out there was where my major impact would be; banner of affirmation; inward tears; committed afresh to be available. p(ma), p(df), p(dr).

**Life Purpose/ Ultimate Contribution/ Effective Methodology**—in and out ministry of developmental training abroad and all over will be a means for fulfilling life purpose.

### 19. 1994 TYPE IV—Repeated Anointing on In and Out Ministry

Workshops over past 4 years; hands laid on Richard and I. Fulfillment of a sense of destiny for Richard with me. Increased anointing in our workshops; much broader impact; yet penetrative. Malaysia/ Singapore—fulfillment of destiny longings of 30 years ago. p(df); indications of things to come—thoughts of Canada, all over U.S., India, repeated influence in Asia, desire to write, intentional mentoring (Simeon concentric circles) p(dr)

**Life Purpose/ Ultimate Contribution/ Effective Methodology**—repeated confirmation of ministry validates sense of destiny.

**Feedback—Constructing Your Personal Destiny Log**

1.  Examine the critical incidents you listed previously in the feedback on critical incidents.

    a.  For each critical incident list the date.

    b.  For each critical incident, if a destiny processing item, identify which Type.

        ___ Type I
        ___ Type II
        ___ Type III
        ___ Type IV

    c.  For each critical incident give the incident some label that helps identify it in your mind.

    d.  For each critical incident describe the incident succinctly enough to remind you of what happened—not necessarily enough detail for others.

    e.  For each critical incident, ask yourself if it helped you understand something about your life purpose, major role, effective   methodology, or ultimate contribution. (For the most part we are primarily concerned with critical incidents which tell us about life purpose).

2.  You should now have a list of items some of which help you learn about life purpose. Seek to describe your life purpose in terms of what these appropriate critical incidents have led you to see. Jot down the idea about life purpose that each of the appropriate incidents suggest.

3.  Now seek to condense the various ideas about life purpose into one coherent statement describing your life purpose.

**ANSWERS------------**

Your choice.

## Personal Life Mandate Syn. Personal Mission Statement, Mission Statement

Introduction — Covey's principle, *Begin With the End in Mind* challenges us as we seek to lead focused lives. It is important that we understand what it is we are shooting for. By deriving an explicit Personal Life Mandate from underlying assumptions and past processing which centers on focal issues we are bringing out into the open concepts to approve, modify, abrogate if necessary, and finally use them to become very intentional about our lives.

Definition — A Personal Life Mandate is a one to three page length description, made up of several paragraphs, which give in essence a person's life time goals in terms of what is known of the focal issues (Life Purpose, Major Role, Effective Methodology, and Ultimate Contribution) and using language which gives further intents toward these issues as well as describing being and doing achievements in harmony with these issues.

Comment — **Life purpose** is usually the dominant focal issue in most lives. It usually forms the topic around which the first paragraph of the Personal Life Mandate is given—called the introductory paragraph.

Comment — Being statements describe inner character or sanctification issues in the life which are intents for development. They underlie the *why* we do what we do and somewhat the *what* of what we do. Life purpose may well relate to the *when* of what we are doing. Doing statements flow from life purpose and ultimate contribution findings. They most relate to the *what* that we are about.

Comment — **Effective  methodologies** describe the major means whereby life purpose or ultimate contributions are realized. These relate to the *how* we operate or the means whereby we achieve or make progress in delivering our ministry.

Comment — **Major Role** recognizes that we may not be able to carry out life purpose and exploit our effective  methodologies unless we adjust our present role.

Comment — **Ultimate contributions** help set the boundaries for what we want to accomplish in terms of the big picture. They will relate to *means* and *ends*.

Comment — The actual writing form of the paragraphs, other than reflecting being and doing and focusing on focal issues can take on any unique form that fits the person and with which the person is comfortable. The basic issue is *does the Personal Life Mandate help the person to be more proactive and deliberate in focusing the life*. If so, the format is good. If not, change it.

Comment — Personal Life Mandates should be revised regularly. The core will change little but there will be clarification throughout life as the focal issues emerge.

Comment — Start with any rough draft Personal Life Mandate. A poor one is better than none. Expect it to be modified, become more specific and helpful as you develop. It will become a means for proactive decision making. Early ministry can be rather exploratory —focal issues are still up for grabs. Further experience will help you focus. Closed doors provide boundaries as focal issues are clarified. So don't be afraid to try things. As you move toward end game play say **yes** and **no** using your Personal Life Mandate as a screen for choosing ministry activity.

## Step 1—Writing Your Introductory Paragraph

| | |
|---|---|
| Introduction | Below is given the description of an introductory paragraph of a personal life mandate shown with several examples. |

Description       An <u>introductory paragraph</u> reflects what is known to date of life purpose and is usually made up of a core sentence, bold-faced, along with explanatory clauses or sentences.

| | |
|---|---|
| Comment | A standard form usually starts, "My purpose is to..." It will boldface the core essence of the life purpose and leave in normal type all other explanatory clauses or other broadening descriptions. |
| Comment | In the earliest formations of an introductory statement it is sometimes helpful to include in parenthesis the numbers of entries from your personal destiny log in the statement at appropriate places where the phrasing represents those destiny items. See example 3. |

Example 1. Personal Life Mandate—Introduction Paragraph: CRJ

**My purpose is to challenge, motivate, and enable**—via study and development of leadership concepts both empirically and from the Scriptures, by teaching of leadership concepts, by modeling of them, by mentoring of select leaders in them, and by providing available resources and materials—**high level leaders all over the world to finish well**.

Example 2. Personal Life Mandate—Introduction Paragraph: Samuel Brengle

**My life purpose is basically two-fold, to lead many non-believers to a personal saving knowledge of Christ and many believers to a holiness experience**[25] that will let them live lives well pleasing to the Lord. God has gifted me to speak publicly with effectiveness before all kinds of audiences. I want to live a consistent holy life so that my message, backed by my life, will carry great power. I will serve the whole body of Christ by promoting this salvation and holiness message in a wide itinerant public pulpit ministry all over the United States and abroad as God leads.

Example 3. Personal Life Mandate—Introduction Paragraph: TGS

In the context of an intimate relationship with God and based in a supportive community, **my purpose will involve** a transient cross-cultural ministry (2 ,5, 10, 11) which will focus on high level influence (1, 4) in the equipping of leadership both at individual and organizational levels. **My ministry will involve** stepping out in faith many times (3, 10), the use of modeling from my own life (6) and will be marked by the unusual blessing of God (7, 8, 9). I will come alongside leaders to encourage them to be who God created them to be, to reach their God given potential, and to minister effectively in their calling. I will endeavor to pursue creativity so that my leadership training will always be innovative for global trends and societal shifts.

Example 4. Personal Life Mandate—Introduction Paragraph: Apostle Paul

**My life purpose is to take the Gospel to Gentiles, primarily where no one else has yet gone, and see them turn from the power of Satan, the Kingdom of Darkness, to the power of Christ, the Kingdom of God.** I will primarily do this through the planting of churches and development of leaders to care for these churches. I recognize that my ministry is pioneer work and will become a model for many others.

---

[25]God called me long ago to serve my own organization so that I want, especially, many from my own organization, The Salvation Army, to experience this holiness experience. But I cannot contain it there. I want many others too to know the power of the Holy Spirit in their lives.

**Commentary On Life Purpose And Personal Life Mandate**

Introduction Since the life purpose is the dominant focal issue it should have a place of prominence in the Personal Life Mandate. The introductory paragraph is usually directed to give life purpose. All else in the Personal Life Mandate explains further how life purpose will work out.

Comment The more succinct and clear is a life purpose, the more likely it is to be interwoven into one's thinking and decision making. One way to make it succinct is to describe the life purpose in core phrases and expanded phases. Using the core phrases gives the succinct basic life purpose. The expanded phrases can clarify it further. One way of doing this is to bold face core phrases and write them in such a way as to make a stand-alone sentence describing life purpose. The expanded phrases can be added to clarify and modify or limit. These would not be boldfaced. So then the succinct life purpose can be read via the bold faced phrases. But the longer version includes the bold face and the added. All of the previous examples used core phrases and expanded phrases or sentences.

Example: **My purpose is to challenge, motivate, and enable**—via study and development of leadership concepts both empirically and from the Scriptures, by teaching of leadership concepts, by modeling of them, by mentoring of select leaders in them, and by providing available resources and materials—**high level leaders all over the world to finish well.**

This statement can be read succinctly and clearly as: **My purpose is to challenge, motivate, and enable high level leaders all over the world to finish well.** Or it can be read with the added clarification.

Comment The life purpose, introductory paragraph, is **the critical portion** of a personal life mandate.

Comment Because the seeds of life purpose are contained in destiny processing I will add basic definitions of the categories of destiny processing which occurs usually early in ministry, through out middles stages, and at the end of ministry.

**Destiny Preparation Process Item** Symbol: P(DP)

Introduction    The Destiny Pattern is a pattern with three aspects. One, God's preparatory work brings a growing awareness of a sense of destiny. Two, the awareness moves to conviction as God gives revelation and confirmation of it. Three, there is movement in accomplishment of that destiny which often culminates in destiny fulfilled. Destiny preparation describes the category of process items which are operative in aspect 1 of the destiny pattern. That is, God's preparatory work in instilling a growing awareness that a leader is going to be used in a special way to accomplish special purposes for God.

Definition      The <u>destiny preparation process item</u> describes a grouping of process items concerning significant acts, people, providential circumstances, or timing, which hint at some future or special significance to a life and, when studied in retrospect, add firmness to a growing awareness of sense of destiny in a leader's life.

Examples        Bertelsen (1985) lists the following specific kinds of destiny preparation process items:

- prophecy
- name
- prayer
- contract (oath)
- parent's sense of destiny for child

- faith act
- contextual items
- mentor
- birth circumstances
- preservation of life
- heritage

Example         A prophecy destiny preparation process item is the prophecy seen in Luke's account of the pre-birth prophecies about John the Baptist and Jesus. A contemporary example is the prophetic words spoken at Peter Kuzmic's birth by a visiting evangelist, "This boy will be a great preacher of the Gospel someday."

Example         Joseph's name signifies answer to prayer by God on Rachel's behalf. The timing of his birth was seen to be controlled by God. God was at work shaping Rachel as well as initiating a plan to later deliver Jacob's family.

Example         Hannah made a contract with God. She wanted a son. God wanted a transition leader.

Example         Moses parents by faith (Hebrews 11:23) saved his life in the small ark which was providentially discovered by Pharaoh's daughter.

**Feedback On Destiny Preparation Process Item**

1.  One danger of exposing a concept like sense of destiny or the destiny pattern is that these concepts might tend to make people overly ambitious. One of my students once said after class that he didn't believe in such a thing as a sense of destiny because it tends to puff up the ego of Christian workers. How would you handle such a criticism? What dangers do you see in introducing such concepts as sense of destiny and the concept of the destiny process item?

2.  Sometimes it is not clear that a destiny preparation process item has happened until some time in the future and one does some retrospective thinking. After some time the happening can be more clearly seen as part of a destiny pattern. Has this happened to you? If so, describe these destiny preparation experiences?

3.  Can you think of incidents from the Bible which illustrate destiny preparation process items for any of the specific items for which I didn't give examples? They are listed here:

    ____ a. contextual items
    ____ b. mentor
    ____ c. birth circumstances
    ____ d. parents (sense of destiny for child)
    ____ e. preservation of life.

Do any you can and give Bible references.

**ANSWERS------------**
See next page.

**Feedback On Destiny Preparation Process Item** continued

ANSWERS------------

1. I'll leave the meat of this answer for discussion. But I will say that if someone feels this way about such concepts I would advise them not to use the concept at all since they would be violating their conscience, which is sin. But I think it would be tragic to miss the added confirmation of God's working in a life, which can come through retrospective reflection on preparation items. I would advise also that one should not neglect a truth simply because it is abused by some.

2. I have identified 4 such experiences. I'll relate one.

| When | Means | Experience | Intent/Impact |
|---|---|---|---|
| 1966 | home Bible Study with a couple | Young Christian, not a charismatic, made a prophetic statement about me which I didn't recognize or understand | • to give me guidance later when I would need it.<br>• to encourage me that God was going to use me in a much wider sphere |

When this preparation process item occurred I did not know of the concept of a *word of prophecy*. As I walked out of a home Bible study, after teaching for about an hour, a young man said to me, "When you get your Doctorate we'll say we knew you when you were just a Bible teacher." At the time, I was an electrical engineer, a lay-leader in a church, with local church sphere of influence. The remark seemed out of context and strange. Yet it stuck with me and I would often think about it. There came a time during conflict processing when the remark came back to my mind with force and served as confirmation in the next step of guidance. I went on to get a doctorate and to a teaching ministry with a wide sphere of influence.

3. a. Paul's birth and early life in Tarsus--the third University city of its time. Roman citizenship.
   b. Gamaliel as a mentor for Paul.

All these in retrospect fall into a pattern of a Jewish leader being prepared to bridge into the Gentile world.

**Destiny Revelation/Confirmation Process Item** Symbol: P(DR)

Introduction    The Destiny Pattern moves through three aspects. One, God's preparatory
work brings a growing awareness of a sense of destiny. Two, the
awareness moves to conviction as God gives revelation and confirmation
of it. Three, there is movement in accomplishment of that destiny which
often culminates in destiny fulfilled. Destiny revelation/ confirmation
describes the category of process incidents or items which are operative in
aspect 2 of the destiny pattern, God's confirming of a destiny. God begins
to reveal more definitely what it may be, or at least give hints that there
will be a destiny, and that the leader will be used in a special way to
accomplish special purposes for God.

Definition    The <u>destiny revelation/confirmation process item</u> describes a grouping of
incidents or process items with an unusual sense of God's presence
working in them, and which are significant acts, people, providential
circumstances, or timing, which confirm a future destiny and perhaps
begin to clarify its nature.

Examples    Bertelsen (1985) lists the following specific kinds of destiny revelation
process incidents or items:

- revelatory act
- revelatory
  dream/vision
- revelatory
  prophecy
- word, obedience,
  integrity,
  faith checks

- all forms of sovereign guidance: double
  confirmation, divine contacts, mentors
- spiritual authority
- divine affirmation,
- destiny insight
- leadership backlash
- power items
- convergence

Example    Moses' experience at the burning bush was a revelatory act in which God
attracted Moses' attention and then revealed to him the next steps in his
destiny.

Example    Joseph's dreams in Genesis 37 are examples of revelatory dreams and
revelatory prophecy.

Example    The voice from heaven in John 12:27-29 illustrates divine affirmation used
as destiny confirmation.

Example    Ananias' vision in Acts 9:10-16 is an example of sovereign guidance given
for Paul (double confirmation) which was destiny revelation.

## Feedback On Destiny Revelation/Confirmation Process Item

1. What destiny revelation incident or item occurs in Acts 16:6-10? Identify it; then tell its basic function in Paul's destiny pattern.

2. Can you think of incidents from the Bible, which illustrate any other of the destiny revelation process items listed? (I realize that you are not yet familiar with some of the process items. But for the ones which are descriptive or self-evident, do this exercise.) Check any you can and give scripture references.

| | | | | |
|---|---|---|---|---|
| ___ a. | revelatory acts, dreams/vision, prophecy | | ___ e. | guidance items: sovereign guidance, double confirmation, divine contacts, affirmation |
| ___ b. | word, obedience, integrity, faith checks | | ___ f. | leadership backlash |
| | | | ___ g. | power items |
| ___ c. | divine affirmation | | ___ h. | convergence |
| ___ d. | spiritual authority affirmation | | | |

3. Later we will come back to this exercise after more of these process items have been defined. But for now can you describe any incidents in your own life which you believe may have been destiny revelation/confirmation?

**ANSWERS------------**

1. Revelatory dream or vision. From Acts 9, 22, and 26 we know that Paul had a destiny to take the Gospel to Gentiles. Here God gives clear guidance as to the next segment of Gentiles to receive the Gospel. This was guidance as well as confirmation to Paul that he is doing the right thing and fulfilling another step in his destiny.

2. c. divine affirmation: the voice on the Mount of Transfiguration; Mark 9:7,8. g. power items: resurrection of Lazarus in John 11.

3. I have identified several. I'll relate one. In a boundary phase in which I needed specific guidance I set aside a day of prayer to get alone with the Lord and seek his specific guidance. I worshipped and prayed and reflected on my past ministry experiences and then asked the Lord to give me specific guidance as to what he wanted me to do. Within the next week I had three unsolicited requests concerning possible ministry situations for me. These along with two I knew about made up five choices. Now the three unsolicited requests in response to specific prayer gave tremendous divine affirmation of destiny. But the major destiny confirmation item that came was a destiny insight. My reflection on past ministry and how God had moved me in boundary times revealed a pattern. All major boundary decisions in the past had reflected an increase in sphere of influence potential. I then ordered the five opportunities in light of this destiny insight and made my decision, which God later further confirmed.

**Destiny Fulfillment Process Item** symbol: P(DF)

| | |
|---|---|
| Introduction | The Destiny Pattern contains three aspects. One, God's preparatory work brings a growing awareness of a sense of destiny. Two, the awareness moves to conviction as God gives revelation of it. Three, there is confirmation and movement toward an accomplishment of that destiny which often culminates in destiny fulfilled. Destiny fulfillment describes the category of process items that are operative in aspect 3 of the destiny pattern—the confirmation and growing sense of awareness of God's completion of a specific destiny. |
| Definition | The <u>destiny fulfillment process item</u> describes a grouping of process items which are significant acts, people, providential circumstances, or timing which represent the completion of destiny processing that has gone on previously. |
| Example | Joseph. See Genesis 30:22-24 for destiny preparation item. See Genesis 37:5-8, 9-11 for destiny revelation. See Genesis 42-47 for destiny fulfillment. |
| Example | Paul. See Acts 9:15,16 for destiny revelation. See Acts 26:19 and all the Pauline epistles for various aspects of destiny fulfillment. |
| Kinds | Bertelsen (1985) lists the following specific kinds of destiny fulfillment process items: |

1. promise realization.
2. divine affirmation
3. obedience process items
4. word process items
5. faith acts
6. prophecy fulfillment.

| | |
|---|---|
| Use | Probably no greater satisfaction, from a ministry standpoint, can be derived than that of destiny fulfillment. To see destiny items occur over a lifetime (including preparation items and various revelation items) and then to see them come to fruition is to know that one's life counted for Christ. Destiny fulfillment is God's *well-done* while still here on earth. It is God's closure on a life that counted. |
| Timing | Ultimate destiny fulfillment occurs late in life, usually in the unique ministry time period. Mini-fulfillments can occur any time in Growth or Unique Ministry (e.g. fulfillment of a prophecy, realization of a promise, etc.). |

**Feedback On Destiny Fulfillment Process Item**

1.  What words indicate a destiny fulfillment process item in John 19:29,30? Trace at least one destiny item from destiny preparation and destiny revelation which show progress leading to this destiny fulfillment item.

    a. words symbolic of destiny fulfillment:

    b. destiny preparation item:

    c. destiny revelation item:

2.  Can you think of incidents from the Bible which illustrate any of the items suggested by Bertelsen as occurring in destiny fulfillment? Choose one, identify, and explain briefly the item.

    ___a. promise realization
    ___b. divine affirmation
    ___c. obedience process items
    ___d. word process items
    ___e. faith acts

3.  Have you experienced incidents indicating destiny fulfillment? Describe.

**ANSWERS------------**

1.  a. It is finished. Jesus had accomplished what the Father had sent him to do. b. See Luke 1:32,33 and Luke 2:33-35. c. John 12:27-33

2.  e. faith acts. See Joseph. Genesis 50:25,26 along with Joshua 24:32

3. Promise realization. In 1967 God affirmed a promise that someday I would be able to visit and preach in a chapel to be constructed at Christian Leader's Training College in Papua New Guinea. Students at Columbia Bible College were raising money to construct this chapel. My wife and I gave sacrificially to this project. In 1983 the promise was fulfilled. It was a moving moment for me, which confirmed God's continued goodness in my life.

**Commentary On Destiny Processing**

| | |
|---|---|
| Bertelsen | Bertelsen (1985), in conjunction with a special research project, did a comparative study of destiny process incidents in the lives of ten Biblical characters. These characters included Abraham, Joseph, Moses, David, Jeremiah, Daniel, Peter, Paul, Isaac and Jacob. All the characters were not studied with equal thoroughness, though all were done well. This study was definitive in terms of the concept, sense of destiny, the formulation of the destiny pattern, and identification of various process items that were observed to fit the destiny cluster. From this study the basic destiny pattern was derived. The various Biblical characters give ample evidence and illustrations of the pattern. |
| Example | Paul's life history follows this pattern. There was the destiny revelation experience on the road to Damascus. The three testimonies about this in Acts 9, 22, and 26 give expanded detail on it (see particularly Acts 26:19). The Galatians 1:15,16 shows retrospective reflection concerning destiny preparation. His closing words in II Timothy 4:6-8 show culmination of his destiny. |
| Comment | Often during aspect 2 of the destiny pattern, it is in retrospect, that a leader sees earlier process items with a sense of destiny focus. The growing conviction of a sense of destiny is significantly re-enforced, which is the major development task of aspect 2 of the pattern. |
| Importance | No leader of any significance, that has been studied, and for which there is ample data, has failed to have one or more important destiny experiences. It is the accumulation of destiny experiences that frequently give one the vision that becomes the ultimate contribution for a life. |
| Comment | We should at least be aware of a variety of ways in which God intervenes in the destiny of a leader. They might well apply in our own lives. They may give us insights as we help develop other leaders. |
| Comment | Later when the mentoring process item is discussed, I will suggest that one thing a mentor can do to help a young emerging leader is to sensitize that leader to sense of destiny experiences. A growing sense of destiny is one of the major lessons seen in effective leader's lives. |
| Major Lesson | EFFECTIVE LEADERS EVINCE A GROWING AWARENESS OF THEIR SENSE OF DESTINY. |

**Commentary on Chapter 3. Moving Toward Life Purpose**

Introduction     Life purpose is the dominant focal issue in a leader's life. Destiny processing provides the seedbed for discovering life purpose. A study of destiny processing will provide insights into life purpose. A synthesizing of these findings allows one to derive a draft of an introductory paragraph of one's Personal Life Mandate.

Comment          The more thorough is a leader's understanding of destiny processing, the easier it will be to identify critical incidents that involve sense of destiny. This chapter has categorized 4 general types of destiny processing: awe–inspiring interventions of God, indirect influences through or from others, circumstantial (providential), apparent repeated blessing of God.

Comment          Further, the chapter pointed out a destiny pattern which involved early destiny processing called destiny preparation, on-going destiny processing called destiny revelation, and culminating items of destiny processing called destiny fulfillment.

Comment          All leaders will have destiny processing but not all leaders recognize this nor do all leaders have Type I experiences. Awareness of this shaping activity of God may indeed awaken a need for some leader to hunger for and want Type I experiences. God can grant this.

Comment          At this point in the manual you have at least an initial sense of your life purpose. Ensuing chapters will help you identify other of the focal issues. As you do so you will continue to add to your Personal Life Mandate.

(This page is deliberately left blank.)

# Chapter 4 Seeing Effective Methodologies

Introduction    While life purpose forms the prime integrating factor around which a focused life operates there has to be a way to deliver ministry to people. It is one thing to have a high sounding life purpose. It is another thing to effectively carry out ministry to people flowing from that life purpose. How do you do that? God frequently gives break–through concepts that allow a leader to do something well. We call these break–through concepts **ministry insights.** We repeatedly find ways to use these ministry insights and when we do they become for us, **Effective Methodologies. Effective Methodologies** then are those ministry insights which fit who we are, help us carry out our life purpose, and become effective vehicles for us to carry out ministry. It is these kinds of breakthroughs that concern us in this chapter.

All leaders have ministry insights. These break–throughs will come all during ministry. We may get them in any of the age brackets. But it is in the latter age brackets [40-50 and 50-60] that we really realize what we have and how powerful they can be if we focus on them. It is in the years 50-60 that we should reflect back and conserve those major breakthrough insights that we have gained in the past by converting them into **Effective Methodologies.** In other words, we should use them to death—especially as we see their purpose in focusing our lives.

Overview    In this chapter you will be introduced to:

- the overall flowchart leading to assessment of a focused life, and where this chapter fits in that assessment,
- the time-line—as it relates to ministry insights,
- the notion of ministry insights and effective methodologies,
- the personal ministry insights log,
- an example of personal ministry insights log,
- step 2 in writing your personal life mandate—using your personal ministry log to write paragraphs that describe some of your ministry insights and how you intend to use them for life purpose.

End Result    By the conclusion of this chapter you will not only have a tentative introductory paragraph reflecting your life purpose (done in the last chapter) but you will have added one or more paragraphs describing your intents for using effective methodologies to your personal life mandate.

**Flowchart—Overview Of Assessment**

# Basic Flow Chart
# For Moving Toward A Focused Life
|
|

Basic shaping of life and basic ministry experience
lead to **indications** of:

In this chapter you are here --->
- life purpose (**LP**),
- effective methodologies (**EM**),
- major role (**MR**),
- ultimate contributions (**UC**).
|
|

which allow the drafting of a **tentative**
**Personal Life Mandate**

In this chapter you are here --->
- intro paragraph—life purpose (**LP**)
- additional paragraphs—intent to use ministry insights as effective methodologies (**EM**)
|
|

And the Setting of **Intermediate Goals**
Along 5 Different Age-Groupings
|
|

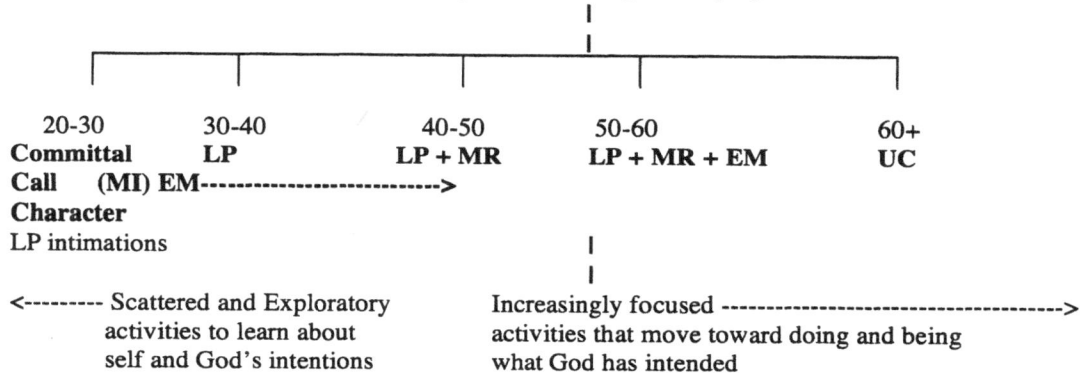

| 20-30 | 30-40 | 40-50 | 50-60 | 60+ |
|-------|-------|-------|-------|-----|
| **Committal** | **LP** | **LP + MR** | **LP + MR + EM** | **UC** |
| **Call**   (MI) EM----------------------> | | | | |
| **Character** | | | | |
| LP intimations | | | | |

|

<--------- Scattered and Exploratory          Increasingly focused ------------------------------------>
activities to learn about                     activities that move toward doing and being
self and God's intentions                     what God has intended
|
|

which results in a tentative rough draft of a Personal Life Mandate
with Appropriate Paragraphs and ideas about the next several years—which will vary
from scattered to focused depending on which age bracket you are
and which will eventually build toward long term goals
|

Resulting in Movement Toward a More
|

# FOCUSED LIFE

## Time-Line And Ministry Insights

Introduction      This chapter will suggest that recognition of special ministry experiences, called ministry insights, will be the seedbed of effective methodologies. The best way to do this is by use of a time-line. All leaders must find ways to use their giftedness and what they have learned about ministry to do ministry well. Again, a time-line is the place to think through and integrate these ministry ideas.

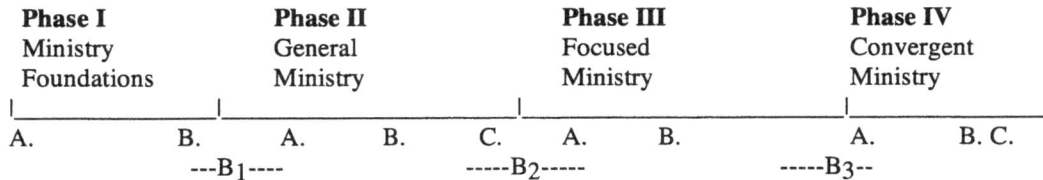

| **Phase I** | **Phase II** | **Phase III** | **Phase IV** |
|---|---|---|---|
| Ministry | General | Focused | Convergent |
| Foundations | Ministry | Ministry | Ministry |

```
|_____|_____|_____|_____|
A.            B.    A.        B.      C.    A.        B.          A.        B. C.
              ---B1----              -----B2-----              -----B3--
```

Where the sub-phases are called:

### Phase I

A. Sovereign Foundations — (13-20 years) —early shaping of character/ personality

B. Leadership Transition (3-6 years) —a time in which first steps in ministry are done

*The initial breakthroughs in how to do ministry usually involve use of giftedness with individuals or small groups. Frequently they have to do with how to present truth from God's word in an effective manner.*

### Phase II

A. Provisional Ministry    (2-6 years) —the first attempts at full time ministry assignments; it is provisional because it might not last, that is, the leader may not stay in ministry.

*Further breakthroughs usually come here and they have to do with the importance of relationships and organizational structures through which we work. Conflict processing usually forces us to learn quickly.*

B. Growth Ministry (6-8 years) —ministry utilizing known giftedness with efficiency; giftedness and role issues are learned; this sub-phase is more for developing the leader than the ministry which is accomplished.

*All kinds of ministry insights come here as we explore further different roles and discover more of our giftedness.*

C. Competent Ministry<— (2-6 years) —>operating out of giftedness in roles that fit that giftedness produces excellent results; still to be determined is the potential level of influence.

*It is here that we begin to use some of the accumulated ministry insights repeatedly. They become effective methodologies.*

### Phase III

A. Role Transition—There is movement toward compatibility between role, giftedness and influence-mix profile. There is shaping of a role more ideally suited to giftedness and challenge toward influence-mix.

B. Unique Ministry—ministering effectively as well as efficiently with giftedness. (Role plus unique may last 3-12 years)

*It is here that we get maximum benefit from effective methodologies. We reflect back and remember some used in the past. We organize our ministry around them. We exploit them.*

### Phase IV

A. Special Guidance—movement toward a role focusing on ultimate contribution

B. Convergent Ministry—fulfilling a sense of destiny/ ultimate contribution

C. Afterglow—fall out effects of a life well lived; spiritual authority dominant

And the boundaries are called: $B_1$ the logistics barrier–moving from non-full-time Christian role to a full time paid Christian role; $B_2$ the strategic barrier/ Doing to Being–recognizing that fulfillment does not come from achievement alone but from ministry which flows out of being; $B_3$ The Convergence Springboard–moving into a focused life role that brings about very effective ministry.

## Sample Time-Line With Hints Toward Effective Methodologies

| I. NAÏVE NATURAL LEADER | II. NATURAL TO SPIRITUAL LEADER | III. DESTINY LEADERSHIP |
|---|---|---|

|---------------|---------------|---------------|

| 1936 | 1964 | 1970 34 | 1974 38 | 1978-1981 Geographical Convergence | 1987-1988 | Present |
|---|---|---|---|---|---|---|
| Age | 28 | 34 | 38 | 43-45 | 51, 52 | |

A. (1936-57)
Great Depression Values,
Sovereign Foundations

A. (1971-74)
The Minors—Educational Technology
Perspectives

A. (1981-87)
The Majors—Developing Content &
Effective Methodology for Teaching;
Researching Leadership and
Developmental Framework

B. (1957-64)
Marriage, Early Career

B. (1974-79)
Authority Lessons, Learning to
Produce Materials

B. (1988-1993)
Influence-Mix Challenge; Expansion
by Taking Concepts Out; Writing via
Barnabus

C. (1964-70)
Transition to Ministry, Home
Bible Study Experience

C. (1979-81)
Broadening—Getting Missiological
Perspective

C. (1994—present)
Reflection and Intentionality Toward
Destiny Fulfillment; Developing
Others To Carry Out My Legacy

## Ministry Insights ... Effective Methodology Indications

1964-1970
  Personal Ministry
  Informal Theorem
  Discipleship Mentor
    1965 Sodality,
    Means For Getting
    Ministry Out
      1968 Slot/
      Filler Insight

1970-72
Materials Preparation; educational
technology insights

    1975 Information Mapping;
    The Organization of
    Information In Materials

      1981ff Many Teaching
      Insights Via O.J.T and
      Reflection; 3 Formations; 4
      Learning Domains;
      N.B. Spiritual Formation;
      Applying Informal
      Theorem in Academic
      Setting; see teaching
      manual for details

1981-1990
Materials Continuum;
Deliberation in Writing;

1986-87 Materials Publishing via
Barnabas Publishers

    1991 Mentoring Intentionality

    1991-1994 Workshop Technology

      1994 Slots/ Filler
Communication Layout; Stump Speech
Layered Concept;

        1994-2005 Bible Centered
        Leadership Concepts,
        especially leadership genre
        and studying Bible for
        leadership findings

**Ministry Insights**
**Effective Methodology Defined**

| | |
|---|---|
| Introduction | A leader usually discovers personal insights on how to do ministry well. Some of these ministry insights become polished and reused frequently so that the leader effectively delivers his/her ministry. Such a concept when exploited over a life time becomes a Effective methodology. Most focused leaders will have several ministry insights or even a cluster of them which form a main means for delivering ministry. |
| Definition | A <u>ministry insight</u> is some breakthrough a leader gets concerning how to personally do ministry well. |
| Definition | A <u>effective methodology</u> is some ministry insight around which the leader can pass on to others the essentials of doing something or using something or being something, that is, a means of effectively delivering some important ministry of that leader which enhances life purpose or moves toward ultimate contribution. It represents repeated use of a ministry insight and recognition that the ministry insight should be used with effectiveness. |
| Example: | I will use personal counseling, one-on-one, with a framework derived from Larry Crabb to help people move to wholeness. |
| Example: | The basic methodology for moving people in literacy is captured in the phrase, each one teach one. This will be the major force of my efforts. If I can motivate those who have just learned to read and are excited about it to teach others I will have a mechanism which can expand exponentially. And I have found some important techniques for doing this. |
| Example: | A workshop format which includes pre-workshop introduction to concepts, intensive application of them at the workshop in a small group interactive setting, and post-workshop application in-depth of some concept will be the main methodology for delivering off campus ministry. |
| Example: | Development of self-study materials for use in supplementing classes and workshops. |
| Example: | A framework for the development of materials along a continuum all the way from definitions of concepts all the way up to classical texts. |
| Example: | Abilities to lead a small group into discovering their uniqueness in spirituality and taking steps to develop it. |
| Example: | Abilities to organize a ministry so that it runs efficiently. |
| Comment | Leaders discover ministry insights, breakthroughs in how to deliver ministry effectively. This will happen as they get varied experience in ministry and learn to use giftedness effectively. Some of these ministry insights will be used for a period of time while a given role is in place and may not come into play again. Others will find repeated use in varied ministry settings. Such repeated use of ministry insights in all kinds of ministry efforts are candidates for effective methodologies. |
| Comment | This methodology becomes a major means which moves people toward results in line with life purposes or ultimate contributions. |

**Feedback On Effective Methodology**

1. Review again the generalized ministry time-line that was given in chapter 1. In your opinion when do you think the most ministry insights are recognized. Order the three most important time periods for getting ministry insights. Use 1 for most, 2 for next most, and 3 for the next. Put 0 beside the time period which is least likely to produce new ministry insights.

____A.  Sovereign Foundations -- (13-20 years)--early shaping of character/ personality
____B.  Leadership Transition (3-6 years)--a time in which first steps in ministry are done
**Phase II**
____A.  Provisional Ministry  (2-6 years) --the first attempts at full time ministry assignments; it is provisional because it might not last
____B.  Growth Ministry (6-8 years)--ministry utilizing known giftedness with efficiency; giftedness and role issues are learned; this sub-phase is more for developing the leader than the ministry which is accomplished.
____C.  Competent Ministry<-- (2-6 years) -->operating out of giftedness in roles that fit that giftedness produces excellent results; still to be determined is the influence-mix profile.
**Phase III**
____A.  Role Transition--There is movement toward compatibility between role, giftedness and influence-mix profile. There is shaping of a role more ideally suited to giftedness and challenge toward influence-mix.
____B.  Unique Ministry--ministering effectively as well as efficiently with giftedness. (Role plus unique may last 3-12 years)
**Phase IV**
____A.  Special Guidance--movement toward a role focusing on ultimate contribution
____B.  Convergent Ministry--fulfilling a sense of destiny/ ultimate contribution
____C.  Afterglow--fall out effects of a life well lived; spiritual authority dominant

2. Under each sub-phase list by topic heading your most important ministry insights.

____(1).  Sovereign Foundations -- (13-20 years):
____(2).  Leadership Transition (3-6 years):
____(3).  Provisional Ministry  (2-6 years):
____(4).  Growth Ministry (6-8 years):
____(5).  Competent Ministry<-- (2-6 years):
____(6).  Unique Ministry--:

**ANSWERS------------**

1.  _1_B. Growth Ministry (6-8 years)
    _2_A. Provisional Ministry (2-6 years)
    _3_B. Leadership Transition (3-6 years)
    _0_C. Afterglow

2.  Your choice.

## Examples of Ministry Insights—CRJ

Introduction     Below are listed some different kinds of ministry insights. Note that they vary quite a bit over a range of topics. But all helped the leader to know more about ministry and how to do it better.

1. **1964 Personal Individual Ministry—Its Power**
   Personal Ministry—Dollar, Trottman, "Where's your man?"
   One to one, discipleship focus, indirect influence, long term influence, habit of looking for people who were hungry to be discipled, informal training methodology, ministry philosophy—always be developing someone, things to do and not to do when working with an individual, spouse jealousy, time commitment, etc.

2. **1964  Committed Small Group—Its Power**
   Dedicated Band—Nav contacts, Lockbourne Air Force Base, saw power of small group really committed, small group pressure, accountability, importance of leader modeling what is being demanded of others.

3. **1965  Entry Unit; Developmental Unit**
   Home Bible studies, vehicles for low key evangelism, evangelistic entry structure, power in word to interest people, structure for second committal beyond the regular, place for gifts to emerge at lowest levels, fishing pool, dispersal structure (church scattered)

4. **1964-1970 Public Non-formal Training**
   Bible Conference Ministry at Reynoldsburg Bible Mission Baptist Church, a structure for utilizing networking power, going beyond provincialism in a local church, cross-pollination, way of promoting study of Bible, use of non-formal training model, a church structured to show importance of mastering the word of God (challenged church membership to read through the Bible each year, one whole day read the Bible through corporately, home Bible classes, Radio Ministry of Bible classes, Bible tapes of many great teachers, Bible Commentaries and other books available, small book store), will see many emerging leaders (since leaders will be word gifted people) thrust forth into full time ministry, Bible teacher models (how, content focus, life, relational presence; some included: George Mundell, Marmion Lowe, Norman Geisler, Herman Hoyt, Joe Temple).

5. **1965,66 Small Group for Training**
   Preacher Boys class, committal (6:00-8:00 a.m. on Saturday mornings), sense of eliteness, went through Pentateuch verse by verse in two years, verse by verse teaching allows for all kinds of ministry philosophy input, knowing the Pentateuch allows an excellent foundation for other parts of the Bible. Out of this insight I have eventually designed many kinds of small groups including mentoring groups.

6. **1965,1966 Informal On-The-Job Ministry Training Approach: Release of Pulpit**
   Most pastors guard their pulpit jealously, opening up the pulpit to developing leaders is an outstanding way of helping them emerge into leadership, Harold Dollar, myself, Max Prouty, Jeff Imbach (great series on the Levitical Offerings), basic communication skills.

## Examples of Ministry Insights—CRJ continued

7.  **1965, 1966 Public Communication Approach: Public Testimony Time**
    Expression deepens impression, brings closure to events, challenges others, allows giftedness to operate at lowest levels, leaders emerge, day of prayer at CBC—brought closure by testimony time.

8.  **1966, 1967 Board of Deacons; Church Government**
    Conflict in holding pastor accountable, danger in putting new Christians on board too early, introduction to many problems in local church ministry, the down side of ministry (Home Bible studies, etc. were the upside), the nitty-gritty details of what it takes to maintain a ministry.

9.  **1967 Sodality on Side**
    L. Thompson sodality; Pastor Thompson had a sodality on the side to promote and do his Radio Bible Ministry; printing of mimeographed materials, outside conference ministry, etc. Sodalities within sodalities are often needed to get around what otherwise would be restrictions to ministry.

10. **1966, 1967 Resource Center**
    Pastor Thompson maintained a book table, track rack, lending book library, lending tape library. Materials for developing people should be available and distributed freely. I could borrow books, tapes, tape recorders, etc.

11. **1967, 1968 Ministry Communicational Approach—Sells' Closure Methodology**
    Clincher phrases, clincher choruses and songs, closure prayer (committal time), always applied truth and made us feel the power of the Spirit applying truth

12. **1967-70 Ministry Communicational Approach; Integrative Overview**
    Hatch integrative overview, symbols capturing concepts, need to communicate overall in a connected step-by-step way.

13. **1971, 1972 JBC: Delivery System**
    Decentralized Formal Training—TEE, problems of producing materials, power in autodidactic materials, freeing up of class time for motivational, etc. problems when philosophy is not followed, the realization that people in ministry do not habitually study and use the word of God

14. **1972, 1973 And Later—Informal Power Structures/ Tactical Versus Strategic**
    What may be correct tactically may not be so strategically. Removed E. V. Thompson from teaching Romans class, his big gun; Imbach taught (brilliant teacher; knew Victorious life teaching), later E. V. was on executive leadership team of mission (and didn't have too good a view of me, affected many decisions about me—including isolation and leaving mission)

15. **1970-1973 JBC—Institutional insights: Indigenous Leadership**
    Importance of indigenous leadership (Guyana), country went socialistic, work permits, on-going ministry, struggle with constituency problem, finances, change in need yet how to change institution.

## Examples of Ministry Insights—CRJ continued

16. **1973-1975 Institutional Insight: Sodality Within Sodality, Worldteam, Miami:**
Sodality, LRC; with a sodality, specific tasks may need to be spun off in a sodality which is quasi-autonomous within a sodality, communication of its purposes and policies and procedures, must be given to parent sodality, need for resourcing missionaries on field, how to produce materials, importance of literary processing and networking power.

17. **1975-1979 Ministry Structures: House Church**
South Dade Bible Chapel, Miami: House Church Structures: renewal effort in Bible Church, essence of house church, plurality of leaders, implementing change as one among many, change dynamics—intervention time (Gene Getz).

18. **1977, 1978 Organizational Power**
Executive leadership team at WorldTeam; small groups not a panacea, executive leadership team supposedly modeling this for whole mission, could not make it work when crunch came.

19. **1981 Philosophical Structures—Ecclesiology**
FTS, Ecclesiology: McGavran paper (authority insights processing), seeing the church in terms of domains and functions, broadening my view on how it may manifest itself.

20. **1981 Organizational Concept; Structural Time**
FTS, Structural time concept: organizational (sodality/modality dynamics and interplay), led to seeing other patterns (Greiner, Flamholtz, Schein, Mintzberg, Adizes, etc.).

21. **1986, 1987 Organizational Paradigm**
FTS, Mintzberg, Adizes—Organizational structures; major paradigms for viewing Christian organizations (sodalities or modalities). See bibliography for Mintzberg and Adizes.

22. **1987, 1988 Organizational Means**
FTS, Power and Spiritual Authority: Mintzberg and Wrong, and DeGeorge, Boards. See bibliography Mintzberg.

23. **1983, 1989 Strategic Planning: Ministry Structures**
JCGI, Vertical Structures, penetration evangelism

24. **1981-1990 Organizational Structures: Networks**
SWM, networking power, importance of knowing people of status all around the world, door openers.
**Effective Methodology**: personal ministry in lives here at SWM will lead to ministry abroad. Look for doors to open to penetrate groups that God wants us to penetrate.

## Examples of Ministry Insights—CRJ continued

25. **1970-1989 Materials Preparation—The Materials Continuum**
    Parables materials for H.S. class; then educational technology training; programmed materials; information mapping. Various kinds of writing; actual development of the continuum. Continuous movement along the continuum; getting partnerships in writing to further proliferate the concepts. **Effective Methodology**: Constantly be aware of where some item is along continuum; update; set out new projects along the continuum.

26. **1990-1994 Cluster Group Training**
    Effective penetration of small groups with leadership concepts; exploring with various kinds of models
    **Effective Methodology**: Choose only situations that allow for penetration designs. The pre/intensive/ post works well. Use it whenever possible. Cluster groups work best where individuals have already been in a mentoring relationship with facilitator.

27. **1990-1994 Power of Mentoring**
    Experimented with various forms of individual mentoring as well as groups; very powerful means of training. Out of this came **Connecting** and **The Mentor Handbook**. See bibliography. **Effective Methodology**: Deliberately mentor—Use all three forms of connecting; select life time mentorees and proactively assess and challenge to growth through letters of intent; use Simeon's circles of intimacy as a guideline.

28. **1994 Boards That Count**
    Principles for evaluating and designing board structures; later this insight deepened with discovery of Carver's book. See bibliography.
    **Effective Methodology**: Focus on one or two organizations and penetrate them with concepts via the general director; serve on board to do this. Help boards do meaningful functions.

## Personal Ministry Insights Log

Introduction    Below is given a suggested layout for keeping a record of your ministry insights.

Description    A <u>ministry insights log</u> is a personal record of ministry insights that have been breakthroughs for ministry for a leader.

Format    A basic format contains Date, label, brief explanation, and reflection toward how the insight is moving toward a effective methodology and helps with focus.

## Format for Personal Ministry Insights Log
1.    Date, Label Pinpointing Essence,
    Brief Explanation
    Reflection toward Effective Methodology or Personal Life Mandate

## Examples Entries of Personal Ministry Insights Log—CRJ

24.    **1981-1990 Organizational Structures: Networks**
    SWM, networking power, importance of knowing people of status all around the world, door openers.
    **Effective Methodology**: personal ministry in lives here at SWM will lead to ministry abroad.  Look for doors to open to penetrate groups that God wants us to penetrate.

25.    **1970-1989  Materials Preparation--the materials continuum**
    Parables materials for H.S. class; then educational technology training; programmed materials; information mapping. Various kinds of writing; actual development of the continuum.  Continuous movement along the continuum; getting partnerships in writing to further proliferate the concepts.
    **Effective Methodology**:  Constantly be aware of where some item is along continuum; update; set out new projects along the continuum;

26.    **1990-1994  Cluster Group Training**
    effective penetration of small groups with leadership concepts; exploring with various kinds of models
    **Effective Methodology**:  Choose only situations that allow for penetration designs.

27.    **1990-1994  Power of Mentoring**
    Experimented with various forms of individual mentoring as well as groups; very powerful means of training.
    **Effective Methodology**:  Deliberately mentor—use all three forms of connecting; select life time mentorees and proactively assess and challenge to growth through letters of intent;  use Simeon's circles of intimacy as a guideline.

28.    **1994  Boards that Count**
    Principles for evaluating and designing board structures.
    **Effective Methodology**:  Focus on one or two organizations and penetrate them with concepts via the general director; serve on board to do this.  Help boards do meaningful functions.

**Feedback on Personal Log for Ministry Insights**

1.  Develop your own ministry insights log. Think back over your previous experience and build your log using the following format: (Do this on separate pages as it may well take 2 or 3 pages.

> 1.  Date, Label Pinpointing Essence,
>        Brief Explanation
>        Reflection toward Effective Methodology or Personal Life

Mandate

> 2.  Date, Label Pinpointing Essence,
>        Brief Explanation
>        Reflection toward Effective Methodology or Personal Life

Mandate

> 3. etc.

2.  Now examine your log and indicate which of these ministry insights are most likely to or ought to become Effective methodologies.

3.  For each of the potential Effective methodologies—identify a descriptive phrase that you could possibly use somewhere in your Personal Life Mandate.

**ANSWERS------------**
Your choice.

**Personal Life Mandate** Syn. Personal Mission Statement, Mission Statement

| | |
|---|---|
| Introduction | Covey's principle, *Begin With the End in Mind* challenges us as we seek to lead focused lives. It is important that we understand what it is we are shooting for. By deriving an explicit Personal Life Mandate from underlying assumptions and past processing which centers on focal issues we are bringing out into the open concepts to approve, modify, abrogate if necessary, and finally use them to become very intentional about our lives. |
| Definition | A <u>Personal Life Mandate</u> is a one to three page length description, made up of several paragraphs, which give in essence a person's life time goals in terms of what is known of the focal issues (Life Purpose, Major Role, Effective Methodology, and Ultimate Contribution) and using language which gives further intents toward these issues as well as describing being and doing achievements in harmony with these issues. |
| Comment | **Life purpose** is usually the dominant focal issue in most lives. It usually forms the topic around which the first paragraph of the Personal Life Mandate is given—called the introductory paragraph. |
| Comment | Being statements describe inner character or sanctification issues in the life which are intents for development. They underlie the *why* we do what we do and somewhat the *what* of what we do. Life purpose may well relate to the *when* of what we are doing. Doing statements flow from life purpose and ultimate contribution findings. They most relate to the *what* that we are about. |
| Comment | **Effective methodologies** describe the major means whereby life purpose or ultimate contributions are realized. These relate to the *how* we operate or the means whereby we achieve or make progress in delivering our ministry. |
| Comment | **Major Role** recognizes that we may not be able to carry out life purpose and exploit our Effective methodologies unless we adjust our present role. |
| Comment | **Ultimate contributions** help set the boundaries for what we want to accomplish in terms of the big picture. They will relate to *means* and *ends*. |
| Comment | The actual writing form of the paragraphs, other than reflecting being and doing and focusing on focal issues can take on any unique form that fits the person and with which the person is comfortable. The basic issue is *does the Personal Life Mandate help the person to be more proactive and deliberate in focusing the life*. If so, the format is good. If not, change it. |
| Comment | Personal Life Mandates should be revised regularly. The core will change little but there will be clarification throughout life as the focal issues emerge. |
| Comment | Start with any rough draft Personal Life Mandate. A poor one is better than none. Expect it to be modified, become more specific and helpful as you develop. It will become a means for proactive decision making. Early ministry can be rather exploratory —focal issues are still up for grabs. Further experience will help you focus. Closed doors provide boundaries as focal issues are clarified. So don't be afraid to try things. As you move toward end game play say **yes** and **no** using your Personal Life Mandate as a screen for choosing ministry activity. |

## Step 2—Describe Your Effective Methodology in Terms of Intents

Introduction  The paragraph(s) representing use of effective methodologies are most diverse of all. Sometimes they are not unique paragraphs but are simply descriptive phrases suggesting intents, which are woven into the other paragraphs. At other times several whole paragraphs give a listing of breakthroughs and the intents for use of them in ministry.

Procedure  Indicate in what way you plan to deliver ministry in terms of unique methodologies either by separate paragraphs or by including descriptive phraseology in the other paragraphs. Go back to your Personal Life Mandate statement thus far. Add to your statement phrases or a new paragraph, which gives some hint at effective methodologies. Sometimes it is better to wait till you have Step 3 Major Role and Step 4 Ultimate Contributions. Then simply weave into what you have, indications of how effective methodology will relate to major role and ultimate contribution.

Format  Those who use a paragraph(s) sometimes have a format, "Some things I have learned about ministering effectively include ..." or "I intend to repeatedly use...which I have found to be a very effective way for me to minister" or "Several things I have learned about making my ministry more effective include: ..."

Example  God has given me some natural abilities which I intend to use more consciously in my ministry. Because I have relational skills I am going to explore much more the use of peer mentoring and peer groups in mentoring.

Example  Several things I have learned about making my ministry more effective include: the deliberate use of two design models—one for assessing what is in focus, and the other for assessing balanced learning in terms of learning domains—for designing any training whether formal, non-formal or informal, whether a public presentation, a single session of input, a workshop, a conference, or an entire course in a formal setting; the special use of motivational techniques in a formal classroom setting like attention getters and closure exercises; the special design of small groups into a formal course situation; the use of ad hoc small groups on the spot to cause reflection and penetration of an idea; a writing continuum to guide me as I prepare materials; the importance of having good written materials to carry cognitive input; the use of in-depth workshops which require pre-work and post-work; the use of a team both for training and in-depth penetration of ideas in a workshop setting; one-on-one personal time in light of an ideation framework—a perspective; the use of informality in all of my ministry efforts; the use of modeling and telling of stories to move the affect; the use of concentric circles of influence to both screen and become increasingly proactive in my mentoring efforts; the use of "by invitation only" small groups for combining mentor efforts; the development of various kinds of helps for supplementing my administrative work as I mentor many people; . I intend to use these various methodologies in a much more conscious way as I fulfill my life purpose of selecting, developing, and releasing quality leaders toward good finishes.

**Step 2—Describe Your Effective Methodology in Terms of Intents** continued

Example      Examine Samuel Brengle's Personal Life Mandate. Note the boldfaced phrases interwoven in other paragraphs. These represent effective methodologies in his ministry intents.

My life purpose is basically two-fold, to lead many non-believers to a personal saving knowledge of Christ and many believers to a **holiness experience**[26] that will let them live lives well pleasing to the Lord. God has gifted me to **speak publicly with effectiveness** before all kinds of audiences. I want to live a consistent holy life so that my message, backed by my life, will carry great power. I will serve the whole body of Christ by promoting this salvation and holiness message in a wide itinerant public pulpit ministry all over the United States and abroad as God leads.

I will fulfill this life purpose through a special itinerant ministry role—a traveling evangelist and holiness preacher—which is not only authorized but supported and financed by my organization, The Salvation Army, who have freed me to minister with effectiveness in this role. I intend always to use my ministry to move people to make **significant decisions**[27] either for Christ or for holiness.

In addition to public ministry I intend at every opportunity, public and private, to promote my two fold message. I will endeavor to have personal ministry whenever and wherever I can. I will always endeavor to minister for results in lives by giving people opportunity to respond to God.

Wherever possible I will develop simple materials that can be used by the common people that I speak to—materials that will help them understand evangelism and holiness.

I want the **fragrance of my life to live on and inspire others to persevere and finish well**.[28]

Example      I intend to repeatedly use the *technique of blessing,* which flows out of my revelatory gifting both in a one-on-one setting and in large groups which I have found to be a very effective way for me to minister hope and see individuals and groups step out in faith, expecting God to work through them.

Example      Two things I have learned about ministry thus far, that I want to explore further, include facilitating techniques in a small group and a methodology for designing serendipity Bible studies in the Psalms. I intend to get more deliberate in my involvement in small groups and in getting more people to study the Psalms for application.

---

[26]God called me long ago to serve my own organization so that I want, especially, many from my own organization, The Salvation Army, to experience this holiness experience. But I can not contain it there I want many others too to know the power of the Holy Spirit in their lives.

[27]I have learned how to use the penitent form, a special form of altar call, to help people actually enter into salvation and holiness. I have learned how in personal conversation to listen to the Holy Spirit and move people toward what He wants to do. I am always seeking to move them to decisions that will affect their lives.

[28]I have come to recognize that a consistent life lived openly and transparently before people, brings impact.

### Example 2. CRJ—Effective Methodology Phrases

Introduction    Again the boldfaced phrases indicate intents for effective methodologies.

My purpose is to challenge, motivate, and enable—via study and **development of leadership concepts** both empirically and from the Scriptures, by teaching of leadership concepts, by **modeling of them**, by mentoring of select leaders in them, and by providing **available resources and materials**—high level leaders all over the world to finish well.

I intend to continue **researching** personal leadership development theory and organizational or church leadership and **write articles, papers, manuals, popular books and texts** which will provide the conceptual frameworks that will challenge, motivate and enable.  I plan to have a strong Biblical emphasis for my leadership findings.  The conceptual framework, my leadership findings, will have powerful force alone to challenge, motivate, and enable—by giving perspective.

In addition to the conceptual framework being developed I will be involved in promoting the ideas via **teaching** them, by **training others to teach them**, and by **sponsoring others to teach** them.  Further I recognize that I must be what I am talking about.  **Modeling** will be a high priority with me.  Therefore I want to live an exemplary life that counts for Christ:

- by centering my life in Christ and hence developing a spirituality flowing from Him,
- by modeling a teaching lifestyle which embodies this spirituality, flows from my giftedness, is in harmony with my destiny as I understand it, and moves me toward convergence and accomplishment of my ultimate contribution set as I know it.

I sense that my teaching style involves **effective methodologies for challenging the affect and volitional as well as the cognitive**.  For me, with my giftedness and influence-mix, this means a **narrow focus on the few**—smaller groups via **seminars** and **workshops** rather than to the large such as are at conferences.  Hence, I know that God will lead me via **networking** to these small groups.  My personal ministry will often provide the connections that will open doors later.

I recognize that for a time I need a base that provides status but that my ministry will not be limited to that base and its geographical area.  For a period of time while I have energy and drive I will best operate from a base but provide my teaching to various parts of the world—with a higher priority on Asia.  During this period of time I must pass the torch on to others and provide them with the best possibility of carrying on what I am about.

My end game ministry will focus more on **enabling others to do what I am about**.  I will concentrate more on operating out of the base and less on decentralized workshops and seminars.  It will allow **personal ministry to fewer leaders on an in-depth basis**—those who will be attracted to spend time with me.  I recognize that I will need a setting that allows for isolation and much research and writing for this end game phase.

I intend to be motivated by the following ultimate contribution set.  The decisions I make about what I do will depend to a large extent on my understanding of these life achievements.  For each of the ultimate contributions I am tentatively describing what it means and how that affects what I am and what I do.

**Final Commentary on Effective Methodology**

Comment   Effective methodology is usually too detailed to include in any explanatory way in the personal life mandate itself. Instead phrases which are meaningful to the originator of the document usually link to implied effective methodologies. Others may or may not make the connection. If you are using your Personal Life Mandate as a means of teaching others then you should probably footnote the phrases about effective methodologies with some further explanation as I did with Samuel Brengle.

Comment   The New Testament Stewardship Model[29] helps us recognize that God gives us abilities, skills, special opportunities to learn, experiences which profit us in ministry. We should use all of what we have and are in effective ways in ministry. The recognition of ministry insights—breakthroughs in ministry—and the effective development of them into *effective methodologies* is simply a recognition of our stewardship responsibilities and that God will bless our use of what He has given us if we trust Him by faith and if we step out and use what He has given us.

---

[29]See Clinton and Clinton, **Unlocking Your Giftedness** for an explanation of the Stewardship Model.

(This page is deliberately left blank.)

# Chapter 5 Toward A Major Role

Introduction

Life purpose forms the prime integrating factor around which a focused life operates. We learned about that in chapter 3. But we must also do ministry effectively which flows from that life purpose. We learned about that in Chapter 4 where we studied ministry insights, that is, breakthroughs in ministry. We recognized that repeated use of those breakthroughs become effective methodologies that fit us. Now we must recognize that not all Christian ministry roles will fit our life purpose and allow us freedom to use our ministry insights. We are not only after efficient ministry insights—we want effective ministry. Effective ministry flows out of a role that not only allows but also enhances our use of effective methodologies—those ministry insights that we use repeatedly. Major role allows for effective ministry. It also meshes with our giftedness and our destiny—life purpose thrusts.

Few leaders ever find an ideal role that exactly fits their life purpose. There are several reasons for this: 1. Few know themselves very well—that is, they don't have an everyday working grasp of their giftedness set. 2. They are forced by economic reasons to take pre-designed roles that do not necessarily fit their uniqueness. 3. They do not even know that they should be adapting a role to make it a major role. 4. It is difficult to bring about change in systems which have predetermined expectations as to roles.

So in this chapter I try to get at some of these basic barriers. I give a brief introduction to giftedness set. If you understand your giftedness set and how it changes over time you are well on your way to the first half of finding your major role. I then talk about adapting a role. Few will find an ideal role. Most major roles are at best compromises. But they allow for the best possibility in moving toward focus in non-ideal situations, which is what most of ministry is.

Overview

In this chapter you will be introduced to:

- the overall flowchart leading to assessment of a focused life and where this chapter fits in that assessment,
- major role defined,
- the time-line—and how giftedness development fits along it,
- the notion of the giftedness set including natural abilities, acquired skills, and spiritual gifts and the connection to major role,
- the notion of focal element of a giftedness set—a major determining factor of role,
- the notion of a Venn diagram—a graphical representation of your giftedness set, and how to do one,
- the process of brainstorming to idealize a role,
- the notion of compromising in a role but majoring on the focusing parts,
- step 3 in writing your personal life mandate—adding paragraphs to your introductory paragraph (life purpose) and your paragraph(s) on unique methodologies so that you can describe the major role that will enable you to effectively use unique methodologies and carry out more fully your life purpose.

End Result

By the conclusion of this chapter you will have $3/4$ of your personal life mandate done— 1. the introductory life purpose paragraph, 2. tentative paragraph(s) giving intents for using unique methodologies, 3. and now tentative paragraphs describing the major role you are moving toward which allow effective use of unique methodologies to carry out life purpose.

**Flowchart—Overview Of Assessment**

# BASIC FLOW CHART
# FOR MOVING TOWARD A FOCUSED LIFE

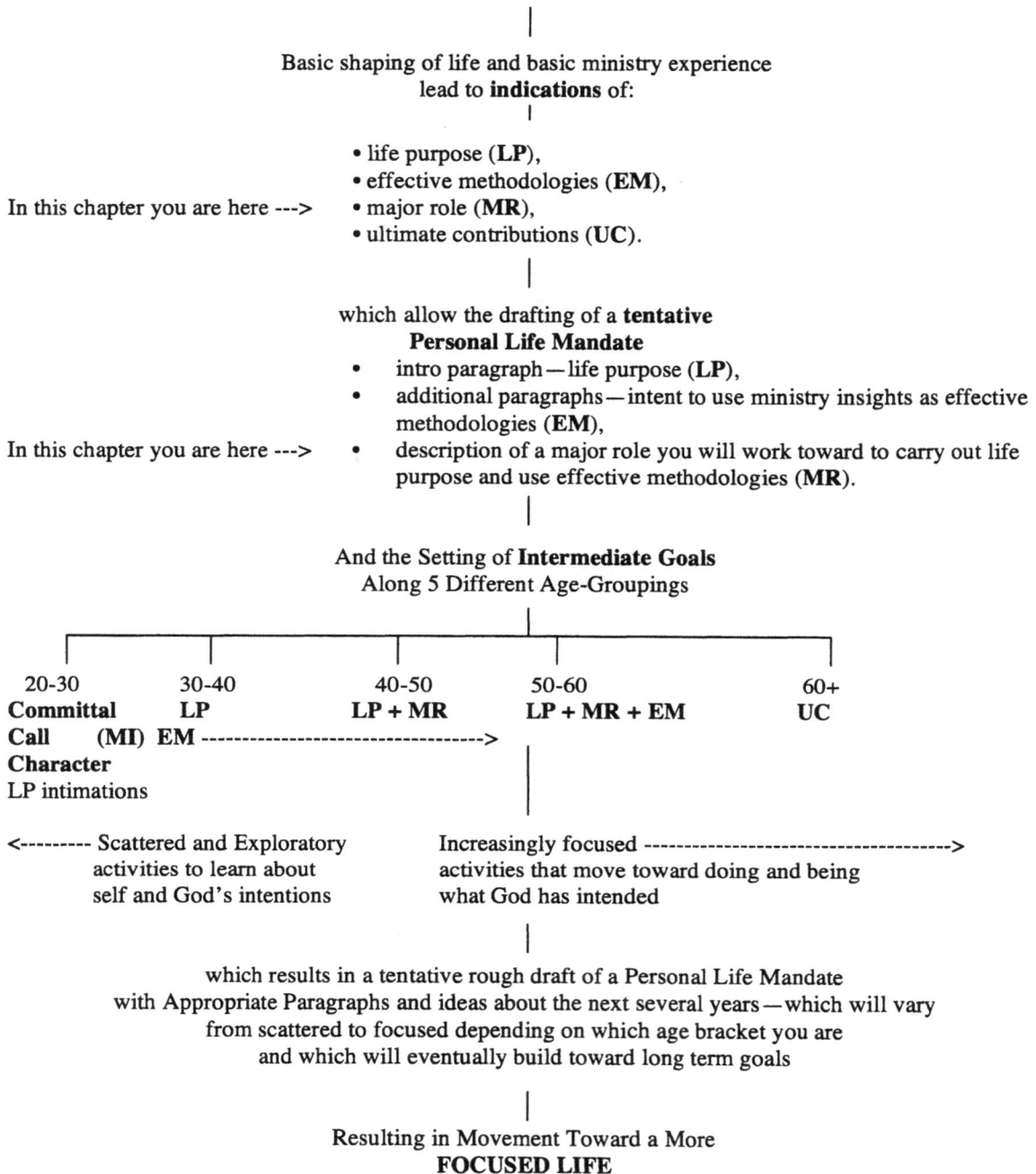

|

Basic shaping of life and basic ministry experience
lead to **indications** of:

|

                                    • life purpose (**LP**),
                                    • effective methodologies (**EM**),
In this chapter you are here --->   • major role (**MR**),
                                    • ultimate contributions (**UC**).

|

which allow the drafting of a **tentative**
        **Personal Life Mandate**
    • intro paragraph — life purpose (**LP**),
    • additional paragraphs — intent to use ministry insights as effective
      methodologies (**EM**),
In this chapter you are here --->   • description of a major role you will work toward to carry out life
      purpose and use effective methodologies (**MR**).

|

And the Setting of **Intermediate Goals**
Along 5 Different Age-Groupings

|

| 20-30 | 30-40 | 40-50 | 50-60 | 60+ |
|-------|-------|-------|-------|-----|
| **Committal** | **LP** | **LP + MR** | **LP + MR + EM** | **UC** |
| **Call**  (MI)  **EM** ------------------------------> | | | | |
| **Character** | | | | |
| LP intimations | | | | |

<--------- Scattered and Exploratory          Increasingly focused -------------------------------------->
        activities to learn about            activities that move toward doing and being
        self and God's intentions            what God has intended

|

which results in a tentative rough draft of a Personal Life Mandate
with Appropriate Paragraphs and ideas about the next several years — which will vary
from scattered to focused depending on which age bracket you are
and which will eventually build toward long term goals

|

Resulting in Movement Toward a More
**FOCUSED LIFE**

**Major Role**     synonym: the platform for my ministry

Introduction     All full time Christian leaders will have some job description (maybe implicit) for their basic work. Someone may be a youth worker on a staff of a large church or may be a visitation pastor on a large church staff. Another may be a Christian education director or a missionary church planter. Whatever the job title there are usually several recognized functions under that, title, which describe the major things that a leader does. There will be other functions the leader does that are not described in the formal job description. As a leader moves toward focus, the job description will usually have to be adapted so that these functions will line up with the leader's life purpose or effective methodologies. Such a role, which enhances focus is called the major role.

Definition     A **major role** is the official or unofficial position, or status/ platform, or leadership functions, or job description that basically describes what a leader does and which allows recognition by others and which uniquely fits who a leader is and lets that leader effectively accomplish life purpose(s).

Components     A major role is made up of the **base component** and **the functional component** where,

| **The Base Component provides:** (the things the leader does that everyone recognizes go with the job) | **The Functional Component:** (the things the leader does because he/she wants to and are usually not recognized as part of the job) |
|---|---|
| 1. the **formal job description** recognized by society and for which the leader gets paid | 1. is the **informal job actually done** which has functions that the leader does to reflect giftedness and carry out life purpose achievements; some of these functions are described by the formal job description while others are informal and reflect giftedness and ministry beyond the described |
| 2. **status**—positions with organizations either church or mission carry credibility which others recognize. This status is often needed in order to carry out functions. Traditional categories recognized include licensed, commissioned, ordained and various levels of official position (rector, bishop, archbishop; assistant pastor, associate pastor, senior pastor; intern, missionary, field superintendent, country leader, etc.) | 2. **comprises the means** for carrying out ministry insights and eventually unique methodologies; these are usually related tightly to **giftedness** and **calling**; preaching ministry, teaching ministry, personal work, administrative work, edification ministries, outreach ministries, etc. |
| 3. **logistics for ministry**—home base out of which to operate; support—emotional, prayer, other resources; finances | 3. describes the **scope or sphere of influence** that is appropriate to the leader which may or may not be covered in the formal job description |
| 4. **Tactical** direction; the everyday basics | 4. **strategic** direction; the long term |

**Examples of Major Role**

Example:     An itinerant public Bible teacher with his own organization at national level who teaches different large groups of 1000 or more in face-to-face ministry on a repetitive basis. The *base component* is provided by his job description as President of National Bible Ministry, Inc, for which he answers to his board. In his base role he has to provide funds for the organization. He will hire, train, and fire, when necessary, the folks who do administrative backup for the organization. He must co-ordinate the board functions and initially helped form the board, which is now self-sustaining. He also runs his own seminars held all over the U.S. as part of the base component. The *functional component* involves his public rhetorician ministry at conferences, his invitations to seminars to teach the Bible, which are held all over the world and his workshops to train Bible teachers and his mentoring of a few specific up-coming Bible teachers.

Example:     A seminary professor who has contacts with leaders from all over the world. His *base component* is given in his job description and contract, which is renewed annually. It involves teaching six classes a year, serving on three committees, and mentoring doctoral students. His *functional component* involves his freedom to minister (via workshops, seminars, conferences) outside the seminary as well as inside it both in classes and via mentoring. The seminary professor does a lot of personal growth mentoring, some with seminary students, and some with leaders outside the seminary. The professor also does a lot of writing of manuals, books, and leadership articles, which he self-publishes. All of these latter things are *functional component* aspects that fit the professor's giftedness and life purpose activity.

Example:     A senior pastor of a flagship church who ministers 50% in the church and 50% outside the church in conferences as a public rhetorician and who has a sodality on the side for producing radio ministry and written materials. The senior pastor has as his *base component* a job description, which he drafts himself each year and presents to a group of men who hold him accountable for ministry and life. The *base component* includes his responsibility to manage 5 top full time leaders who run various programs in the church. His *base component* also lists his public ministry responsibilities. This pastor does not do counseling nor visitation. Both of these functions are filled by 2 of the 5 leaders reporting to him. This pastor majors in his public rhetorician ministry—both as part of his *base component* and to a large degree, his *functional component*.

Comment     Major role does not emerge strategically till mid-40s, after 10-15 years of varied kinds of ministry experiences with a variety of roles. Experience helps force the need for focus and prioritizing of ministry functions.

### 5 Components of A Tailor-Made Major Role

Introduction      Most roles held by leaders are not, technically speaking, major roles. Major Roles are formed by adapting normal roles, by adding *functional component* items, so as to fit a leader's giftedness, destiny and life purpose flowing from it, and a leader's effective methodologies which flow from ministry insights discovered along the way. It will at the same time provide the stability and recognition and finances needed to exist and follow one's calling.

     Some essential components must be in place. In real life, one will seldom have all of the components in their ideal form. Instead there will be compromises that allow some of the component but usually not all of it.

### 5 Components

The five component which make up an effective major role include:

1. a suitable **ministry base** (*base component* providing a recognized job, stability, finances),
2. a **job description** which covers the major thrusts of the recognized job (*base component*),
3. **ministry compatible with giftedness** (*functional component* primarily but also must have some of this in the *base component*),
4. **Freedom** to proactively **choose ministry,** which enhances focus and to refuse that which does not (*functional* primarily, occasionally happens in *base*)
5. a **respected status** which enables effective entrance to ministry situation, bespeaks of spiritual authority, and gives a good hearing (usually this requires recognition by society of the role and is primarily done by the *base component*—sometimes secondarily by the *functional component*).

Comment      A major role is characterized by the fact that it enhances giftedness and allows use of effective methodologies that complement life purpose. It will also enable the leader to leave behind special contributions or ultimate contributions. And finally, it will also screen out ministry functions, which detract from a focused life.

Comment      A major role will usually have to be adapted. Neither churches nor Christian organizations define such a role to fit a person. They hire to positions or qualifications rather than hiring people and defining the position in terms of the people. That is, they have a tendency to use people rather than enhance their development. The major role that is tailor made for a leader, that is adapted from some other role will almost always be a combination of formally recognized issues (the *base component*) and informal ones done implicitly (the *functional component*).

## 10 Questions That Help Clarify a Major Role

Introduction          Below are given some questions to help prompt you toward discerning major role issues. They are grouped around destiny issues, i.e. Life purpose, giftedness issues (and the extent of that influence), legacy issues, i.e. Ultimate contribution thinking).

### Life Purpose Related:

1. Will I be **bi-vocational** (secular job plus ministry) or **vocational** (full time being paid for ministry) or **neither** (finances provides some other way)? If bi-vocational, which will dominate my priorities the secular or ministry vocations? If bi-vocational one will usually one will be primary and the other secondary).

2. Will I operate from a **pastoral base** (church—modality) or **missionary base** (sodality—Christian organization) or some combination? Mono-cultural, cross-cultural or some combination?

3. Geographically, will I be **local** or **itinerant** or some **combination**?

### Giftedness and Sphere of Influence of That Giftedness

4. Will my ministry be directed dominantly toward the **inward aspects** (pastoral, teaching, governments, exhortation, prophecy, leadership—that is, mainly edification ministries building up the body of Christ once people are in the Kingdom) of the great commission, or the **outward aspects** (apostleship, evangelism, faith, exhortation, prophecy, leadership—that is, directed to getting people into the Kingdom of God) of the great commission or some combination?

5. At what level is my **potential influence** most appropriate: Type A (local internal influence), Type B (local external influence), Type C (local/ regional influence), Type D (national influence), Type E (international influence)?

### Ultimate Contribution Focused

6. Will my ministry be largely concerned with **personal modeling** or **ministry modeling** or some **combination** or **neither**? What base component best fits with this? How can functions best be carried out to reflect this?

7. Will my ministry be dominantly **large public** or **dominantly smaller and more personal** or some combination? What base component best fits with this? How can functions best be carried out to reflect this?

8. Will my ministry be **catalytic** in nature breaking new ground (Pioneer, change person, artist)? What base component best fits with this? How can functions best be carried out to reflect this?

9. Will my ministry be **organizational** (either founding new organizations, or stabilizing them)? What base component best fits with this? How can functions best be carried out to reflect this?

10. Will my ministry be dominantly **working with ideas**—that is, theoretical in nature (researcher, writer) or practical working with ideas (writer, promoter) or some combination? What base component best fits with this? How can functions best be carried out to reflect this?

### 4 Things To Do In Light of The Base + Functional Definition of Major Role

Introduction     In addition to answering the 10 questions which prompt you to think about major role and the five step guidelines here are 4 things you can do. You should do these 4 activities and process them with someone who is much further along in ministry. These activities are getting at the underlying issues of a major role.

### 4 Things To Do To Help Get at Underlying Issues of Base + Function Thinking

| Item | Label | Procedure |
| --- | --- | --- |
| 1. | Function | Describe functions you need to do to carry out giftedness and life purpose things, especially those things that bring you joy and invigorate you with life. |
| 2. | Credibility | Identify what kind of base would provide credibility to do these functions. |
| 3. | Finances | How or what finances will you need? What type of base is needed for this? That is, what base role will give you financial stability but will also allow some of the function listed in step 1. |
| 4. | Compromises | What compromises must you make because you cannot get the ideal situation you need? That is, what base role has things you don't like but allows some of what you do like? For how long can you do this? Both in terms of carrying out the base role with integrity and doing the things you really like. Can you eventually get those things you like to do recognized as part of what your are required to do? |

**Feedback On Major Role**

1. The terminology is significant—**Major role**. All Christian workers have a role. But when I use **Major role**, I am indicating,
   ___ a. an important well paid position recognized as such in the Christian world,
   ___ b. a starring position that has tremendous visibility,
   ___ c. a descriptive label of the functions that a leader has come to prioritize as most important and which reflects life purpose and effective methodologies; Oh, by the way, it may be the name of some recognized Christian full-time role; it may not. MAJOR means it is a focal role that is being emphasized and not just some ordinary role.
   ___ d. none of the above.

2. The single most important determinant of major role and that, which must be well known by the leader, if that leader is to move to focus in the life is,
   ___ a. giftedness
   ___ b. destiny processing
   ___ c. successful experience
   ___ d. none of the above.

3. In your opinion, what do you think might be the major factors that keep a leader from realizing a major role?

4. One major drawback to teaching a concept like major role to a younger leader is,
   ___ a. they may be tempted too early to refuse job descriptions or functions they don't like under the excuse of saying no in order to become focused. Young leaders all the way up to the 40s should get varied experience in order to better identify major role. Early extensive exploration will lead to later pinpointing.
   ___ b. they may become frustrated and give up if they think they can not reach a major role due to circumstances or factors seemingly prohibiting them.
   ___ c. the inability to recognize the difference between the notion of a formal ministry role with its recognized name, like Pastor, and the concept itself which describes functions of a non-existent formal role.
   ___ d. all of the above.

**ANSWERS-----------**
1. _√_ c. 2. _√_ a.

3. The question called for your opinion. Your answers may well be as right as my own. (1) A leader may identify too prominently with a formal role and its expectations by the constituency being served and providing finances for the role; (2) can not economically fund the optimum role, hence must do other things not in focus for financial reasons; (3) a lack of knowledge, of both the major role concept or even that roles should be adapted to fit ministry flowing out of one's being. (4) It is often easier to flow and react to things that happen rather than trying to proactively make them happen. Such a habit will usually preclude someone from adapting toward a major role.

4. _√_ d. At least I think all of them are possible.

## Time-Line And Hints About Major Role

Introduction   As you learn about giftedness and as you experience different ministry assignments you will soon recognize that in some roles you will discover barriers to operating more fully out of who you are. In other roles you will find moments of excitement as you see the assignment flowing out of who you are (we call this discovering mini-convergences). In the early stages, it is necessary to try out many varying ministry assignments in order to really discover your giftedness and which roles your giftedness best matches. It is normal to see mismatches in giftedness and role in these early stages because your giftedness is not yet fully known. It will take time and experience to see this. But eventually as you experience a number of mini-convergences over time and as you get a better understanding of your giftedness you will know what is the ideal role for you. This ideal role will be one that you will work toward by adapting the role you do have. It is helpful to trace across your time-line each discovery of information (giftedness and role), which helps you understand something of your major role.

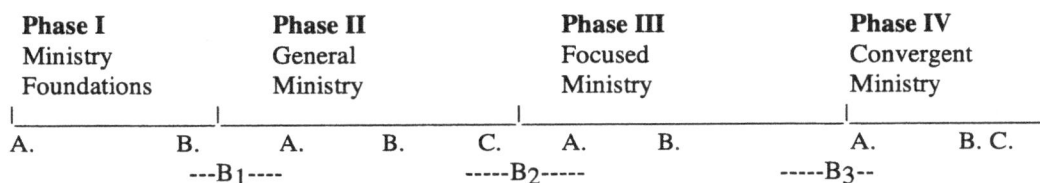

| **Phase I** | | **Phase II** | | | **Phase III** | | **Phase IV** | | |
|---|---|---|---|---|---|---|---|---|---|
| Ministry | | General | | | Focused | | Convergent | | |
| Foundations | | Ministry | | | Ministry | | Ministry | | |
| I_____I | | I_____I_____I | | | _____I | | I_____I | | |
| A. | B. | A. | B. | C. | A. | B. | A. | B. | C. |
| | ---B₁---- | | | -----B₂----- | | | -----B₃-- | | |

### Phase I

A. Sovereign Foundations — (13-20 years) — early shaping of character/ personality
B. Leadership Transition (3-6 years) — a time in which first steps in ministry are done

*Very little will be learned here about major role. You will perhaps enjoy some aspect of your transitional ministry, which may lead you to suspect certain gifts and even a role that allows that gift to be used. Most likely what you find here will be an attraction to someone you admire in ministry. That attraction will follow the like-attracts-like giftedness pattern. You will then upon reflection have some hints as to giftedness.*

### Phase II

A. Provisional Ministry (2-6 years) — the first attempts at full time ministry assignments; it is provisional because it might not last, that is, the leader may not stay in ministry.

*Here you will discover more of giftedness—both what you have and what you don't have. You will learn more of what roles you don't fit than what roles you do fit.*

**Time-Line And Hints About Major Role** continued

B.  Growth Ministry (6-8 years)—ministry utilizing known giftedness with efficiency; giftedness and role issues are learned; this sub-phase is more for developing the leader than the ministry which is accomplished.

*Here you are exploring both ministry roles and who you are. You are discovering much. You do not usually have much control over roles but you certainly have feelings about what roles you would like and those you don't like. You are beginning to recognize the focal element of your giftedness set.*

C.  Competent Ministry<— (2-6 years) —>operating out of giftedness in roles that fit that giftedness produces excellent results; still to be determined is the potential level of influence.

*Here you recognize your giftedness set and the kind of role you would like to be in to be effective.*

### Phase III

A.  Role Transition—There is movement toward compatibility between role, giftedness and influence-mix profile. There is shaping of a role more ideally suited to giftedness and challenge toward influence-mix.
B.  Unique Ministry—ministering effectively as well as efficiently with giftedness. (Role plus unique may last 3-12 years)

*Here you are operating in a role, which does enhance who you are. You may still need to adapt it in order to proactively see focus. But you will make sure that you do those things which really illustrates ministry flowing out of being for you—you will have a base component and a functional component so that ministry does flow out of being for you.*

### Phase IV

A.  Special Guidance—movement toward a role focusing on ultimate contribution
B.  Convergent Ministry—fulfilling a sense of destiny/ ultimate contribution
C.  Afterglow—fall out effects of a life well lived; spiritual authority dominant

### Sample Time-Line/Giftedness Development: Hints Toward Major Role—CRJ

Introduction    Below is given a sample time-line which displays helpful information suggesting what a major role might be.

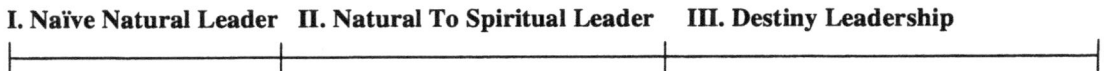

**I. Naïve Natural Leader    II. Natural To Spiritual Leader    III. Destiny Leadership**

| | | | |
|---|---|---|---|
| 1936 | 1970  1974 | 1981 | Present |

|  | 1964    1970 | | 1978 1981 | 1987  1988 |  |
|---|---|---|---|---|---|
|  | B1 Bell Labs to | | B2 Geographical | B3 Toward |  |
|  | Bible Teacher | | Convergence | Focused Ministry |  |
| Age | 28    34    38 | | 43-45 | 51,52 |  |

A. (1936-1957) A Godly Mother

A. (1971-1974) Playing in The Minors, Educational Technology Base

A. (1981-1987) Playing in The Majors Effective methodologies in teaching, content for leadership emergence framework of teaching Develops

B. (1957-64) Marriage, Early Career

B. (1974-1979) Authority Lessons

B. (1988-1993) Influence Mix Expands—Starting to Get Materials Written and Out

C. (1964-1970) Transition To Ministry

C. (1979-1981) Broadening the Base of Teaching Material

C. 1994-  Proactive Movement Toward Focused Life; Teaching of Teachers Who Can Develop Leaders

**Giftedness Develops**

Natural Leadership
  Athletic Ability
    Analytical Skills
      Teacher Gift

Analytical Skills Buttressing Teaching
Exhortation Gift emerges
Writing Skills begin
                    Word of Wisdom seen

Research Skills develop
Writing skills expand
Teaching, Exhortation Become efficient
Analytical Skills About Leadership Honed
Leadership Skills develop/ especially in terms of conceptual understanding

**Major Role Indications**

| 1965-1967 | 1970-71 | 1975 | 1981 Teacher of | 1981-1990 | 1991-1994 ff |
|---|---|---|---|---|---|
| Bible Teacher | Full Time Worker | Writing of | Leadership; Life | Researcher, Leader | International |
| Mentor Discipler | Missionary | Materials begins | Long Development | Trainer at High | Influence as |
|  | Teacher | Trainer of Leaders | Concepts Emerge | Level; Publishing | Trainer of Leaders; |
|  |  |  | Materials | of Material | Development of |
|  |  |  | Publishers Begins | Expands | Leadership |
|  |  |  |  |  | Materials and |
|  |  |  |  |  | Publishing |
|  |  |  |  |  | Expands; writer; |
|  |  |  |  |  | researcher; Mentor |
|  |  |  |  |  | Focus—Coach, |
|  |  |  |  |  | Teacher, Sponsor, |
|  |  |  |  |  | Model |

## THE GIFTEDNESS SET[30]

| Introduction | Because our thinking is shaped by our understanding of the stewardship model, we recognize that we will have to be accountable to God for everything that He has entrusted to us. Accountability will be measured in part by our faithfulness, our growth and development and the results of our ministry. The giftedness set accounts for the three components that make up the set: natural abilities, acquired skills, and spiritual gifts. |
|---|---|
| Definition | The Giftedness Set refers to the threefold collection of giftedness elements: natural abilities, acquired skills, and spiritual gifts. |
| Definition | Natural abilities refer to those capacities, skills, talents or aptitudes which are *innate* in a person and allow him/her to accomplish things. |
| Examples | analytical bent, persevering attitude, relational aptitude |
| Definition | Acquired skills refer to those capacities, skills, talents or aptitudes which have been *learned* by a person in order to allow him/her to accomplish something. |
| Example | writing, oral motivational skills, frameworks for thinking and analysis |
| Definition | A spiritual gift is a *God-given* unique capacity imparted to each believer for the purpose of releasing a Holy Spirit empowered ministry via that believer. |
| Example | discernings of spirits, kinds of healings, teaching, exhortation, prophecy |
| Comment | Natural abilities may be reflected in a spiritual gift. That is, a spiritual gift may relate to or be based on a previously recognized natural ability. The Holy Spirit releases the gift through the individual in such a way that his/her natural ability is enhanced with the power of the Spirit. |
| Comment | Acquired skills often act as enhancements to either natural abilities and/or spiritual gifts. It is in the area of acquired skills that we can focus our growth and development efforts. Once we begin to identify our natural abilities and spiritual gifts, we can be intentional about learning skills that we need in order to enhance our effectiveness. |
| Comment | Sometimes there may be no direct correlation between natural abilities and spiritual gifts, e.g. a person prior to conversion and empowerment by the Holy Spirit may have had no teaching bent but subsequently begins to teach with power. Often it is difficult to say if something is natural or acquired or a combination of both. The giftedness awareness continuum helps us relate natural abilities, acquired skills, and spiritual gifts. |
| Comment | Each of these elements of the giftedness set, natural abilities, acquired skills, and spiritual gifts are defined with much more detail in my book, **Unlocking Your Giftedness**. |

---

[30]A set is a mathematical concept describing a collection of items—in this case the items, which allow a leader to accomplish ministry.

**FEEDBACK ON GIFTEDNESS SET**

1.  Check any of the following which reflect correct teaching on giftedness.
____a.  Spiritual gifts represent the most important element in the giftedness set.
____b.  Most leaders have only one of the elements of the giftedness set.
____c.  Natural abilities never are reflected in a spiritual gift--the two are distinct.
____d.  Acquired skills often act as enhancements to either natural abilities or spiritual gifts.
____e.  None of the above were given in the teaching on giftedness.


2.  Why does our approach to giftedness differ from the usual approach which focuses only on spiritual gifts?


3.  Sometimes there may be no direct correlation between natural abilities and spiritual gifts and at other times there can be relationships.

    a.  That is, sometimes a spiritual gift appears which seems not to fit in with the background and natural abilities of a person. Can you think of a Biblical illustration of this?


    b.  Or, sometimes a spiritual gift seems to build upon a persons background and natural abilities of a person. Can you think of a Biblical illustration of this?


**ANSWERS----------**

1. d
2. Because our thinking is shaped by our understanding of the stewardship model, we recognize that we will have to be accountable to God for everything that He has entrusted to us. Accountability will be measured in part by our faithfulness, our growth and development and the results of our ministry. The giftedness set takes into account the three components that make up the set: natural abilities, acquired skills, and spiritual gifts. Spiritual gifts are important to us too. The majority of leaders will have spiritual gifts as the focal element of their set. However, we are concerned with developing the whole person so that their ministry flows out of who they are, that is, who God made them to be.
3.  a.  Peter
    b. Paul

## THE FOCAL ELEMENT

Introduction    As we studied various leader's giftedness sets, we discovered that each one was unique. We also discovered that usually one of the three components was more dominant that the other two. Our initial assumption about leaders and giftedness was that the spiritual gifts would be the dominant element. As we studied the giftedness sets of various leaders, we discovered that any one of the three elements could be the dominant element. We call the dominant element the **focal element**. It is the recognition of this dominant element and seeing the synergistic[31] relationship of the other two which truly frees up a leader to minister out of being. The giftedness set and especially the notion of the focal element are two of the most liberating concepts in all of our teaching.

Definition    **The <u>focal element</u> refers to the element of a person's giftedness set that is dominant and to which the other two elements operate in a supportive way which enhances the dominant element.**

Example    Philip Bliss, important evangelistic song leader and hymn composer during the mid 1800s—**natural abilities** were his focal element.

Example    G. Campbell Morgan, leading Bible Expositor during the first half of the 20th Century—**spiritual gifts** (teaching, prophetical and exhortation) were his focal element.

Example    Henry Venn, mission statesperson—19th century, **acquired skills** (organizational frameworks).

Comment    It is possible to be an effective leader and have any of the three elements as the focal element. Philip Bliss who was used by God as a songwriter had **natural abilities** as the focal element. Acquired skills in music enhanced his natural musical abilities. God released the gift of exhortation and evangelism through the lyrics that he wrote. God uses other leaders whose focal element is in **acquired skills** in powerful ways. Counselors who have been trained in certain counseling methodologies often have acquired skills as their focal element. The counseling methodology, an acquired skill, usually dominates how they operate in ministry. Their spiritual gifts and natural abilities will flow through that methodology. Also, leaders who have primarily administrative or organizational positions often have their acquired skills dominate how they operate in ministry. Usually they have learned certain management paradigms or tools, which they use to operate in ministry.

Comment    A common wrong assumption about leaders is that their spiritual gifts should dominate in their ministry. In many circles, certain spiritual gifts are required or projected on to leaders. If you are a leader, then you should be able to _____ (fill in the blank). This creates difficulty for those leaders whose gifting does not match the expected ones. Often, they move on to other groups or places that affirm who they are.

Comment    The focal element usually remains the same throughout the entire time of ministry. The exception to this occurs when spiritual gifts are late in being identified (late bloomer or late adult conversion).

---

[31]Synergism and its related words (synergistic, synergistically) all refer to a process in which items work together to produce a united effort which is greater than just the sum of the individual efforts.

## FEEDBACK ON THE FOCAL ELEMENT

1.  Consider the two following possibilities:

    a.  A leader with a focal element of natural abilities supported by spiritual gifts and acquired skills. For example: creative musical ability dominates though there is a strong natural ability (charismatic kind of person) to lead, strong helps gift, music theory is part of acquired skills.

    b.  A leader with a focal element of acquired skills supported by natural abilities and spiritual gifts. For example: a person with an organizational framework with strong tendencies toward strategic planning, job analysis and descriptions, goal setting, accountability, etc. supported with an innate ability to put things in order, and a spiritual gift of teaching.

Now suppose that each of these persons is put into a ministry ambiance in which leaders who are affirmed, supported, and given the best ministry assignments have spiritual gifts dominant—for example: prophecy. Natural abilities and acquired skills are not even acknowledged as being important.

What do you think will happen to the leader of situation a? the leader of situation b? How will the leader in each case view what is happening? How will the leadership over them view the situation?

2.  What is the basic problem we are dealing with in situations a and b?

**ANSWERS------------**

1.  In both cases the leaders will probably either attempt to get the spiritual gift of prophecy or minister as if they had it or will be frustrated and eventually leave the ministry situation and move to an environment more suited to who they are. Leader "a" will most likely try to fit in and sublimate creative music drives to giving supportive atmosphere for the prophetical ministry. But creativity in music will be thwarted. Leader "b" will be even more frustrated than leader "a." For the prophecy ambiance will usually have associated with it an intuitive approach to planning or organizational matters or none at all. Leader "b" will see the lack of coordinated purpose, no accountability. He/she will want to organize things, will see the need for structures, etc. In both cases, leadership will see both leader "a" and "b" as weak leaders who do not hear from God and cannot minister with power.

2.  We are dealing with the concept of **gift projection**, that is, the tendency of strong gifted leaders to lay expectations (even guilt trips) on followers to operate in the same gifts in which these leaders are strong. Leaders with strong evangelism gifts want all to have evangelism. Leaders with strong teaching gifts want all to teach the Bible like they do. Leaders with healing gifts want all followers to be able to heal. This is not a new problem. Paul dealt with it in the Corinthian church in which gift projecting by some leaders (tongues) was taking place. The end result of gift projections is that those emerging leaders without the necessary gifts being projected are made to feel like second class leaders—self-image is affected.

## SUMMARY LISTING OF GIFT DEFINITIONS

Introduction       Very shortly now you will be asked to display your giftedness set. I assume that you have an intuitive grasp of your natural abilities and acquired skills and can identify the most important items. But perhaps you may want some help in terminology describing your spiritual gifts—a most important part of the giftedness set. For a detailed description of each gift given below and how to develop it—See Clinton and Clinton, **Unlocking Your Giftedness**, 1994. Hopefully, most leaders studying the focused life will have a fairly good understanding of their giftedness set.

**Gift**                                            **Definition**

**The 7 Word Cluster Gifts**

**teaching**       A person who has the <u>gift of teaching</u> is one who has the ability to instruct, explain, or expose Biblical truth in such a way as to cause believers to understand the Biblical truth. **CENTRAL THRUST - TO CLARIFY TRUTH**

**exhortation**    The <u>gift of exhortation</u> is the capacity to urge people to action in terms of applying Biblical truths, or to encourage people generally with Biblical truths, or to comfort people through the application of Biblical truth to their needs. **CENTRAL THRUST - TO APPLY BIBLICAL TRUTH**

**prophecy**       A person operating with <u>the gift of prophecy</u> has the capacity to deliver truth (in a public way) either of a predictive nature or as a situational word from God in order to correct by exhorting, edifying or consoling believers and to convince non-believers of God's truth. **CENTRAL THRUST - TO PROVIDE CORRECTION OR PERSPECTIVE ON A SITUATION**

**apostleship**    The <u>gift of apostleship</u> refers to a special leadership capacity to move with authority from God to create new ministry structures (churches and para-church) to meet needs and to develop and appoint leadership in these structures. **CENTRAL THRUST - CREATING NEW MINISTRY**

**pastor**         The <u>pastoral gift</u> is the capacity to exercise concern and care for members of a group so as to encourage them in their growth in Christ which involves modeling maturity, protecting them from error and disseminating truth. **CENTRAL THRUST - CARING FOR THE GROWTH OF FOLLOWERS.**

**evangelism**     The <u>gift of evangelism</u> in general refers to the capacity to challenge people through various communicative methods (persuasion) to receive the Gospel of salvation in Christ so as to see them respond by taking initial steps in Christian discipleship. **CENTRAL THRUST - INTRODUCING OTHERS TO THE GOSPEL.**

**ruling**         A person operating with <u>a ruling gift</u> demonstrates the capacity to exercise influence over a group so as to lead it toward a goal or purpose with a particular emphasis on the capacity to make decisions and keep the group operating together. **CENTRAL THRUST - INFLUENCING OTHERS TOWARD VISION.**

## SUMMARY LISTING OF GIFT DEFINITIONS continued

<u>Gift</u>                              <u>Definition</u>

### The 8 Power Cluster Gifts

| | |
|---|---|
| **word of wisdom** | The <u>word of wisdom</u> gift refers to the capacity to know the mind of the Spirit in a given situation and to communicate clearly the situation, facts, truth or application of the facts and truth to meet the need of the situation.<br>**CENTRAL THRUST - APPLYING REVELATORY INFORMATION** |
| **word of knowledge** | The <u>word of knowledge</u> gift refers to the capacity or sensitivity of a person to supernaturally perceive revealed knowledge from God which otherwise could not or would not be known and apply it to a situation.<br>**CENTRAL THRUST - GETTING REVELATORY INFORMATION** |
| **faith** | The <u>gift of faith</u> refers to the unusual capacity of a person to recognize in a given situation that God intends to do something and to trust God for it until He brings it to pass.<br>**CENTRAL THRUST - A TRUSTING RESPONSE TO A CHALLENGE FROM GOD.** |
| **gifts of healings** | The <u>gifts of healings</u> refers to the supernatural releasing of healing power for curing all types of illnesses.<br>**CENTRAL THRUST - RELEASING GOD'S POWER TO HEAL.** |
| **workings of powers** | The workings of powers, gift of miracles, refers to the releasing of God's supernatural power so that the miraculous intervention of God is perceived and God receives recognition for the supernatural intervention.<br>**CENTRAL THRUST - THE RELEASING OF GOD'S POWER TO GIVE AUTHENTICITY.** |
| **discernings of spirits** | The <u>discernings of spirits gift</u> refers to the ability given by God to perceive issues in terms of spiritual truth and to know the fundamental source of the issues and to give judgment concerning those issues; this includes the recognition of the spiritual forces operating in the issue.<br>**CENTRAL THRUST - A SENSITIVITY TO TRUTH AND ITS SOURCE.** |
| **tongues** | The <u>gift of tongues</u> refers to a spontaneous utterance of a word from God in unknown words (to the individual giving the word) to a group of people.<br>**CENTRAL THRUST - SPEAKING A MESSAGE IN AN UNKNOWN TONGUE.** |
| **interpretation of tongues** | The <u>gift of interpretation of tongues</u> refers to the ability to spontaneously respond to a giving of an authoritative message in tongues by interpreting this word and clearly communicating the message given.<br>**CENTRAL THRUST - INTERPRETING A MESSAGE GIVEN IN TONGUES.** |

### SUMMARY LISTING OF GIFT DEFINITIONS continued

| <u>Gift</u> | <u>Definition</u> |
|---|---|

#### <u>The 4 Love Cluster Gifts</u>

**gifts of governments**

The <u>gifts of governments</u> involves a capacity to manage details of service functions so as to support and free other leaders to prioritize their efforts.
<u>**CENTRAL THRUST**</u> - **SUPPORTIVE ORGANIZATIONAL ABILITIES.**

**giving**

The <u>gift of giving</u> refers to the capacity to give liberally to meet the needs of others and yet to do so with a purity of motive which senses that the giving is a simple sharing of what God has given to you.
<u>**CENTRAL THRUST**</u> - **A SENSITIVITY TO GOD TO CHANNEL HIS RESOURCES TO OTHERS.**

**mercy**

The <u>gift of mercy</u> refers to the capacity to both feel sympathy for those in need (especially the suffering) and to manifest this sympathy in some practical helpful way with a cheerful spirit so as to encourage and help those in need.
<u>**CENTRAL THRUST**</u> - **THE EMPATHETIC CARE FOR THOSE WHO ARE HURTING.**

**gifts of helps**

The <u>gifts of helps</u> refers to the capacity to unselfishly meet the needs of others through very practical means.
<u>**CENTRAL THRUST**</u> - **THE ATTITUDE AND ABILITY TO AID OTHERS IN PRACTICAL WAYS.**

### Explaining the Venn Diagram

Introduction   A Venn Diagram (Venn was a mathematician who developed this means of showing relationships between sets and elements of sets) is a special way to picture items and relationships between them.

Description   **A Venn Diagram of a giftedness set** represents with symbols a given person's understanding of giftedness including which elements are more dominant and which less including areas of common overlap between elements as well as non-overlap.

Comment   This diagram communicates information in three different ways.

Symbols: We use three different symbols to display giftedness.

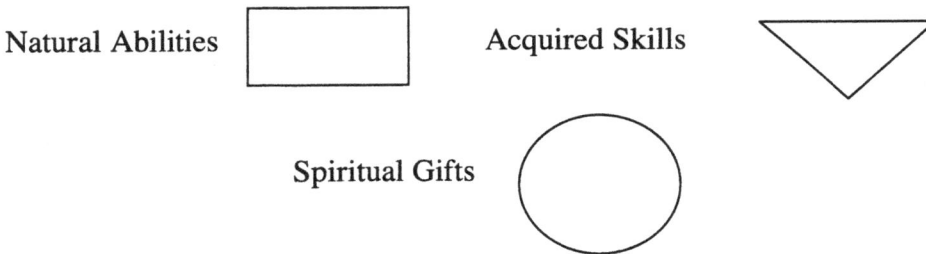

Natural Abilities     Acquired Skills

Spiritual Gifts

Size:   The size of the symbols is important. Bigger size denotes more importance. Smaller size denotes lesser importance. For example:

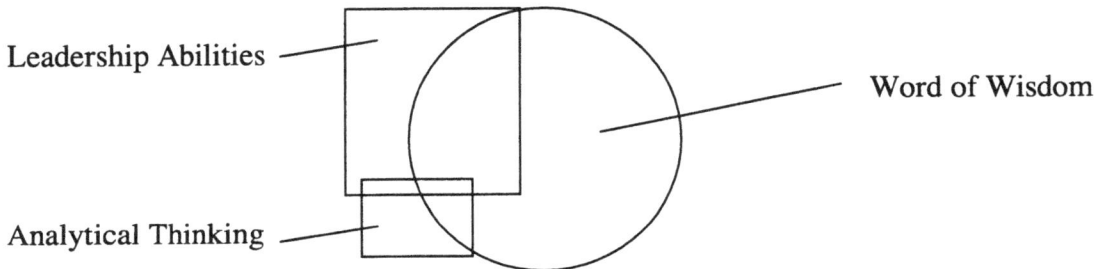

Leadership Abilities     Word of Wisdom

Analytical Thinking

In this example, there are two natural abilities listed and one spiritual gift. The leadership abilities are being displayed as more important than the natural ability of clear thinking. The word of wisdom gift is larger than the leadership abilities and the analytical thinking natural ability. It is the most important. The natural abilities are next most important.

Spacing: Spacing is the most complex feature of a Venn diagram. When you space the symbols on the diagram you are showing the relationship between the symbols. If two elements of the giftedness set are seen as working together, they would be placed in such a way as to demonstrate the relationship. Overlap means that some of both occur simultaneously. Where there is no overlap it means that the item also occurs alone. The most important elements are the largest ones and are placed in the center of the diagram.

**Explaining the Venn Diagram**

For example:

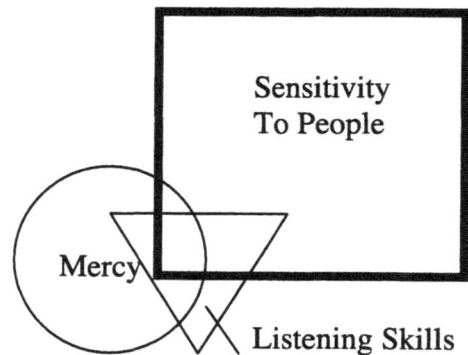

In this example, this person is demonstrating a relationship between three different elements of the giftedness set. The dominant feature is the natural ability called, sensitivity to people. It is placed in the center of the diagram and is the largest symbol. The spiritual gift of mercy enhances the operation of this natural ability in ministry situations. God takes the person's natural sensitivity and empowers this with His Holy Spirit and releases the love of God in the situation. This person has acquired some skills in the area of listening. One would summarize this diagram by saying that this person uses his/her natural ability to release a spiritual gift usually through listening to others.

Here's another example:

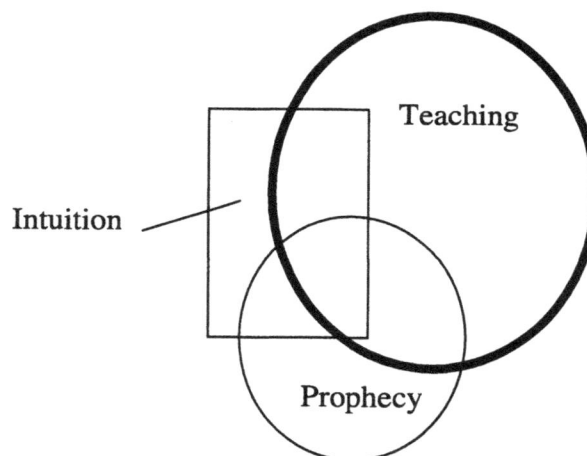

In this example the person is demonstrating that there are three elements that relate closely. The spiritual gifts work hand in hand together. There is a large amount of teaching that is not prophetical. But there is a strong overlap between teaching and prophecy meaning the teaching has strong admonition or correction and/or could be actual teaching on prophecy. The teaching gift is dominant but has a prophetic touch to it. The natural ability of intuition influences both the teaching and the prophetic gifts. But there is a large part of intuition which takes place out of the teaching and prophetic context.

**Example of Venn Diagram of Giftedness Set**
**Samuel Logan Brengle—** (1860-1936) **Salvation Army Worker**

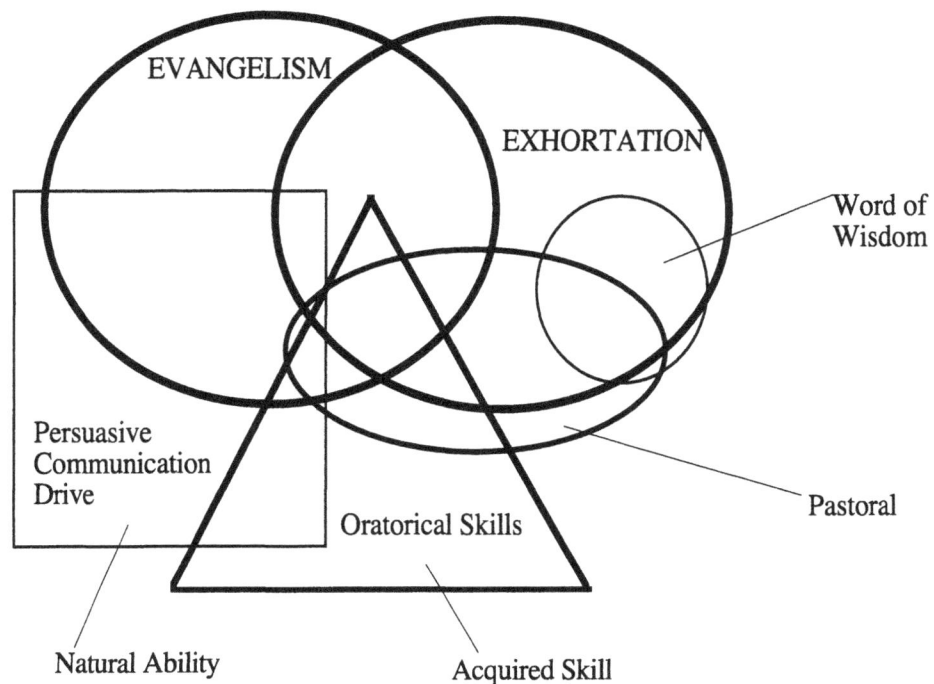

Brengle's giftedness set is given above in diagram form. Spiritual gifts were the focal element. His major natural ability (voice, motivational ability, core communication drive) and his acquired skills (many in the area of public communication) strongly supported his spiritual gifts. Evangelism and Exhortation were twin dominant spiritual gifts in his gift-cluster. Development of these were dominantly via on-the-job experience. His convergent role was ideally suited to this giftedness set.

**Example of Venn Diagram of Giftedness Set**
**G. Campbell Morgan—** (1863-1945) **Bible Teacher and Pastor**

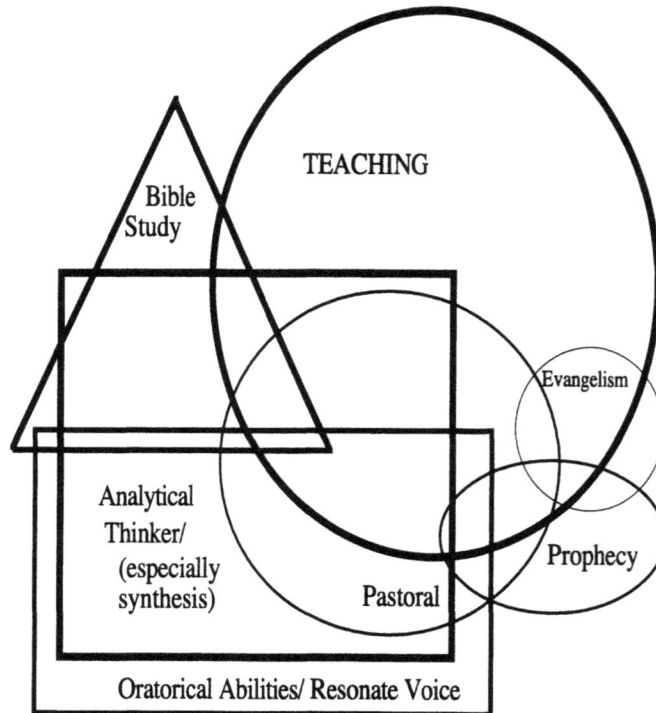

Spiritual gifts are the focal element. His gift-mix includes teaching, pastoral, Spiritual gifts are the focal element. His gift-mix includes teaching, pastoral, prophecy and evangelism. Within spiritual gifts his teaching gift is the dominant gift of the gift-mix. Evangelism was more dominant early in his leadership transition period. It gradually paled before his teaching ministry though he never lost his desire to see people related to God through Christ. Even his strong Bible teaching gift was used occasionally to see people come to Christ. Prophecy was occasionally used, usually from the pulpit in crisis times.

Two natural abilities are worth commenting on. He has a strong analytical natural ability which flows into his Bible study skills that he was able to acquire over his lifetime. This ability fit hand in glove with his Bible study skills which he acquired and his teaching gift. His analytical ability, sharpened by his basic training increased all throughout his life. He had an oratorical bent even as a little child. He was probably strongly conditioned in this from his early visits to hear preachers. He eventually had a resonant voice which strongly enhanced his public ministry. His natural ability at speaking, especially his resonate voice, formed part of the motivational drive for a public ministry role.

These Bible study skills included synthesis and analysis of large units: Bible as a whole, sections of Bible, individual Bible books, various contextual size units in books. He acquired word study skills both in Hebrew and Greek. His Bible study skills developed fundamentally in his first four pastorates (Stone, Rugely, Westminster Road, and New Court). He perfected these, particularly applying synthesis abilities to his Bible study skills, in his first Northfield ministry and his Westminster Chapel days. His early ministry assignments in the rural pastorates were conducive to development of Bible study skills. Starting with the Westminster Road Pastorate his Bible teaching gift began to dominate and continued to do so increasingly in the years to come.

Morgan's giftedness was a dominant factor in movement toward a focused life.

**Example of Venn Diagram of Giftedness Set**
**Robert Jaffray—** (1873-1945) **Missionary Pioneer**

Without a doubt Jaffray's giftedness set was the most significant factor in pushing Jaffray toward a focused life. We minister out of what we are. Along with character, giftedness strongly defines who we are. For Jaffray this was central. His giftedness set dominated his ministry. Without question, spiritual gifts are the focal element of the giftedness set. Apostleship dominates the gift-mix of spiritual gifts. Jaffray's apostleship gift dominated his life. His natural abilities (attitudes) synergistically fit this dominant gift. He used two acquired skills--use of materials and the Bible School to further contribute to his overall giftedness set. This is one of the tighter giftedness diagrams. This is a very focused life in terms of giftedness.

You can get a hint of two very important unique methodologies when you look at his acquired skills.

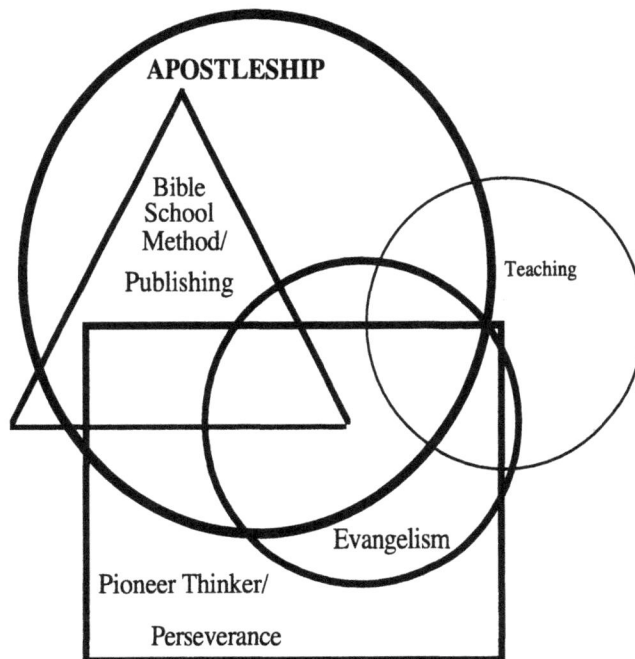

Two questions you should ask yourself when you see a Venn diagram like this. Assuming that it is somewhat indicative of the person then ponder the two following questions. If you were a leader who had this person assigned to you, would such a diagram help you place this leader? What would be a major role that would allow this person to minister effectively?

**Example of Venn Diagram of Giftedness Set**
**Henrietta Mears— (1890-1963) Teacher and Recruiter of Emerging Leaders**

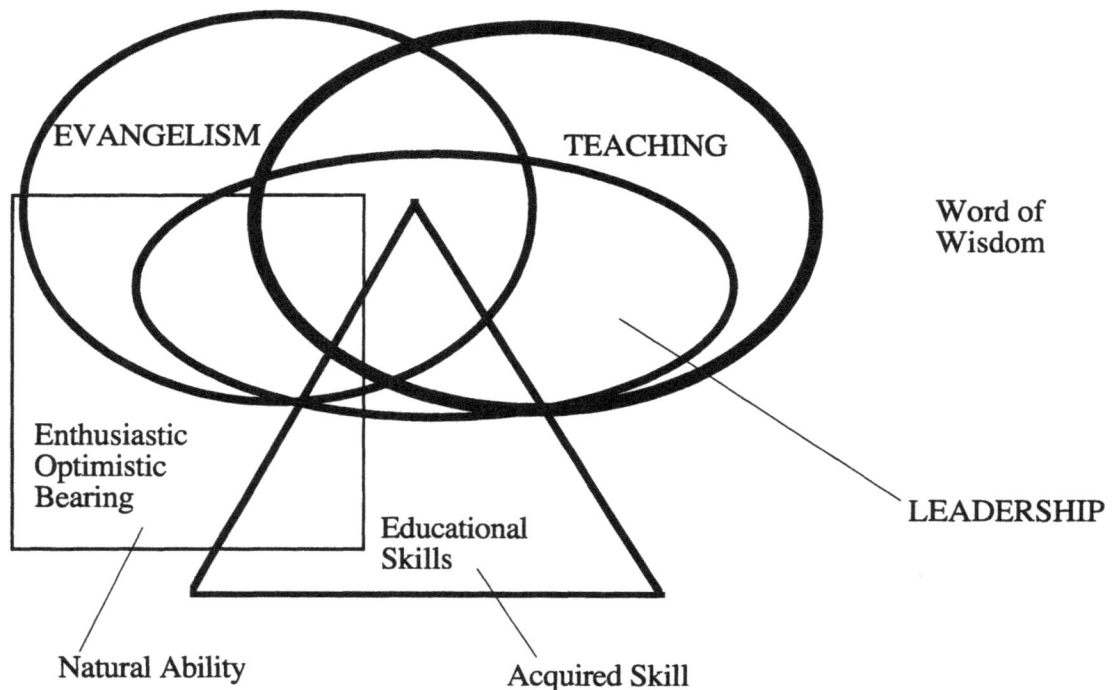

This gift-mix is unusual for two reasons. One, it is somewhat rare for a teacher to be so evangelistically gifted. Teachers dominantly edify and usually do not see many come to Christ personally. Evangelists usually see people come to Christ but can't do much to edify them. Henrietta Mears did both and did it powerfully. Two, she had a strong spiritual gift of leadership which shows up in her motivational ministry. Both in teaching and evangelism she was a powerful motivation. This is a very tight diagram and symbolizes a very synergistic gift-cluster. Such a profile will have a highly focused life—if there is a role which enhances it. And there was for Miss Mears.

Again ask yourself the two questions. Assuming that the Venn Diagram is somewhat indicative of teacher Mears then ponder the two following questions. If you were a leader who had this person assigned to you, would such a diagram help you place this leader. What would be a major role that would allow this person to minister effectively?

## Drawing Your Venn Diagram

### Step 1: Gathering Your Data

At this point you should have identified the most important elements of your giftedness set. List them here. Summarize as best you can your natural abilities and acquired skills. See page 227 for your summary of spiritual gifts.

Your Natural Abilities:

Your Acquired Skills:

Your Spiritual Gifts:
(List only your primary gifts)

### Step 2: The Focal Element

Before you can actually start drawing your giftedness diagram, you need to decide which element is the focal element or the element that dominates your giftedness. Whichever element it is, you will make it the biggest. Occasionally there will be two elements which are equally important but this is not common.

### Step 3: Determining the Relationships and Importance of each part.

Begin with the focal element. Determine how dominant each component is. For example, if spiritual gifts are the focal element, then look at your list of gifts and determine which one of those is dominant and make it the biggest. Then decide how the other gifts relate to that gift. When you overlap symbols the overlap area indicates that all the items that are overlapping operate together. Then move to the other two elements of the giftedness set and repeat the process.

### Step 4: Begin Drawing Your Diagram

By now you should have assigned some degrees of importance and some degree of relationship between the various components of your giftedness set. Begin drawing and start with your focal element. Make the dominant component the largest and place it in the center. Then begin to add the other components according to the importance and relationships as you see them. It will probably take you two or three tries so do the first few in pencil.

### Step 5: Get Feedback

Once you have drawn a rough draft. Contact some people who know you and have observed you in ministry. Share your diagram with them. Talk through the relationships of the various components and describe how you see the importance of each component. Get feedback. As you share the diagram and talk about it, you will see more or learn more. You may want to modify your diagram based on what you have learned.

### Step 6: Prepare Your Final Draft

Once you have gotten some feedback, you can draw your final draft. Recognize that giftedness development is not static. Your giftedness set will change over the years as you grow and mature. From time to time, review your giftedness set and modify it as you see fit.

**Feedback—Doing Your Venn Diagram for Giftedness Set**

1.  Follow the steps for doing a Venn diagram.[32]  Put your Venn Diagram below:

**ANSWERS------------**

Your choice.  Explain what a Venn Diagram is to some friend who knows you well. Then ask that person to look at your Venn Diagram and tell you what he/she sees. This will help you recognize whether you have communicated well in the diagram as well as getting some feedback on your giftedness from a concerned friend.

---

[32]If you really need help on natural abilities and acquired skills, see Clinton and Clinton (1994), **Unlocking Your Giftedness**, chapter 4 which gives a listing of categories and suggested items for both natural abilities and acquired skills.

### How To Think About A Major Role—5 Step Guidelines

Introduction    Knowing your giftedness set and knowing your ministry assignments, especially roles that fit and roles that did not fit, will allow you to think constructively about a future major role that puts it all together. Always we must remember that we are not choosing just for ourselves our desires but that we are seeking what God has for us because He has created us and uniquely gifted us. We want to flow with how and what God has made us for.

Procedure    1.    Use the time-line and plot along it any hints as to roles that were satisfying.
2.    For each role described above, in a one-line statement say what about that role you would like to see in an idealized role or what you hope to avoid.
3.    Now identify your present location and giftedness set.
4.    For your giftedness set at present and from your description of what you would like to see and what you would like to avoid, describe a role that you already know exists that contains at least some of what you have described.
5.    Being Realistic About Major Role. If you are in the:

20-30 age bracket: Don't worry about major role at all—just seek to move toward those roles that attract you and give excitement about ministering.

30-40 age bracket: Identify the most positive satisfaction you have yet experienced in a ministry assignment. Also identify the most negative thing you have learned, that is, what you want to avoid in a ministry role. Now consider your present ministry assignment or your next anticipated one. Can you see in it the positive thing? Can you avoid the negative? Can you adapt to better make the role fit what you have learned. If you cannot, then assume God has some major lessons to teach you through the assignment. And simply learn and wait till God opens the opportunity for movement toward a more compatible role.

40-50 age bracket: Here you must proactively do all you can to adapt your present role to fit the many lessons about yourself—role and giftedness—that you have learned. Seek God in prayer as to how to do this. It may involve a serious change strategy, which will take several years to work out. It may involve asking God for a new assignment more compatible with who you are. In any case you must be proactive in both identifying your major role and moving toward it. But remember, any step forward that enables better focus is practical. Rarely do we get all of what we want in an ideal major role. Any step forward is good.

50-60 age bracket: You should have a major role that at least fits most of who you are by this time. Simply proactively use it to further your life purpose and use your unique methodologies effectively and repeatedly.

**Feedback on Realistic Major Role**

1.  Use the time-line below as a guide.  Date the various sub-phases with your own
    specific dates when you entered the sub-phase. Locate along this time-line each major
    assignment (give it a label).  You may want to also locate along the time-line any
    discovery of or effective use of gifting.

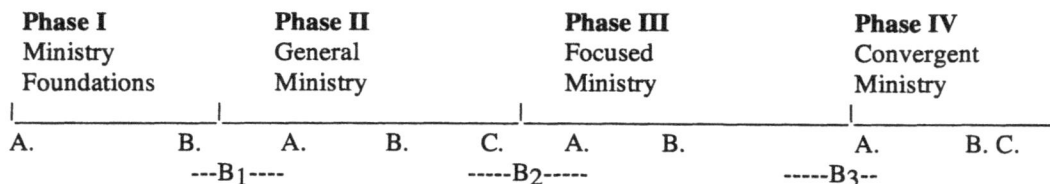

| **Phase I** | | **Phase II** | | | **Phase III** | | **Phase IV** | |
| --- | --- | --- | --- | --- | --- | --- | --- | --- |
| Ministry | | General | | | Focused | | Convergent | |
| Foundations | | Ministry | | | Ministry | | Ministry | |

|_____|_____|_____|_____|

A.              B.      A.       B.       C.     A.         B.          A.          B. C.
            ---B₁----              -----B₂-----            -----B₃--

2.  For each major assignment list the most positive thing you learned about a role.

    a. positive thing that I would like to see again in a role (add more if you need them):

    ministry assignment 1.

    ministry assignment 2.

    ministry assignment 3.

    ministry assignment 4.

b. negative thing that I would like to avoid in a role (add more if you need them):

    ministry assignment 1.

    ministry assignment 2.

    ministry assignment 3.

    ministry assignment 4.

3.  Now locate on the time-line where you are at present and put on it your present
    understanding of your giftedness set—in summary form.  Focal element:  Spiritual
    Gifts:  Natural Abilities:  Acquired Skills:

4.  Now describe how you would like to see your present role changed in a very small
    way to move toward what you have learned in question 2 above and question 3.

5.  Now think big. If you could do what ever you wanted in creating a major role to fit
    what you have learned in 3 and 4 above, what would it be?  Describe as best you can
    an ideal major role.

**ANSWERS------------**
    All of these are your choices.  But you may be helped to talk them over with a friend who knows you
well.

## PERSONAL LIFE MANDATE  syn. Personal Mission Statement

| | |
|---|---|
| Introduction | E.T. Hall's basic principle (seen in **The Silent Language**) of moving from the implicit to the explicit proves extremely valuable when one attempts to utilize Covey's principle, *Begin With the End in Mind*. When we seek to lead focused lives it is important that we understand what it is we are shooting for. By deriving an explicit personal life mandate from underlying assumptions and past processing which centers on focal issues we are bringing out into the open concepts in order to approve, modify, abrogate if necessary, and finally use them to become very intentional about our lives. |
| Definition | A <u>personal life mandate</u> is a one to three page length description, made up of several paragraphs, which give in essence a person's life time goals in terms of several paragraphs centered on what is known to date of the focal issues (Life Purpose, Major Role, Effective Methodology, and Ultimate Contribution) and using language which reflects development along being and doing lines. |
| Comment | <u>Life purpose</u> is usually the dominant focal issue in most lives. It usually forms the topic around which the first paragraph of the personal life mandate is given. |
| Comment | Being statements describe inner character or sanctification issues in the life. They under lie the *why* we do what we do and somewhat the *what* of what we do. Sometimes as life purpose develops it may well relate to the *when* of what we are doing. |
| Comment | Doing statements flow from life purpose and ultimate contribution findings. They most relate to the *what* that we are about. |
| Comment | Effective methodologies describe the major means whereby life purpose or ultimate contributions are realized. These relate to the *how* we operate or the means whereby we achieve or make progress in delivering our ministry. |
| Comment | Ultimate contributions help set the boundaries for what we want to accomplish in terms of the big picture. They will relate to *means* and *ends*. |
| Comment | The actual writing form of the paragraphs, other than reflecting being and doing and focusing on focal issues can take on any unique form that fits the person and with which the person is comfortable. *The basic issue is, "Does the personal life mandate help the person to be more proactive and deliberate in focusing the life?"* If so, the format is good. If not, change it. |
| Comment | Personal life mandates should be revised regularly. The core of them will probably remain the same but there will be clarification throughout life as the focal issues become specific. |
| Comment | Start with the best personal life mandate you can get. Even a poor one is better than none. Then expect it to be modified, to become more specific and helpful as you develop and to become a means for proactive decision making as you move more into the end game. Opening game and middle game activity can be rather exploratory--focal issues are still up for grabs. As you go your experience will help you focus and closed doors provide boundaries as focal issues are clarified. So don't be afraid to try things. As you move toward end game play the personal mission statement becomes more of a vital mandate for focusing your life. |
| Comment | Start with any rough draft Personal Life Mandate. A poor one is better than none. Expect it to be modified, become more specific and helpful as you develop. It will become a means for proactive decision making. Early ministry can be rather exploratory —focal issues are still up for grabs. Further experience will help you focus. Closed doors provide boundaries as focal issues are clarified. So don't be afraid to try things. As you move toward end game play say **yes** and **no** using your Personal Life Mandate as a screen for choosing ministry activity. |

### Step 3 in Writing Your Personal Life Mandate

Introduction    Below is given the description of paragraph(s) of a personal life mandate, which describes major role shown with several examples.

Description    **Major role paragraphs** reflect what is known to date of giftedness and a matching role that enhances that giftedness. It is usually made up of a description of what role you feel will move you more to focus.

Comment    A standard form usually starts, "I hope to ..." or "in terms of my giftedness set and my past role experience I know that ..." and then describe what you know including the kind of role that you are moving toward in order to better use the ministry break throughs you have learned and which better fits your giftedness. The description is very tentative in the age bracket 20-30s (probably one tentative paragraph) and somewhat clearer in the 30-40s (probably only one paragraph but a better description) and very clear in the 40-50 bracket (at least in anticipation).

Comment    Sometimes there is clarification of what it will take to move from the present role to a better role fitting focus. What must be done in the future to adapt a role is important information. Sometimes there is a description of added skills or development of giftedness that will better fit that ideal role.

Example 1. Personal Life Mandate—Introduction Paragraph and Major Role Paragraphs—FLM

My life purpose is to demonstrate a special vulnerability to God which reflects the reality and faithfulness of God to personally relate to people and to intervene in their lives for His purposes, their welfare, and setting the agenda for people's lives. I want to demonstrate that He is trustworthy, wise, loving, and intricate in His plans for us. I know I am to do this via personal modeling—especially being transparent about my own vulnerability and how God has used that in my own life to transform me into the image of Christ. He has renewed me and constantly is doing so in repeated experiences both personally and ministry related. I want to engender this same kind of renewal, first of all, in my own Anglican denomination, and secondly in other situations and groups to whom God may lead me. I want to penetrate any of these groups with ministry, which demonstrates the powerful presence of the Holy Spirit. I want to take many individuals and groups through the same paradigm shift I myself have gone through—that of knowing personally the work of the Holy Spirit in my life and ministry.

I believe the role that will allow me best to do this is basically five-fold:

1. I must be vitally in touch with **parish ministry.** I could operate either on a large parish staff with lots of freedom for outside ministry or in a parachurch organization which has good connections with parish ministry. I need to be grappling with and seeing what I want to preach on, teach on and model out there happening in local situations. I realize that part of my effectiveness *out there* depends on my faithfulness and God's shaping in a *local scene*. How can I tell others they need this renewal in their churches if I myself do not see it in local situations?

## Step 3 in Writing Your Personal Life Mandate continued

Example 1. FLM continued

2. **Roving Apostolic Ministry**. I must reproduce vital Holy Spirit led and empowered ministry with groups and individuals *out there*. I am energized when I am ministering in locales that the Holy Spirit has led me to. Part of this outside ministry is focusing on bringing the renewal that I mentioned in my life purpose. Part of this outside ministry is focusing on training others to do this renewal. Part of this outside ministry is modeling what I mean by renewal. Part of this outside ministry has to do with my own faith and the risk of having to trust God to time and time work. I need this.
3. **Change Agent**. I must proactively focus on being a person of change. I realize that if I am indeed to bring about renewal in the denomination and groups that I must increasingly prioritize what I do so that it will bring lasting results. I must target key individuals and churches throughout the denomination. I must do personal mentoring of these key individuals and seek out ways to impact these key churches.
4. **Writer**. I must capture the spirit of my renewal movement in some major writing projects. I need written materials both to stimulate and attract people to the movement as well as capture the ideas. I need also to facilitate the development of follow-up training materials to conserve the gains I make in situations. I am particularly interested in writing for leaders: expose leader values, priorities, leadership styles and skill-sets. I want to motivate, encourage teach, and model through my writings.
5. **Organizational Entrepreneur**. I must begin to organize my outside ministry into an organization which can perpetuate the movement of renewal much more systematically and with more effectiveness. I must attract people to me who can help me with this as this is not my strength.

Example 2. Samuel Brengle

My life purpose is basically two-fold, **to lead many non-believers to a personal saving knowledge of Christ** and **many believers to a holiness experience** that will let them live lives well pleasing to the Lord. God has gifted me to speak publicly with effectiveness before all kinds of audiences. I want to live a consistent holy life so that my message, backed by my life, will carry great power. I will serve the whole body of Christ by promoting this salvation and holiness message in a wide itinerant public pulpit ministry all over the United States and abroad as God leads.

I will fulfill this life purpose through a special itinerant ministry role--a traveling evangelist and holiness preacher — which is not only authorized but supported and financed by my organization, The Salvation Army, who have freed me to minister with effectiveness in this role.

In addition to public ministry I intend at every opportunity, public and private, to promote my two fold message. I will endeavor to have personal ministry whenever and wherever I can. I will always endeavor to minister for results in lives by giving people opportunity to respond to God.

### Feedback—Doing Step 3

1. From your exercises done in this chapter think through and describe one or more paragraphs that reflect what you know about role and where you want to go with it. In other words write the paragraphs that you will add to your Personal Life Mandate to reflect the focal issue of major role.

**ANSWERS------------**
You may find this exercise difficult at present due to your placement in the age brackets. Perhaps a more fruitful exercise is to go through several example lives like those of Samuel Brengle, G. Campbell Morgan, Robert Jaffray, etc. found in **Focused Lives**. Go to the portion of life representing your age bracket and see if you can construct for those lives this same assignment. You have the added advantage of looking at their whole life before you.

### Final Commentary on Major Role

Comment        Don't be hasty in trying to find an ideal role. Your major responsibility in life is simply to obey God. If you are hearing from God and obeying Him He will help you see and make decisions that will lead to roles that better fit focus for you.

Comment        On the one hand I have said don't be hasty. But on the other hand I want you to learn all you can about who you are and roles that fit you. You are responsible for who you are and who God is making you to be. You are responsible for being a good steward of what you have. Wise decision making which moves toward a major role leading to focus is certainly compatible with following God. For He has uniquely made you and is shaping you for His purposes. Ministry flows out of being. Giftedness is a major part of that beingness.

Comment        Without dreams of what we can be, few of us will ever get there.

(This page is deliberately left blank.)

# Chapter 6 Leaving A Legacy

Introduction    Life purpose forms the prime integrating factor around which a
focused life operates.  Effective methodologies represent those precious
ministry insights that fit who you are and allow you to deliver efficient
ministry.  Major role represents the best fit between your giftedness and
the job that you must do.  This major role allows for effective use of
effective methodologies and the satisfaction of fulfilling life purpose.  The
final realization of this process is the accomplishment of life
achievements—both in being and doing.  At the end of our lives we want
to leave behind both tangible and intangible results from our life work.
We call these results—**ultimate contributions**.

All leaders leave behind results of their life work.  Most do not do so
deliberately.  It just happens.  Sometimes they miss doing or being
something that they should have.  Perhaps with intention they could have
left behind God-intended legacies had they been aware.  This chapter
exposes you to categories of lasting legacies that have been derived from
comparative study of effective leaders.  Most present day leaders can
identify readily with these lasting legacies. Intuitively they can identify a
set of two to five of these legacies that both appeal to them and seem to be
items that can be achieved.  Once these are recognized there can be
proactive decision making in terms of how major role and effective
methodologies can be focused toward end of life results.

Overview    In this chapter you will be introduced to:

- the overall flowchart leading to assessment of a focused life and where
  this chapter fits in that assessment,
- the time-line—and related information about ultimate contribution,
- the notion of ultimate contribution—including 13 prime types—and
  the ideal notion of the ultimate contribution set,
- several sample time-lines with critical incidents pointing to ultimate
  contribution,
- the notion of a Venn diagram which portrays your tentative ultimate
  contribution set (your collection of intended lasting legacies),
- the practical suggestions of intermediate goals setting around this
  ultimate contribution set,
- step 4 in writing your personal life mandate—using your Venn
  diagram to guide you in intermediate goal setting that takes your
  Personal Life Mandate into realizable activities for the immediate
  future.

End Result    By the conclusion of this chapter you will have your tentative Personal
Life Mandate and some ideas for working it out in the near future.

**Flowchart—Overview Of Assessment**

# BASIC FLOW CHART
# FOR MOVING TOWARD A FOCUSED LIFE
|

|

Basic shaping of life and basic ministry experience
lead to **indications** of:

- life purpose (LP),
- effective methodologies (EM),
- major role (MR),

In this chapter you are here --->    • ultimate contributions (UC).
|

|

which allow the drafting of a **tentative**
**Personal Life Mandate**
- intro paragraph—life purpose (**LP**),
- additional paragraphs—intent to use ministry insights as effective
methodologies (**EM**),
- description of a major role you will work toward to carry out life
purpose and use effective methodologies  (**MR**).

In this chapter you are here --->   • Venn diagram of your hoped for legacies which give you long term
guideposts that will result from your increased prioritization
toward
the focused life (**UC**).
|

|

and you are here --->       And the Setting of **Intermediate Goals**
Along 5 Different Age-Groupings

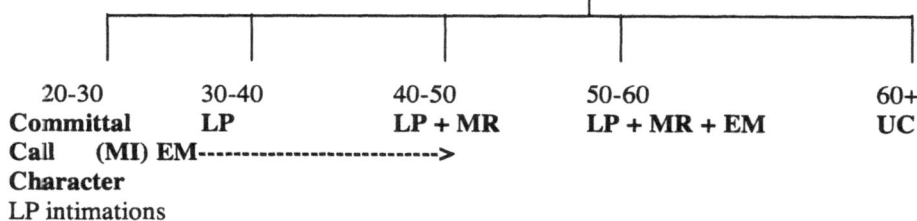

| 20-30 | 30-40 | 40-50 | 50-60 | 60+ |
|---|---|---|---|---|
| **Committal** | **LP** | **LP + MR** | **LP + MR + EM** | **UC** |
| **Call**  (MI) EM----------------------------> | | | | |
| **Character** | | | | |
| LP intimations | | | | |

<-------- Scattered and Exploratory            Increasingly focused ------------------------------------>
activities to learn about            activities that move toward doing and being
self and God's intentions            what God has intended
|

which results in a tentative rough draft of a Personal Life Mandate
with Appropriate Paragraphs and ideas about the next several years—which will vary
from scattered to focused depending on which age bracket you are
and which will eventually build toward long term goals
|

Resulting in Movement Toward a More
**FOCUSED LIFE**

## Time-Line And Hints About Ultimate Contribution

Introduction          This chapter will suggest that over their lifetimes leaders are led by God toward
                      achievements in harmony with who He has made them to be and in terms of the strategic
                      direction He has given them. There are two kinds of results: 1. specific achievements
                      unique to the individual leader and 2. those lasting achievements, called ultimate
                      contributions. Comparative study has identified 12 prime categories that generally
                      describe some important legacies left behind by effective leaders who finished well. It is
                      helpful to trace out how strategic direction indicated early on and confirmed these
                      ultimate contributions. The time-line is helpful for that.

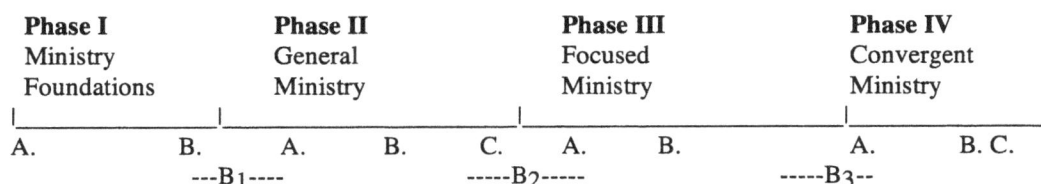

| **Phase I** | **Phase II** | **Phase III** | **Phase IV** |
|---|---|---|---|
| Ministry | General | Focused | Convergent |
| Foundations | Ministry | Ministry | Ministry |

```
|_____|_____|_____|_____|
A.          B.    A.      B.      C.   A.      B.        A.       B. C.
      ---B₁----              -----B₂-----          -----B₃--
```

### Phase I
A.   Sovereign Foundations — (13-20 years)—early shaping of character/ personality
B.   Leadership Transition (3-6 years)—a time in which first steps in ministry are done
     *Discovery Pattern: Some leaders at this juncture or in provisional ministry happen on to an important
     need and as a result give their lives to meet that need. This is a need-centered motivational pattern.
     A person is drawn to a cause and gives his/her life to do something about that cause.*
     *Destiny Pattern: A leader has a mystical experience with God in which direction for all of life is
     given. That direction will naturally lead into what must be accomplished. This is a divine centered
     pattern. A very few leaders get this early in or before leadership transition or in early provisional
     ministry. This is a rare pattern.*

### Phase II
A.   Provisional Ministry   (2-6 years) —the first attempts at full time ministry assignments; it is
     provisional because it might not last, that is, the leader may not stay in ministry.
B.   Growth Ministry (6-8 years)—ministry utilizing known giftedness with efficiency; giftedness and role
     issues are learned; this sub-phase is more for developing the leader than accomplishing ministry.
C.   Competent Ministry<— (2-6 years) —>operating out of giftedness in roles that fit that giftedness
     produces excellent results; still to be determined is the potential level of influence.
     *The Drift Pattern: A person is led in a step-by-step guidance fashion. There is no purposeful
     deliberate attempt to have an ultimate contribution. The person simply follows what he/she thinks is
     God's guidance. Each major guidance decision will probably lead to some new accomplishment that
     will be the focus of efforts until God gives guidance for the next phase—a usual pattern for most.*
     *The Deliberate Pattern: As a leader grows he/she begins to understand more about himself/ herself
     and that leader begins to deliberately move toward training or roles that will enhance development
     and focus efforts. In the focusing of efforts, the ultimate contribution(s) become clear. This is an
     analytical, logical pattern centering on assessment of a person and a meaningful life that will
     contribute. A few leaders enter this pattern usually toward the competent but increasingly so in unique
     ministry.*

### Phase III
A.   Role Transition—There is movement toward compatibility between role, giftedness and influence-mix
     profile. There is shaping of a role more ideally suited to giftedness and toward influence-mix.
B.   Unique Ministry—ministering effectively as well as efficiently with giftedness. (Role plus unique may
     last 3-12 years)

### Phase IV
A.   Special Guidance—movement toward a role focusing on ultimate contribution
B.   Convergent Ministry—fulfilling a sense of destiny/ ultimate contribution
C.   Afterglow—fall out effects of a life well lived; spiritual authority dominant

**Sample Time-Line With Hints Toward Ultimate Contribution, CRJ**

| I. NAÏVE NATURAL LEADER | | II. NATURAL TO SPIRITUAL LEADER | | | III. DESTINY LEADERSHIP | |
|---|---|---|---|---|---|---|

`|----------------|----------------|----------------|`

| 1936 | 1964 | 1970 | 1974 | 1978-1981 Geographical Convergence | 1987-1988 | Present |
|---|---|---|---|---|---|---|
| | | 34 | 38 | | | |
| Age | 28 | 34 | 38 | 43-45 | 51, 52 | |

| A. (1936-57) Great Depression Values, Sovereign Foundations | A. (1971-74) The Minors—Educational Technology Perspectives | A. (1981-87) The Majors—Developing Content & Effective Methodology for Teaching; Researching Leadership and Developmental Framework |
|---|---|---|
| B. (1957-64) Marriage, Early Career | B. (1974-79) Authority Lessons, Learning to Produce Materials | B. (1988-1993) Influence-Mix Challenge; Expansion by Taking Concepts Out; Writing via Barnabus |
| C. (1964-70) Transition to Ministry, Home Bible Study Experience | C. (1979-81) Broadening—Getting Missiological Perspective | C. (1994—present) Reflection and Intentionality Toward Destiny Fulfillment; Developing Others To Carry Out My Legacy |

**Ultimate Contribution Indications** ...................................................➤

| | | |
|---|---|---|
| 1964-1970 Union Life **SAINT**; **MENTOR/** Discipler | 1973 **WRITER** (Puzzles...) 1975 **WRITER** (Spiritual Gifts) | 1981ff; 1989 **RESEARCHER** Life Long Development; Bible Centered Leadership |
| | | 1987 **WRITER** (TML) |
| | | 1989 **MENTOR**: Spiritual Guide; Counselor; Contemporary Model; Sponsor; Teacher |
| | | 1990ff **STYLISTIC PRACTITIONER** |

**Ultimate Contribution**        synonym: lasting legacy
**Ultimate Contribution Set**    synonym: group of lasting legacies

Introduction     An **ultimate contribution** is a legacy that a leader will leave behind after
                 life is over. Leaders usually have several of these. As a leader ages he/she
                 recognizes the shortness of time left in ministry, especially when
                 compared with the time already gone by. This usually brings on a
                 reflection as to what to do that will really count in the remaining years.
                 The concept of ultimate contribution is very useful in channeling that kind
                 of thinking productively. In fact, even younger leaders who reflect this
                 way can begin to proactively move toward these legacies much earlier in
                 their ministries.

Definition       An ultimate contribution is a lasting legacy of a Christian worker for which he
                 or she is remembered and which furthers the cause of Christianity by one or
                 more of the following:
                 - setting standards for life and ministry,
                 - impacting lives by enfolding them in God's kingdom or
                   developing them once in the kingdom,
                 - serving as a stimulus for change which betters the world,
                 - leaving behind an organization, institution, or movement that
                   will further channel God's work,
                 - the discovery of ideas, communication of them, or promotion
                   of them so that they further God's work.

Definition       The ultimate contribution set is the collection of ultimate contribution
                 categories that a given leader will leave behind at the end of life.

Types            Thirteen categories defined in the following table include: saint, stylistic
                 practitioner, family, mentor, public rhetorician, pioneer, change person,
                 artist, founder, stabilizer, researcher, writer, promoter.

Example          Samuel Brengle: saint, public rhetorician, promoter, mentor counselor, and
                 writer

Example          Henrietta Mears: mentor, promoter, founder, writer, public rhetorician

Example          FLM: stylistic practitioner, stabilizer, mentor, writer, saint

Example          CRJ: stylistic practitioner, mentor, researcher, saint, writer

**Ultimate Contribution** continued

Comment          Categories include the following:

| Type | Basic Notion |
| --- | --- |
| **CHARACTER:** | |
| SAINT | A Model life, not a perfect one, but a life others want to emulate. |
| STYLISTIC PRACTITIONER | A Model ministry style which sets the pace for others and which other ministries seek to emulate. |
| FAMILY | Promote a God-fearing family, leaving behind children who walk with God carrying on that Godly-heritage. |
| **MINISTRY:** | |
| MENTOR | A productive ministry with individuals, small groups, etc. |
| PUBLIC RHETORICIAN | A productive public ministry with large groups. |
| **CATALYTIC:** | |
| PIONEER | A person who starts apostolic ministries. |
| CHANGE PERSON | A person who rights wrongs and injustices in society and in church and mission organizations. |
| ARTIST | A person who has creative breakthroughs in life and ministry and introduces innovation. |
| **ORGANIZATIONAL:** | |
| FOUNDER | A person who starts a new organization to meet a need or capture the essence of some movement or the like. |
| STABILIZER | A person who can help a fledgling organization develop or can help an older organization move toward efficiency and effectiveness. In other words, help solidify an organization. |
| **IDEATION:** | |
| RESEARCHER | Develops new ideation by studying various things. |
| WRITER | captures ideas and reproduces them in written format to help and inform others. |
| PROMOTER | Effectively distributes new ideas and/or other ministry related things. |

### Historical Examples Of Ultimate Contributions

Introduction    Below are given several examples taken from my comparative study of eight effective leaders as detailed in **Focused Lives**.

| Prime Type | Major Thrust of the Type | Historical Example |
|---|---|---|
| 1. Saint | A Model life, not a perfect one, but a life others want to emulate. | Samuel Brengle, R. C. McQuilkin |
| 2. Stylistic Practitioner | A model ministry style; a flagship church or ministry organization which effectively delivers the ministry output of a leader. | A. J. Gordon, G. Campbell Morgan |
| 3. Family | Promote a God-fearing family, leaving behind children who walk with God carrying on that Godly-heritage. | A. J. Gordon |
| 4. Mentor | A productive ministry with individuals. | Henrietta Mears, Charles Simeon |
| 5. Public Rhetorician | A productive ministry with large public groups. | G. Campbell Morgan, Samuel Brengle |
| 6. Pioneer | Founds apostolic type works. | Henrietta Mears, Robert Jaffray |
| 7. Change Person | Rights wrongs and injustices in society | A. J. Gordon |
| 8. Artist | Creative breakthroughs. | Henrietta Mears, A. J. Gordon |
| 9. Founder | Starts new organizations. | R. C. McQuilkin, L. E. Maxwell |
| 10. Stabilizer | Solidifies organizations. | G. Campbell Morgan, R. C. McQuilkin |
| 11. Researcher | Develops new ideation. | G. Campbell Morgan, A. J. Gordon |
| 12. Writer | Captures new ideation for use of others. | G. Campbell Morgan, Henrietta Mears |
| 13. Promoter | Distributes effectively new ideation. | L. E. Maxwell, Samuel Brengle |

## Feedback On Ultimate Contribution

1.   Note the groupings of the major categories of ultimate contributions.
     ___ a.   **Character contributions** (saint and stylistic practitioner)--the essential nature of this grouping is modeling which impacts others.
     ___ b.   **Ministry Output** (mentor influencing by relationships with many; influencing by strong public preaching or teaching)
     ___ c.   **Catalytic Work** (recognizing needs and bringing about change to meet those needs by pioneering something, by correcting things, by introducing new and different ways of seeing and doing things)
     ___ d.   **Organizational Work** (by starting new organizations, by making organizations more effective)
     ___ e.   **Ideation—Analytical Work** (by discovering new helpful ideas, by writing about ideas so as to influence, by promoting ideas so that they can be used)

     Which of these groupings is most or least appealing to you? Place a M (for most) in space beside the most important category and an L (for least).

2.   Glance at the table given below. Supply from your own experience the name of someone who fits at least three of the categories.

| Prime Type | Major Thrust of the Type | Personal Example Seen |
|---|---|---|
| 1. Saint | A Model life, not a perfect one, but a life others want to emulate. | |
| 2. Stylistic Practitioner | A model ministry style; a flagship church or ministry organization which effectively delivers the ministry output of a leader. | |
| 3. Family | Promote a God-fearing family, leaving behind children who walk with God carrying on that Godly-heritage. | |
| 4. Mentor | A productive ministry with individuals. | |
| 5. Public Rhetorician | A productive ministry with large public groups. | |
| 6. Pioneer | Founds apostolic type works. | |
| 7. Change Person | Rights wrongs in society | |
| 8. Artist | Creative breakthroughs. | |
| 9. Founder | Starts new organizations. | |
| 10. Stabilizer | Solidifies organizations. | |
| 11. Researcher | Develops new ideation. | |
| 12. Writer | Captures new ideation for use of others. | |
| 13. Promoter | Distributes effectively new ideation. | |

**ANSWERS-----------**
1. Your choice. For me it is a toss-up between two for most. _M_ e. **Ideation—Analytical Work** (by discovering new helpful ideas, by writing about ideas so as to influence, _M_ b. **Ministry Output** (mentor influencing by relationships with many). For least, again it is a toss-up between two; _L_ c. **Catyltic Work** _L_ d. **Organizational Work**
2.   Your choice. But notice carefully what categories you noted people in. For there is a basic principle that like-attracts-like. The ones you note intuitively without thinking are probably those you are most attracted to and may give a hint at your own categories.

### Ultimate Contribution Patterns—Which For Focused Life?

| | |
|---|---|
| Introduction | Leaders enter in to an understanding of their lasting legacies in different ways. Below are given four patterns labeled, described, and some examples of them. As you read through them be aware of people you have known who fit the different patterns. Think about yourself! Which pattern describes you? |

### Four Patterns Leading to Ultimate Contributions

| Pattern | Example | Description |
|---|---|---|
| 1. Destiny | Paul the Apostle<br>Samuel Brengle | This leader has a mystical experience with God in which direction for all of life is given. That direction will naturally lead into what must be accomplished. This is a divine centered pattern. |
| 2. Deliberate | Rufus Anderson<br>Henry Venn<br>R. C. McQuilkin | As this leader grows he/she begins to understand more about himself/ herself and that leader begins to deliberately move toward training or roles that will enhance development and focus efforts. In the focusing of efforts, the ultimate contribution(s) become clear. This is an analytical, logical pattern centering on assessment of a person and a meaningful life that will contribute. |
| 3. Discovery | Frank Laubach<br>C. F. Andrews<br>Alexander Duff | This leader happens on an important need and gives his/her life to meet that need. This is a need-centered motivational pattern. A person is drawn to a cause and gives his/her life to do something about that cause. |
| 4. Drift | Kenneth Strachan<br>A. J. Gordon<br>Hudson Taylor | This leader is led in a step-by-step guidance fashion. There is no purposeful deliberate attempt to have an ultimate contribution. The person simply follows what he/she thinks is God's guidance. Each major guidance decision will probably lead to some new accomplishment that will be the focus of efforts until God gives guidance for the next phase. |

| | |
|---|---|
| Comment | It is the intent of this chapter to make some people aware of the destiny pattern and hence move toward a focused life with divine authority. It should do the same for some discovery type leaders. This chapter should also alert some drift pattern leaders toward the deliberate pattern. At the same time a leader who consciously walks in day-by-day sensitive fellowship with the Spirit can trust God that the drift pattern will move him/her toward ultimate contributions in line with focus. |
| Comment | In other words all of these patterns are acceptable patterns. But some drift leaders may miss focus and hence should be open to moving toward the deliberate pattern. |

### Feedback on Ultimate Contribution Patterns

1. For each of the 4 destiny patterns, see if you can suggest some leader (historical or contemporary) you have known who fits that category.

| Pattern | Your Example | Description |
|---------|--------------|-------------|
| 1. Destiny | | This leader has a mystical experience with God in which direction for all of life is given. That direction will naturally lead into what must be accomplished. This is a divine centered pattern. |
| 2. Deliberate | | As this leader grows he/she begins to understand more about himself/ herself and that leader begins to deliberately move toward training or roles that will enhance development and focus efforts. In the focusing of efforts, the ultimate contribution(s) become clear. This is an analytical, logical pattern centering on assessment of a person and a meaningful life that will contribute. |
| 3. Discovery | | This leader happens on an important need and gives his/her life to meet that need. This is a need-centered motivational pattern. A person is drawn to a cause and gives his/her life to do something about that cause. |
| 4. Drift | | This leader is led in a step-by-step guidance fashion. There is no purposeful deliberate attempt to have an ultimate contribution. The person simply follows what he/she thinks is God's guidance. Each major guidance decision will probably lead to some new accomplishment that will be the focus of efforts until God gives guidance for the next phase. |

2. Which of the four are you?

| Pattern | Which are You? |
|---------|----------------|
| 1. Destiny | |
| 2. Deliberate | |
| 3. Discovery | |
| 4. Drift | |

**ANSWERS-----------**
Your choice.

**How To Do a Venn Diagram of Your Ultimate Contribution Set**

Introduction        The instructions for doing a Venn Diagram for Ultimate Contribution Set are essentially the same as that for your giftedness set given in chapter 5 with the exception that only an oval (circle/ oblong) symbol is used to represent each ultimate contribution. It is the size and placement of the figure that gives the information. Sometimes leaders will do the figure in dotted lines if they are tentative about it.

## Step 1: Gathering Your Data

Glance at the table listing and defining the ultimate contributions. When a leader glances at all 13 it usually the case that almost immediately the leader can eliminate 5 or 6. He/she knows that those will never be part of the life achievement. Now for the remaining items select in priority order which ones best fit you. The top 2 or 3 you may want to call fairly certain and the rest as possiblities. It may help at this point if you go back to your time-line and think through the ones you have selected to see where you have indications from God's shaping activity that lends credibility to your selection.

## Step 2: Select the Most Dominant Ultimate Contribution

Decide which of the ultimate contributions is the most important to you. Whichever one it is, you will make it the biggest and center it on the page. Occasionally there will be two elements which are equally important but this is not common.

## Step 3: Determining the Relationships and Importance of each part.

Now add the other contributions to the diagram. Decide how the other contributions relate to that dominant contribution. When you overlap symbols the overlap area indicates that all the items that are overlapping operate together.

## Step 4: Begin Drawing Your Diagram

Go ahead and finish your initial draft. You have to make some effort. It will probably take you two or three tries so do the first few in pencil.

## Step 5: Get Feedback

Once you have drawn a rough draft. Contact some people who know you and have observed you in ministry. Share your diagram with them. Talk through the relationships of the various contributions and describe how you see the importance of each contribution. Get feedback. As you share the diagram and talk about it, you will see more or learn more. You may want to modify your diagram based on what you have learned.

## Step 6: Prepare Your Final Draft

Once you have gotten some feedback, you can draw your final draft. Recognize that this is a tentative diagram. As you move into your 50s you will become more and more certain about it. Be prepared then, from time-to-time to revise this diagram.

**Sample Venn Diagram for Samuel Brengle/ Explanation**

Introduction    Below is given Samuel Brengle's Venn Diagram for ultimate
                contributions. In addition I have described that set and shown also his
                specific contributions in order that you might have perspective on both
                kinds of contributions.

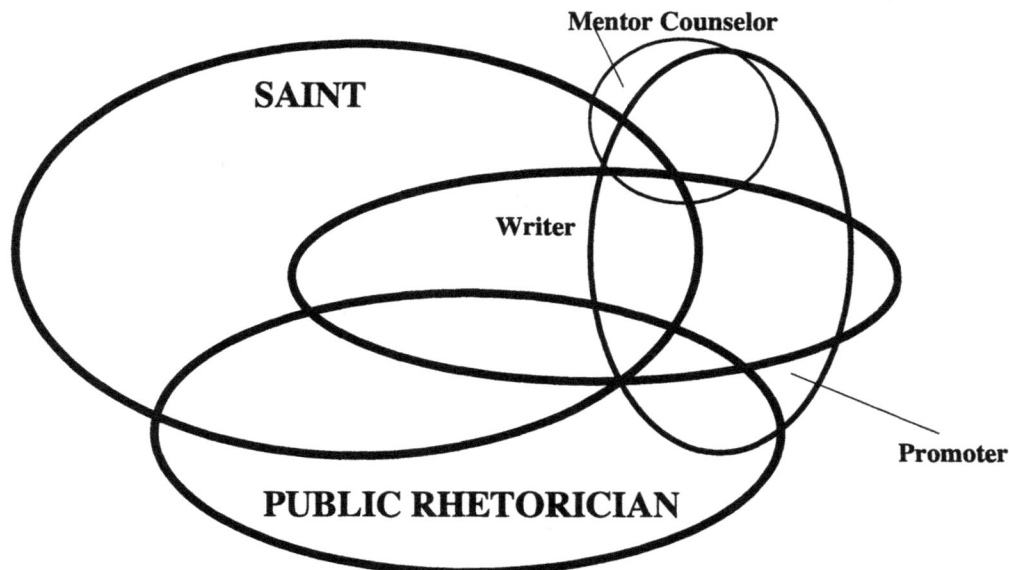

**Description of Ultimate Contribution Set**

He was a **saint**. His dominant contribution was his model of a holy life.
Sensitivity to God, obedience to God, and a life devoted wholly to pleasing God were an
inspirational stimulus to all who knew him and to all of us who profit through study of
his life. He demonstrates the reality of living a life above the controlling authority of sin.
He shows that God is real and can change a life.

But he was a **public rhetorician** who led many people to Christ through his
public ministry. He led many people to experience the holiness powergate and opened
for them the possibility of living a holy life. His pulpit work was both effective in itself
and in the model he left for those who want to communicate effectively in the power of
the Spirit. He merges oratorical natural abilities and acquired skills with powerful
evangelism and exhortation spiritual gifts. His most powerful pulpit material as been
revised and published in the form of written material. So though we do not capture the
affect and volitional power of his public ministry we do have much of its cognitive
content. His sermon, the Atonement, was a major contribution in a moment of time and
will have eternal results which we shall yet see someday.

He was a **writer**. His written achievements captured life experiences-- personally
with God and from public ministry. His was not theoretical treatment of subjects but an
experiential understanding of them. These writings were part of his activity to promote
holiness and sensitivity to God. They were dominantly for the common person, the
seeker or Christian needing help in his audiences. But it is amazing to see, from
testimonies, just how much these practical writings also helped leaders.

**Sample Venn Diagram for Samuel Brengle** continued

He was a **mentor** who related to people personally and gave good counsel. His personal ministry was probably as powerful as his public ministry. His spiritual gifts of evangelism, exhortation, and word of wisdom were powerful in private ministry. He dealt well with individuals in formal and informal times of counseling. His servant leadership is probably seen best in his giving of himself to others in individual ministry. As Hall says he was instant out of season as well as in season.

He was a **promoter**. The dominant idea he promoted was holiness—*to insist upon holiness of heart and life.* He advocated a holiness paradigm through which people could enter into that experience. He was strongly focused in this. This was the focal element and probably the more dominant of his two pronged life purpose--evangelism and holiness.

### Listing of Brengle's Unique/ Special Contributions

Brengle's specific contributions to the cause of Christ and the on-going of the Christian movement include at least the following:

1. He led many people to know Christ as their personal Savior.
2. He led many people to experience the Holy Spirit's power for living.
3. He pioneered a new ministry role within The Salvation Army, which role was passed on after his retirement.
4. He left behind materials in written form to promote holiness.
5. He modeled the foundational ministry pattern--faithfulness in ministry assignments.
6. He showed that even in short term assignments (his longest assignment before National Spiritual Special was 3 years or less ) a leader can have effective ministry if he/she concentrates on developing available leadership.
7. He modeled a focused life with two focal issues dominant--major role and life purpose.
8. He is an ideal type of a leader who finished well.

**Sample Venn Diagram for Henrietta Mears**

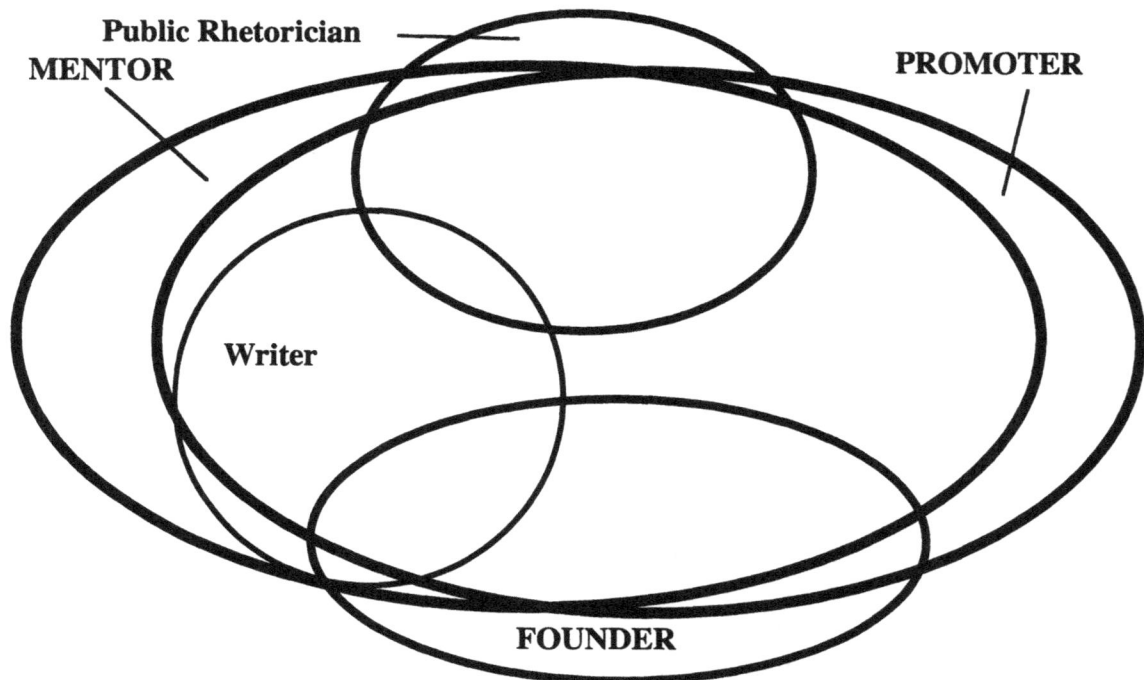

**Explanation of Mears Set**

The **Mentor** and **Promoter** ultimate contributes dominate what she left behind. Her ministry was very personal. She recruited, trained and released so many leaders. She promoted (remember her motivational bent) Sunday Schools, Bible Teaching, and leadership. She **Founded** a powerful Christian Education Department, a publishing company, and a retreat ministry. She **Wrote** Sunday School materials, teacher training materials, and Bible materials. Her speaking ministry, including an on-going Bible teaching ministry to collegiates and conference ministries, as well as her speaking around the world on her trips was significant. She was an outstanding **Public Rhetorician**, but it didn't dominate her ministry.

**Sample Venn Diagram for FLM/ Listing of Goals To Move Toward It**

Introduction    Here is the ultimate contribution set of a contemporary leader. Note the stimulating thinking toward deliberate proactive movement as described by the questions to probe goals flowing from the diagram.

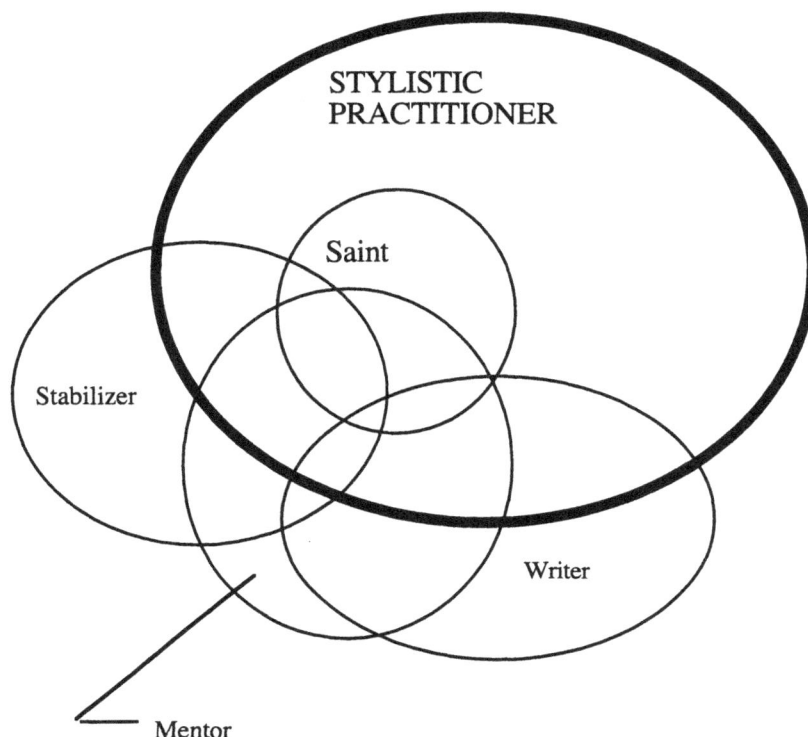

I have devised a set of key questions to help me think through my goals that flow from this ultimate contribution set. All are prefaced with a header, **ASK GOD**, which reminds me and forces me to model what I mean about being vulnerable to God for His setting of the agenda.

1. **Ask God.** What organizations should I be penetrating in order to move people and groups toward renewal as I have experienced it?
2. **Ask God.** What should be my strategy with these organizations? How should I help them?
3. **Ask God.** How can I be more deliberate in penetrating individual leaders? How can I be more pro-active in mentoring them? How can I be a more effective mentor?
4. **Ask God.** What does God want me to do with my writing? How does my writing fit with my other tasks? What kinds of materials would enable my ministry to continue after me? Should I recruit others to work with me in it? Can I effectively mentor-sponsor others in writing?
5. **Ask God.** Do I need to set up a parachurch organization? How am I to be financially stable?

**Sample Venn Diagram for CRJ**

Introduction    Below is given the Venn Diagram for another contemporary leader. What kind of major role would fit this end of life achievement pattern?

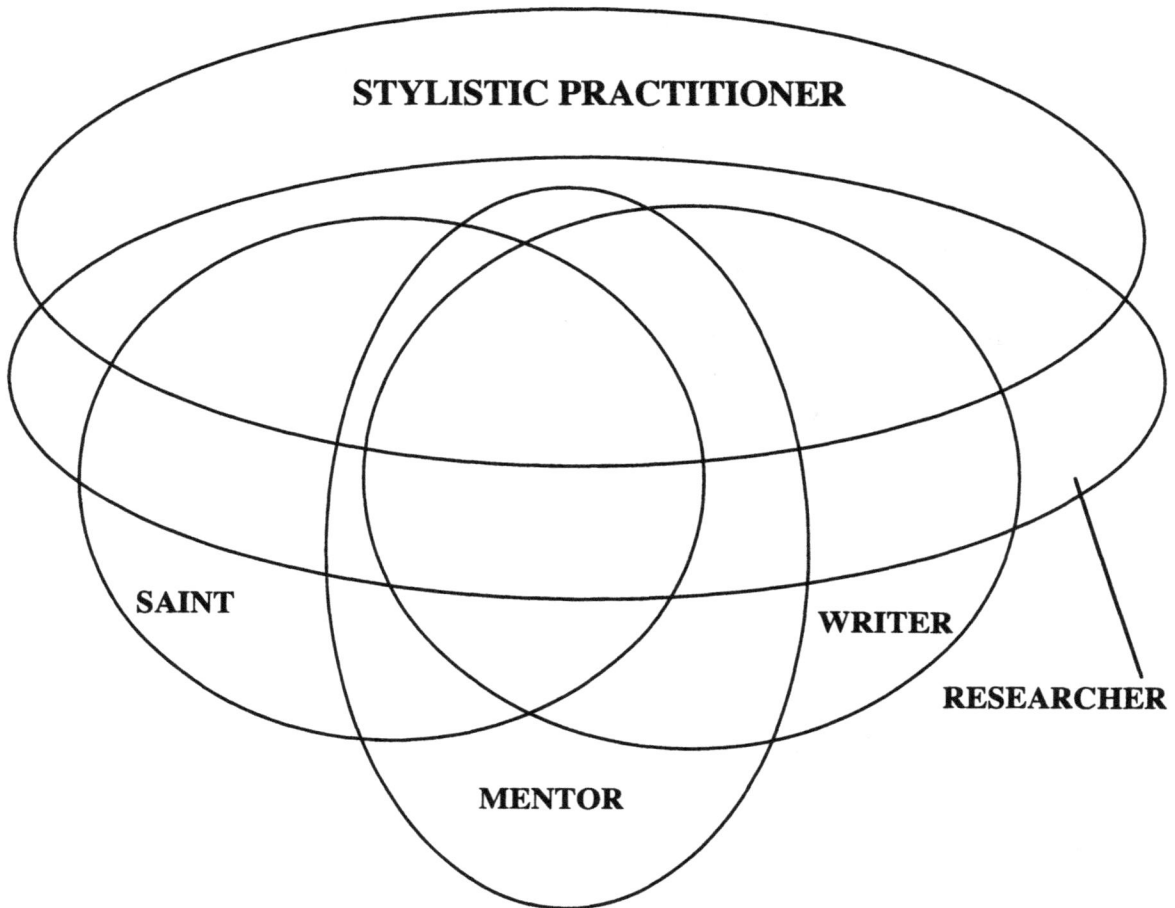

**STYLISTIC PRACTITIONER**

**SAINT**

**WRITER**

**RESEARCHER**

**MENTOR**

Proverbs 10:7  The memory of the righteous will be a blessing...

Comment     What do you think is the import of the verse?  Why included on the Venn Diagram?

**Personal Life Mandate**     Synonym: Personal Mission Statement, Mission Statement

| | |
|---|---|
| Introduction | Covey's principle, *Begin With the End in Mind* challenges us as we seek to lead focused lives. It is important that we understand what it is we are shooting for. By deriving an explicit Personal Life Mandate from underlying assumptions and past processing which centers on focal issues we are bringing out into the open concepts to approve, modify, abrogate if necessary, and finally use them to become very intentional about our lives. |
| Definition | A <u>Personal Life Mandate</u> is a one to three page length description, made up of several paragraphs, which give in essence a person's life time goals in terms of what is known of the focal issues (Life Purpose, Major Role, Effective Methodology, and Ultimate Contribution) and using language which gives further intents toward these issues as well as describing being and doing achievements in harmony with these issues. |
| Definition | <u>Life purpose</u> is usually the dominant focal issue in most lives. It usually forms the topic around which the first paragraph of the Personal Life Mandate is given—called the introductory paragraph. |
| Comment | Being statements describe inner character or sanctification issues in the life which are intents for development. They underlie the *why* we do what we do and somewhat the *what* of what we do. Life purpose may well relate to the *when* of what we are doing. Doing statements flow from life purpose and ultimate contribution findings. They most relate to the *what* that we are about. |
| Comment | **Effective methodologies** describe the major means whereby life purpose or ultimate contributions are realized. These relate to the *how* we operate or the means whereby we achieve or make progress in delivering our ministry. |
| Comment | **Major Role** recognizes that we may not be able to carry out life purpose and exploit our effective methodologies unless we adjust our present role. |
| Comment | **Ultimate contributions** help set the boundaries for what we want to accomplish in terms of the big picture. They will relate to *means* and *ends*. |
| Comment | The actual writing form of the paragraphs, other than reflecting being and doing and focusing on focal issues can take on any unique form that fits the person and with which the person is comfortable. The basic issue is *does the Personal Life Mandate help the person to be more proactive and deliberate in focusing the life*. If so, the format is good. If not, change it. |
| Comment | Personal Life Mandates should be revised regularly. The core will change little but there will be clarification throughout life as the focal issues emerge. |
| Comment | Start with any rough draft Personal Life Mandate. A poor one is better than none. Expect it to be modified, become more specific and helpful as you develop. It will become a means for proactive decision making. Early ministry can be rather exploratory —focal issues are still up for grabs. Further experience will help you focus. Closed doors provide boundaries as focal issues are clarified. So don't be afraid to try things. As you move toward end game play say **yes** and **no** using your Personal Life Mandate as a screen for choosing ministry activity. |

**Step 4 in Writing Your Personal Life Mandate**

Introduction | Below is given the description of paragraph(s) of a personal life mandate which describes the inclusion of ultimate contribution as shown with several examples.

Description | <u>Ultimate contribution paragraphs</u> reflect what is known to date of end of life achievements—that is, expected results, lasting legacies.

Comment | Three things make up the ultimate contribution paragraph:
1. The descriptive introduction.
2. The Venn Diagram depicting the ultimate contribution set.
3. The description of goals that may lead to accomplishing of the ultimate contribution set or at least proactively move in that direction.

Comment | A standard form usually starts, "I know that if I am to leave behind a lasting legacy..." then follows a description of intents.

Comment | The goals are described in various ways. Sometimes they are in terms of probing inquiries. Sometimes they are in terms of projects that will bring growth. They can be in any form as long as they help the leader move closer to focus.

Example | **FLM**—I know that if I am to leave behind a lasting legacy of renewal in my own denomination that I must become much more focused and proactive about it. In seeking to do this I know that God will constantly affirm me, renew me personally, and give me great satisfaction. I intend to be motivated by and to set specific goals toward fulfillment of the following ultimate contributions set (my lasting legacies I want to leave behind).

Example | **CRJ**—My end game ministry will focus more on enabling others to do what I am about. I will concentrate more on operating out of the base and less on decentralized workshops and seminars. It will allow personal ministry to fewer leaders on an in-depth basis--those who will be attracted to spend time with me. I recognize that I will need a setting which allows for isolation and much research and writing for this end game phase. I intend to be motivated by the following ultimate contribution set. The decisions I make about what I do will depend to a large extent on my understanding of these life achievements. For each of the ultimate contributions I am tentatively describing what it means and how that affects what I am and what I do.

**Intermediate Goals**
**Growth Projects**

Introduction      Statement of intermediate goals and growth projects leading toward
                  accomplishment can be almost any form. The key is, "Do they help you
                  think about what you want to achieve and move you toward it?" As you
                  move into the 60s age bracket this will become increasing the major effort
                  of your movement toward focus. If you are in your 20-30s or 30-40s don't
                  even worry about this step. If you are in your 40s tentatively begin to
                  identify and modify your major role to move in the direction of enhancing
                  ultimate contributions. If you are in your 50s you should be seriously
                  thinking about this. Focused activities should be carrying out this.

Example           **FLM**—I have devised a set of key questions to help me think through my
                  goals that flow from this ultimate contribution set. All are prefaced with a
                  header, ASK GOD, which reminds me and forces me to model what I
                  mean about being vulnerable to God for His setting of the agenda.

                  1. **Ask God.** What organizations should I be penetrating in order to move
                     people and groups toward renewal as I have experienced it?
                  2. **Ask God.** What should be my strategy with these organizations? How
                     should I help them?
                  3. **Ask God.** How can I be more deliberate in penetrating individual
                     leaders? How can I be more pro-active in mentoring them? How can I
                     be a more effective mentor?
                  4. **Ask God.** What does God want me to do with my writing? How does
                     my writing fit with my other tasks? What kinds of materials would
                     enable my ministry to continue after me? Should I recruit others to
                     work with me in it? Can I effectively mentor-sponsor others in
                     writing?
                  5. **Ask God.** Do I need to set up a parachurch organization? How am I
                     to be financially stable?

**Feedback—Doing Step 4 Thinking About Ultimate Contribution**

1. From your exercises done in this chapter think through and describe one or more paragraphs that reflect what you know about ultimate contribution and where you want to go with it. In other words write the paragraphs that you will add to your Personal Life Mandate to reflect ultimate contribution.

ANSWERS-----------

You may find this exercise difficult at present due to your placement in the age brackets. Perhaps a more fruitful exercise is to go through several example lives like those of Samuel Brengle, G. Campbell Morgan, Robert Jaffray, etc. found in **Focused Lives**. Go to the portion of life representing your age bracket and see if you can construct for those lives just what they might have known about ultimate contribution. You have the added advantage of looking at their whole life before you.

### Final Commentary on Ultimate Contribution

| | |
|---|---|
| Comment | As was the case with major role your main responsibility in life is not aiming for an ultimate contribution set—your major responsibility in life is simply to obey God. If you are hearing from God and obeying Him he will help you see and make decisions that will lead to your ultimate contribution that fits focus for you. |
| Comment | On the one hand I have said don't be hasty. But on the other hand I want you to learn all you can about who you are and the legacies you desire to leave behind. You are responsible for who you are and who God is making you to be and do. You are responsible for being a good steward of what you have and what you ought to achieve. Wise decision making which moves toward lasting legacies appropriate to your focus is certainly compatible with following God. For He has uniquely made you and is shaping you for His purposes. Ministry flows out of being. And you were created with God's purposes in mind. |
| Comment | Remember Moses' admonitions: |
| **Psalm 90:12** | **LORD, let us learn to wisely apply ourselves so that our lives might count.** |
| **Psalm 90:17** | **And let the beauty of the Lord our God be upon us. Yes, LORD, establish our life work.** |
| | Let me paraphrase it in terms of the focused life. |
| **Psalm 90:12** | **Teach us to use our time well so that our lives count.** |
| **Psalm 90:17** | **Establish what we have done so that it lives on.** |
| Comment | He certainly wanted his life to count. And he wanted to have what he did be established and left behind as a lasting legacy. |

(This page is deliberately left blank.)

# Chapter 7 Moving Toward Focus

At this point we have covered all four of the focal life issues:

1. **life purpose**—that burden-like calling, a task or driving force or achievement, which motivates a leader to fulfill something or to see something done.
2. **effective methodologies**—ministry insights around which the leader can pass on to others the essentials of doing something or using something or being something, that is, a means of effectively delivering some important ministry of that leader which enhances life purpose or moves toward ultimate contribution.
3. **major role**—that official or unofficial position, or status/ platform, or leadership functions, or job description which basically describes what a leader does and which allows recognition by others and which uniquely fits who a leader is and lets that leader effectively accomplish life purpose(s).
4. **ultimate contribution**—that lasting legacy of a Christian worker for which he or she is remembered and which furthers the cause of Christianity.

Now I want to give perspective about your discovering these focal issues in your own life. I want you to recognize that the focused life is a lifetime perspective. Along the way you will pick up indications of what focus will be someday for you. So you explore. You learn both positively and negatively about focus and being detracted from focus. You do not expect a perfection or an ideal focus at any time in your life. There will always be scatter activities. But you will increasingly learn to recognize and avoid these as you move more toward focus.

What does it mean to be making progress toward focus? This past year I have been mentoring several people in the different age brackets with a view toward understanding more about what it means for each one of them to be moving toward focus at that given stage in their life. This chapter will seek to point out some of what I have learned. I will share with you my mentoring efforts with these people.

The chapter's intents are several. I want to take away the sense of helplessness of some who believe that focus is never going to be possible. I want, as well, to give some intermediate goals that help assure others that they are all right just where they are and doing just what they are doing. They are making progress. I want to take away the pressure that you must be in focus and must be there now. I want you to see that you are moving toward focus. Be patient. It will come. If I have learned three things for sure in my mentoring it is this: 1. You must give people hope about focus; 2. You must point out any symptoms of focus that are there with a view toward increasingly movement toward it; 3. You must set goals for three to five year periods ahead which will help develop people so that as focus unfolds they are better prepared for it—no matter which direction it might take.

By the end of this chapter you will:

* recognize some of the items that indicate movement toward focus for the different age brackets (20-30, 30-40, 40-50, 50-60, 60+)
* recognize some suggestions for moving more toward focus for the age bracket you are in.

**Flowchart—Overview Of Assessment**

# BASIC FLOW CHART
# FOR MOVING TOWARD A FOCUSED LIFE

|

Basic shaping of life and basic ministry experience
lead to **indications** of:
- life purpose (LP),
- effective methodologies (EM),
- major role (MR),
- ultimate contributions (UC).

|

which allow the drafting of a **tentative**
**Personal Life Mandate**
made up of paragraphs like:

- an introductory paragraph—**life purpose (LP)**,
- additional paragraphs—intent to use ministry insights as **effective methodologies (EM)**,
- description of a **major role** you will work toward to carry out life purpose and use effective methodologies  (**MR**).
- Venn diagram of your hoped for legacies, **ultimate contributions**, which give you long term guideposts that will result from your increased prioritization toward the focused life (**UC**).

|
|

You are here ------>             And the Setting of **Intermediate Goals**
Along 5 Different Age-Groupings

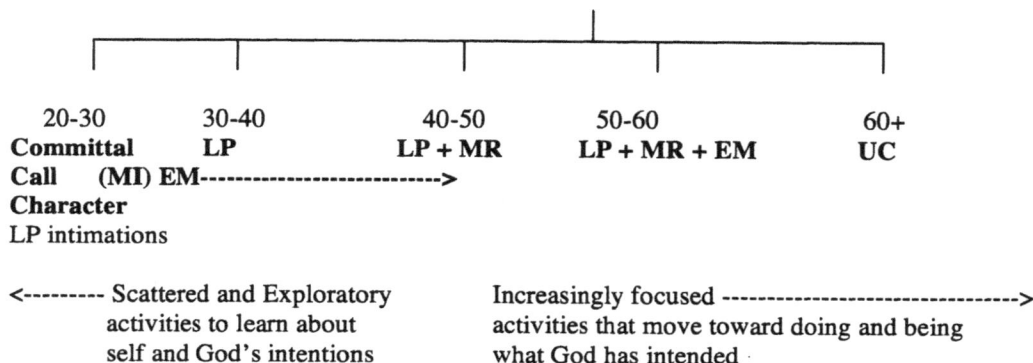

|

| 20-30 | 30-40 | 40-50 | 50-60 | 60+ |
|---|---|---|---|---|
| **Committal** | **LP** | **LP + MR** | **LP + MR + EM** | **UC** |
| **Call**  (MI) | EM------------------------> | | | |
| **Character** | | | | |
| LP intimations | | | | |

<--------- Scattered and Exploratory          Increasingly focused -------------------------------->
activities to learn about             activities that move toward doing and being
self and God's intentions             what God has intended

|

And you are here----> which results in a tentative rough draft of a Personal Life Mandate
with Appropriate Paragraphs and ideas about the next several years—
which will vary
from scattered to focused depending on which age bracket you are
and which will eventually build toward long term goals

|

And you are here ----->           Resulting in Movement Toward a More

|

# FOCUSED LIFE

**Where We Are Headed in this Chapter**

Introduction     We are simply taking our definition of a focused life with the included age brackets beside each concept and expanding the notion. For each of the age brackets we will give comments on what it means for focus to be there.

Definition       A <u>focused life</u> is

Age 20-30        • a life **dedicated** to exclusively carrying out God's unique purposes through it,

Age 30-40        • by identifying the focal issues, that is, the **life purpose, effective**
Age 40-50        **methodology,  major role**, or **ultimate contribution** which allows

Age 50-60        • an **increasing prioritization** of life's activities around the focal issues, and

Age 60+          • results in a **satisfying** life of **being** and **doing**.

Comment          Note how each of the major concepts of the definition comes into play dominantly for a given age group.  The 20-30 year olds should make sure that they have really **dedicated** themselves to exclusive service for God (by a specific calling, an anointing, a Lordship committal, a willful committal to leadership, etc.).  Age 30-40 should **clarify life purpose** and then seek to see any other one of the focal issues identified.  Age 40-50 should clarify **major role** and tie down any remaining focal issue previously unidentified.  Age 50-60 must SAY YES and SAY NO, that is, they must **prioritize** to make the most of what they have already learned about focal issues.  Age 60+ should finish well, confirming and accomplishing ultimate contributions that will lead to a satisfying life.

Comment          We will now take each of these age brackets and talk about them in terms of what focus means and what progress toward focus means. Then I will give an example of a Personal Life Mandate for each age bracket. Finally, I will give you some ideas of how I work as a mentor with age brackets 30-40, 40-50, 50-60, and 60+.

Comment          When I give these age brackets I am thinking developmentally more so than chronological. That is, a given 17 year old person may be 25 years old developmental wise and vice versa. For the most part emerging leaders can use the notion of chronological age as you think of these age brackets but be aware that some folks are accelerated in their development and some folks may be retarded in their development.

**Symptoms Of Movement Toward Focus—Age 20-30**

Introduction    The table below lists some things for assessing 20-30 year olds for focus.

Comment    Leaders can be chronologically different from the ages given and still fit developmentally in this bracket. Frequently, an accelerated teenager may be in this bracket. A delayed 30 year old, who entered ministry from a secular career may be here developmentally.

**Assessment Table—Intermediate Progress Toward a Focused Life, 20-30**

| Age | Efforts Toward Focus | Symptoms of Focus |
|-----|----------------------|-------------------|
| 20-30 | ESTABLISH FOUNDATIONS FOR FOCUS.<br>1. Respond to God as He challenges you to an all out commitment to do whatever He wants you to do. He will challenge. The challenge may be the seeds of a call or a step toward a call or an all out call.<br>2. Respond to God's efforts to build character. Foundational character shaping will open you to the next steps toward focus—ministry exploration.<br>3. Explore various kinds of ministry activities to learn more about who you are in terms of giftedness.<br>4. Expect sense of destiny experiences even if you don't know all of what they mean—e.g. Joseph's dreams. These will give you assurance that God is going to use you, the foundation for a focused life.<br>5. Operate implicitly toward your life purpose by giving yourself to what God calls. You may be able to articulate indications about life purpose or you may not but you know you are doing something now that counts. | • Inward promptings at meetings as speakers present needs for ministry in the world—like, does God want me to do that?<br>• Inward promptings as you read materials—like I would like to do that, I want to be a part of something like that.<br>• Learning to recognize Holy Spirit convictions to change life habits and get perspective about how to live for God.<br>• Being challenged to take part in ministry activities, knowing that faithfulness in little things will lead to the next things.<br>• A sense that response to God in some of the above ways will probably give early indications of what you may want to give your life to, always with a view that it will be clarified later on, but knowing God is with you now.<br>• You will get early ministry insights of how to do ministry. These later will move toward effective methodologies. |

Comment    One of the best things you can do about focus at this stage in your life is to get good perspective. Get mentor help in coaching, counseling and teaching. Wise outside perspective on developing yourself will be the best foundation toward focus.

### Symptoms of Movement Toward Focus—Age 30-40

Introduction    The table below, for the age bracket 30-40, lists some things I use to assess focus in a life for that age range. These include symptoms of focus and what should be your efforts to move toward focus. Leaders can be chronologically different from the ages given and still fit developmentally in this bracket. That is, a younger person may be accelerated and fit here. An older person may be delayed and fit here. I am mentoring one leader who is in the early 30s chronologically but is developmentally toward the late 30s.

### Assessment Table—Intermediate Progress Toward a Focused Life, 30-40

| Age | Efforts Toward Focus | Symptoms of Focus |
|---|---|---|
| 30-40 | ESTABLISH CORE LIFE PURPOSE AND RECOGNIZE SEEDS OF EFFECTIVE METHODOLOGIES. Here you must make first attempts at explicitly drafting a Personal Life Mandate—that is, write up your first draft introductory paragraph about life purpose. Your Personal Life Mandate at this point will have your rough draft introductory paragraph and perhaps some paragraphs describing ministry insights and how you intend to explore ministry activities and use those insights. | • Destiny revelation experiences which will clarify life purpose. <br>• Doors blocked and open which give guidance and take you toward ministry which you sense will be fulfilling. <br>• Personal and ministry affirmation experiences from God that you are on the right track. <br>• An increasing understanding of your giftedness and seeing results from it. <br>• Sometimes extreme frustration if you are in a social base pattern which is putting off your direct ministry while you build and fulfill social base responsibilities—especially seen by word gifted people who are heavily involved in parenting and know that there word ministry lies more fully in the future. <br>• Again a sense of impatience for those who have for whatever reason moved into a delaying pattern. <br>• A sense of snail pace development because of mismatch in role placement. <br>• Satisfaction that some of what you are doing is really counting. |

Comment    The age bracket 30-40 is the time period when most frustration is felt about the focused life. Sometimes it is not yet clear what the ministry role will really be. Sometimes it is clear that there will be a long delay before there is sensed progress toward focus. Delays may come because of choices, like parenting, or clearing some major obstacles (finances, debt, etc.) or for some other reason. Perhaps there has not been a satisfactory ministry experience or roles desired have been blocked. It is in this age bracket that what is clear must be the central hope and not what is unclear. Clarification of life purpose can give hope while you patiently wait for God to clarify guidance toward more meaningful role. Especially when things are unclear the best approach is to rest in what is clear and focus on intermediate goals of development of ministry perspective and skills—these can be used no matter how the strategic direction toward role works out.

### Symptoms Of Movement Toward Focus—Age 40-50

| Introduction | The table below, for the age bracket 40-50, lists some things I use to assess focus in a life for that age range. Leaders can be chronologically different from the ages given and still fit developmentally in this bracket. That is, a younger person may be accelerated and fit here. An older person may be delayed and fit here. I myself am a delayed pattern. I am mentoring one leader who is chronologically in mid-30s but developmentally is early 40-50. I am mentoring one person who is early 50s chronologically but is early 40s developmentally in terms of major role. |
|---|---|

### Assessment Table—Intermediate Progress Toward a Focused Life, 40-50

| Age | Efforts Toward Focus | Symptoms of Focus |
|---|---|---|
| 40-50 | ESTABLISH BASIC PARAMETERS OF YOUR MAJOR ROLE. ESTABLISH SEVERAL EFFECTIVE METHODOLOGIES. Here you are beginning to add the Synergizing Elements that will allow life purpose to bud, bloom and flower. You will be revising the Personal Life Mandate to include other discoveries of focal issues. You may well both clarify the life purpose as you have known it in your 30s or add to it other major thrusts. Frequently, leaders with strong destiny, powerful giftedness, and an expanding sphere of influence will have multi-thrust life purposes. It is not uncommon to have two or three major thrusts in your life purpose. But in particular, major role is the important discovery in this age group. As you know more of who you are becoming in terms of destiny, giftedness, and influence you well sense the need for a role that will enhance what you know about your life purpose. In addition, you will be turning previous ministry insights toward effective methodology as you sense the power in the concepts. | • Experiencing power as you use ministry insights. • Recognizing that you need to find better means for using those ministry insights. • Being led into ministry forays which utilize your giftedness and give you ideas about role adaptation. • Sometimes a sense of anticipation that something big is going to happen in the near future. • Sometimes negative preparation for leaving a secure role but one which will not let you develop to fullness. • Experiencing the symptoms of a major boundary.[33] • Recognition that your present role can be adapted to allow functions that will move toward some new thrust in life purpose that has been added. • A yearning for something more and the sense that you may be missing it. • A major destiny experience which involves renewal and recommittal to life purposes. • Beginnings of clarification of ultimate contribution components. |

| Comment | The frustration is less in this age bracket because the leader is much clearer on purpose and knows that a role must be adapted to give impetus to accomplishment of life purpose. And there is some sense that proactive movement toward the role is possible. |
|---|---|

---

[33]See J. Robert Clinton's ARTICLE on *Boundary Analysis*, in **The Leadership Emergence Theory READER**, which gives a thorough analysis of boundary activity. A boundary is a time of transition from a major development phase to another.

### Symptoms Of Movement Toward Focus—Age 50-60

Introduction        Here we are not talking about movement toward focus but focusing. Leaders can be chronologically different from the ages given and still fit developmentally in this bracket. That is, a younger person may be accelerated and fit here. I know some young 40 year olds who are already here ministry speaking. Conversely, an older person may be delayed and fit here. For example, developmentally speaking, that is, leadership wise, I am a delayed pattern and though I am in my late 50s chronologically, I am in the early 50s developmentally speaking.

### Assessment Table—Intermediate Progress Toward a Focused Life, 50-60

| Age | Efforts Toward Focus | Symptoms of Realization |
|---|---|---|
| 50-60 | THE CHALLENGE: TO PROACTIVELY FOCUS ON MAXIMIZING THE FOCUSED LIFE. It is clear now what the focused life is for you. You have a firm grasp of your Life Purpose even if it is multi-faceted. You have used powerfully a number of ministry insights and have now firmly established them as effective methodologies. You have even sensed fairly clearly the ultimate contributions that flow out of your Life Purpose and your giftedness. You know that your effective methodologies are moving toward achievement of some of those ultimate contributions. There are three secrets of the focused life that are important for you and which you know must be yours. One, the ultimate secret of the focused life is intimacy with God. You are being drawn to that more and more as the basis of your ministry (not achieving success—which you are readily doing). Two, you now are learning to say NO to opportunities not lining up with focus. Three, you are saying YES very proactively to making your focused life happen. The is the prime time for you. And you are making the most of it. | • A role which allows more of giftedness to be productive than at any time in the past.<br>• Confidence in accomplishing ministry, that is, effective use of effective methodologies.<br>• More available ministry opportunities that you can effectively fill.<br>• A confident ability to say No to ministry, which although good, is not primary to your focus.<br>• An amazing sense of God working through you and accomplishing things toward your life purpose.<br>• A driving need to proactively create what must be in order to realize more of life purpose.<br>• Many repetitive moments of satisfaction in what God is doing through you.<br>• Clarity of ultimate contributions.<br>• A growing sense that what you are doing is counting toward your ultimate contribution.<br>• Increasingly knowing the importance of intimacy with God and having repetitive moments of that intimacy. |

Comment        Though you may have accomplished much during the 20 or so years of ministry leading up to this you will sense an acceleration of achievement during this period. Much more will be accomplished with much less self-activation. You will sense God's powerful presence with you and will see things happen that you only hoped for in earlier years. This is the most focused time of the focused life. It is the apex of your life. You will sense the promise of Joshua 23:10, except in a spiritual sense.

### Symptoms Of Movement Toward Focus—Age 60+

Introduction     The table below highlights end of life guidelines. Remember, a younger person may be accelerated and fit here. An older person may be delayed and fit here. The Lord willing, if I continue to develop as I am, I will be late 60s chronologically when I hit this stage developmentally.

### Assessment Table—Intermediate Progress Toward a Focused Life, 60+

| Age | Efforts Toward Focus | How to Finish the Focused Life |
|-----|----------------------|-------------------------------|
| 60+ | 1. CONSERVE THE EFFORTS OF YOUR FOCUSED LIFE.<br>2. MAKE SURE YOU ARE REALIZING YOUR ULTIMATE CONTRIBUTION SET.<br>3. FINISH WELL.<br><br>The threefold goals just given recognize that your best ministry efforts have peaked. You no longer have the strength to do all that you are capable of doing. But you have a long track record on which you can now depend in order to reap all that you have done. You need to make sure that you leave behind the end of life legacies that God has been pointing out to you. You need to go back over your life time and where ever possible encourage those who in the past were part of your ministry. You need now to encourage them to follow through on the values you have imparted to them. You need to encourage them to go on and achieve for themselves their focused lives. You need to bless them with a message of prophetic hope for their own lives. And most of all you need to finish well. On the one hand, what you have done will in some senses be denigrated if you have a poor finish. On the other hand, what you have done will be elevated to new heights if you finish well. | • Demonstrate the finishing well characteristics:<br>1. Maintain a **vibrant personal relationship** with God right up to the end.<br>2. Maintain a **learning posture** and learn from various kinds of sources—especially life itself.<br>3. Portray **Christ-likeness in character** as evidenced by the fruit of the Spirit: love, joy, peace, long-suffering, gentleness, goodness, faithfulness, appropriate humility, and self-control.<br>4. **Live out truth** in life so that convictions and promises of God are seen to be real. Dress with time-tested and life-proven truth and promises as garments of praise to God. Leave behind a track record that God's Word is true. He can be trusted to honor his truth in lives.<br>5. Leave behind one or more **ultimate contributions.** This is in addition to numerous specific contributions.<br>6. Walk with a growing **awareness of a sense of destiny** and see some or all of it fulfilled.<br>• Wishful thinking about returning and seeing the lasting results of your earlier ministry.<br>• Desire to renew contact with and to bless and encourage some of the leaders you have helped select and develop in the past,<br>• Formally pass on the torch for your ministry aspirations to younger leaders so that they are blessed and encouraged to go on with your work—frequently you will have already done this informally but now you want others to recognize this in those heritage leaders.<br>• Be vulnerable and give public testimony to a life of satisfaction in order to model and encourage younger leaders. |

Comment     During these years you must be willing to receive honor for what God has done through your life and in turn to give resounding testimony to God's faithfulness in doing it. Your end-of-life modeling will do almost as much in some ways as your peak time during the 50-60 age bracket.

## Sample Personal Life Mandate, TGS — Age 30-40

My life purpose will involve a transient cross-cultural ministry, which will focus on high level influence in the equipping of leadership both at individual and at organizational levels. My ministry will involve stepping out in faith and many times using modeling from my own life. I know, often, my ministry will be marked by unusual blessing of God.

I know that to carry out my ministry I will need to develop toward an effective trainer who has Spiritual Authority,

- and can operate comfortably (design and/or participate) in a public ministry involving workshops, seminars, and conferences as well as,
- have an effective mentoring ministry (relational ministry) with individuals and in small groups.

I know also that I am to be a part of organizational influence, probably at a consulting level. I know that God frequently gives me strategic organizational input and I want to be able to speak this input into organizational situations to bring life and direction. It is unclear as yet but I may well start or stabilize several organizations over my lifetime.

Over the next several years I want to develop effectiveness as a trainer and pick up organizational skills. I already have small group skills and can influence small groups as well as train leaders for them. I already have found ways of designing and carrying out cross-cultural orientation and training for taking a group of emerging leaders into different cultures. I already have skills at leading and designing Bible studies for groups. In addition, I have learned how to design and teach several kinds of Bible studies. I have designed and taught integrated series.

My social base situation, single or married is uncertain at this time. In any case I want to prepare myself for ministry along the lines I have described above so that in either case of social base I can effectively fulfill that for which I am and have been called to in ministry.

I have some indications already of ultimate contributions but I will not be focusing on these in the next 10 years as far as I can see.

**Sample Personal Life Mandate, WNR—Age 40**

My life purpose involves selecting, developing, and releasing of young leaders into ministry. My basic means of developing and releasing of them will be via a local church on-the-job training program which involves much mentoring, actual coaching practice and teaching. This training will be individualized and have a strong value based component as well as cross-cultural component. These young leaders will be taken on forays as teams beyond the confines of our local church to utilize seminars and workshops to train other young leaders. The scope of these training forays will be worldwide. I know because of my destiny processing that intimacy with God will be a large component of my values training with these young leaders. And I too must model and experience this intimacy that I will teach and impart to these younger leaders.

My role will be multi-faceted. I will operate out of a local church as a trainer, teacher, and roving apostolic facilitator of church plants. My public ministry will involve workshops, seminars, and large conferences as well as pulpit series in local churches from time-to-time. I will also be involved in mentoring and in the training of mentors both in a local church and in distance situations. I will consult with parachurch organizations about their orientation and training programs for the younger upcoming leaders. I will also have a writing influence which spreads leadership materials far and wide. I will have an itinerant public Bible teaching ministry in order to expose leadership values and model a Bible centered ministry. I also will stimulate worship both by modeling of it and by a contemporary music ministry which involves capturing my own and others pilgrimages with God. I intend to spread Biblical truth in music by writing and producing music for publication and distribution.

One of my effective methodologies involves a triad of components: worship, input, and ministry involving the presence of the Holy Spirit. I have learned how to hear from God in situations involving this triad and to see God work mightily in the groups. I have also learned developmental frameworks which allow me to speak into lives individually in terms of career guidance. I have also learned how to design training for a variety of situations: local church, workshops, seminars, large conferences.

I am not totally clear on my ultimate contribution set though I do have a tentative diagram. I have had a large number of unusual destiny experiences with God which have also confirmed some of my ultimate contribution set. But at this point I am concentrating on developing the above described multi-faceted role and using my effective methodologies as much as I can. I have already sensed the powerful presence of God increasingly in my ministry forays and know that what I am doing at present is counting. I also feel that just out ahead of me is a ministry that will break wide open. I anticipate this and am walking in faith awaiting it as I faithfully minister with what I already know.

## Sample Personal Life Mandate, FLM—Age 55

My life purpose is to demonstrate a special vulnerability to God which reflects the reality and faithfulness of God to personally relate to people and to intervene in their lives for His purposes, their welfare, and setting the agenda for people's lives. I want to demonstrate that He is trustworthy, wise, loving, and intricate in His plans for us. I know I am to do this via personal modeling--especially being transparent about my own vulnerability and how God has used that in my own life to transform me into the image of Christ. He has renewed me and constantly is doing so in repeated experiences both personally and ministry related. I want to engender this same kind of renewal, first of all, in my own Anglican denomination, and secondly in other situations and groups to whom God may lead me. I want to penetrate any of these groups with ministry which demonstrates the powerful presence of the Holy Spirit. I want to take many individuals and groups through the same paradigm shift I myself have gone through--that of knowing personally the work of the Holy Spirit in my life and ministry.

I believe the multi-faceted role that will allow me best to do this is basically five-fold:

1. I must be vitally in touch with **parish ministry.** I could operate either on a large parish staff with lots of freedom for outside ministry or in a parachurch organization which has good connections with parish ministry. I need to be grappling with and seeing what I want to preach on, teach on and model out there happening in local situations. I realize that part of my effectiveness *out there* depends on my faithfulness and God's shaping in a *local scene.* How can I tell others they need this renewal in their churches if I myself do not see it in local situations?
2. **Roving Apostolic Ministry.** I must reproduce vital Holy Spirit led and empowered ministry with groups and individuals *out there.* I am energized when I am ministering in locales that the Holy Spirit has led me to. Part of this outside ministry is focusing on bringing the renewal that I mentioned in my life purpose. Part of this outside ministry is focusing on training others to do this renewal. Part of this outside ministry is modeling what I mean by renewal. Part of this outside ministry has to do with my own faith and the risk of having to trust God to time and time work. I need this.
3. **Change Agent**. I must proactively focus on being a person of change. I realize that if I am indeed to bring about renewal in the denomination and groups that I must increasingly prioritize what I do so that it will bring lasting results. I must target key individuals and churches throughout the denomination. I must do personal mentoring of these key individuals and seek out ways to impact these key churches.
4. **Writer**. I must capture the spirit of my renewal movement in some major writing projects. I need written materials both to stimulate and attract people to the movement as well as capture the ideas. I need also to facilitate the development of follow-up training materials to conserve the gains I make in situations. I am particularly interested in writing for leaders: expose leader values, priorities, leadership styles and skill-sets. I want to motivate, encourage teach, and model through my writings.
5. **Organizational Entrepreneur**. I must begin to organize my outside ministry into an organization which can perpetuate the movement of renewal much more systematically and with more effectiveness. I must attract people to me who can help me with this as this is not my strength.

I know that if I am to leave behind a lasting legacy of renewal in my own denomination that I must become much more focused and proactive about it. In seeking to do this I know that God will constantly affirm me, renew me personally, and give me great satisfaction. I intend to be motivated by and to set specific goals toward fulfillment of the following ultimate contributions set (my lasting legacies I want to leave behind).

**Sample Personal Life Mandate, FLM — Age 55** continued

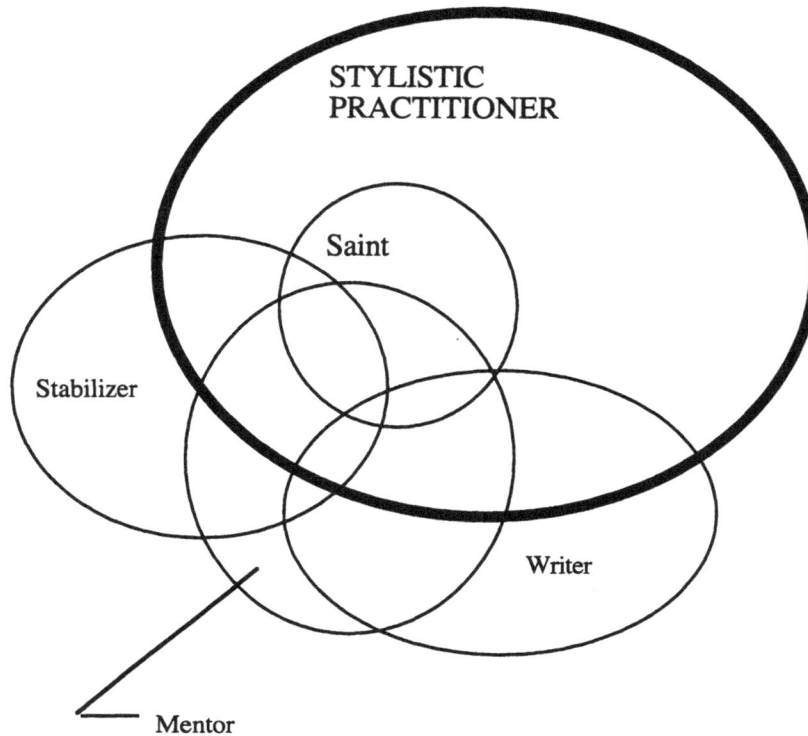

I have devised a set of key questions to help me think through my goals that flow from this ultimate contribution set. All are prefaced with a header, ASK GOD, which reminds me and forces me to model what I mean about being vulnerable to God for His setting of the agenda. I am developing these goals now.

1. **ASK GOD.** What organizations should I be penetrating in order to move people and groups toward renewal as I have experienced it?
2. **ASK GOD.** What should be my strategy with these organizations? How should I help them?
3. Ask God. How can I be more deliberate in penetrating individual leaders? How can I be more pro-active in mentoring them? How can I be a more effective mentor?
4. **ASK GOD.** What does God want me to do with my writing? How does my writing fit with my other tasks? What kinds of materials would enable my ministry to continue after me? Should I recruit others to work with me in it? Can I effectively mentor-sponsor others in writing?
5. **ASK GOD.** Do I need to set up a parachurch organization? How am I to be financially stable?

### Sample Personal Life Mandate, CRJ—Age 60

My purpose is to challenge, motivate, and enable--via study and **development of leadership concepts** both empirically and from the Scriptures, by teaching of leadership concepts, by **modeling of them**, by mentoring of select leaders in them, and by providing **available resources and materials**--high level leaders all over the world to finish well.

I intend to continue **researching** personal leadership development theory and organizational or church leadership and **write articles, papers, manuals, popular books and texts** which will provide the conceptual frameworks that will challenge, motivate and enable. I plan to have a strong Biblical emphasis for my leadership findings. The conceptual framework, my leadership findings, will have powerful force alone to challenge, motivate, and enable--by giving perspective.

In addition to the conceptual framework being developed I will be involved in promoting the ideas via **teaching** them, by **training others to teach them**, and by **sponsoring others to teach** them. Further I recognize that I must be what I am talking about. **Modeling** will be a high priority with me. Therefore I want to live an exemplary life that counts for Christ:

- by centering my life in Christ and hence developing a spirituality flowing from Him,
- by modeling a teaching lifestyle which embodies this spirituality, flows from my giftedness, is in harmony with my destiny as I understand it, and moves me toward convergence and accomplishment of my ultimate contribution set as I know it.

I sense that my teaching style involves **effective methodologies for challenging the affect and volitional as well as the cognitive**. For me, with my giftedness and influence-mix, this means a **narrow focus on the few**--smaller groups via **seminars** and **workshops** rather than to the large such as are at conferences. Hence, I know that God will lead me via **networking** to these small groups. My personal ministry will often provide the connections that will open doors later.

Several things I have learned about making my ministry more effective include: the deliberate use of two design models—one for assessing what is in focus, and the other for assessing balanced learning in terms of learning domains—for designing any training whether formal, non-formal or informal, whether a public presentation, a single session of input, a workshop, a conference, or an entire course in a formal setting; the special use of motivational techniques in a formal classroom setting like attention getters and closure exercises; the special design of small groups into a formal course situation; the use of ad hoc small groups on the spot to cause reflection and penetration of an idea; a writing continuum to guide me as I prepare materials; the importance of having good written materials to carry cognitive input; the use of in-depth workshops which require pre-work and post-work; the use of a team both for training and in-depth penetration of ideas in a workshop setting; one-on-one personal time in light of an ideation framework—a perspective; the use of informality in all of my ministry efforts; the use of modeling and telling of stories to move the affect; the use of concentric circles of influence to both screen and become increasingly proactive in my mentoring efforts; the use of "by invitation only" small groups for combining mentor efforts; the development of various kinds of helps for supplementing my administrative work as I mentor many people; . I intend to use these various methodologies in a much more conscious way as I fulfill my life purpose of selecting, developing, and releasing quality leaders toward good finishes.

I recognize that for a time I need a base which provides status but that my ministry will not be limited to that base and its geographical area. For a period of time while I have energy and drive I will best operate from a base but provide my teaching to various parts of the world--with a higher priority on Asia. During this period of time I must pass the torch on to others and provide them with the best possibility of carrying on what I am about.

My end game ministry will focus more on **enabling others to do what I am about**. I will concentrate more on operating out of the base and less on decentralized workshops and seminars. It will allow **personal ministry to fewer leaders on an in-depth basis**--those who will be attracted to spend time with me. I recognize that I will need a setting which allows for isolation and much research and writing for this end game phase.

I intend to be motivated by the following ultimate contribution set. The decisions I make about what I do will depend to a large extent on my understanding of these life achievements. For each of the ultimate contributions I am tentatively describing what it means and how that affects what I am and what I do.

**Sample Personal Life Mandate, CRJ—Age 60,** continued

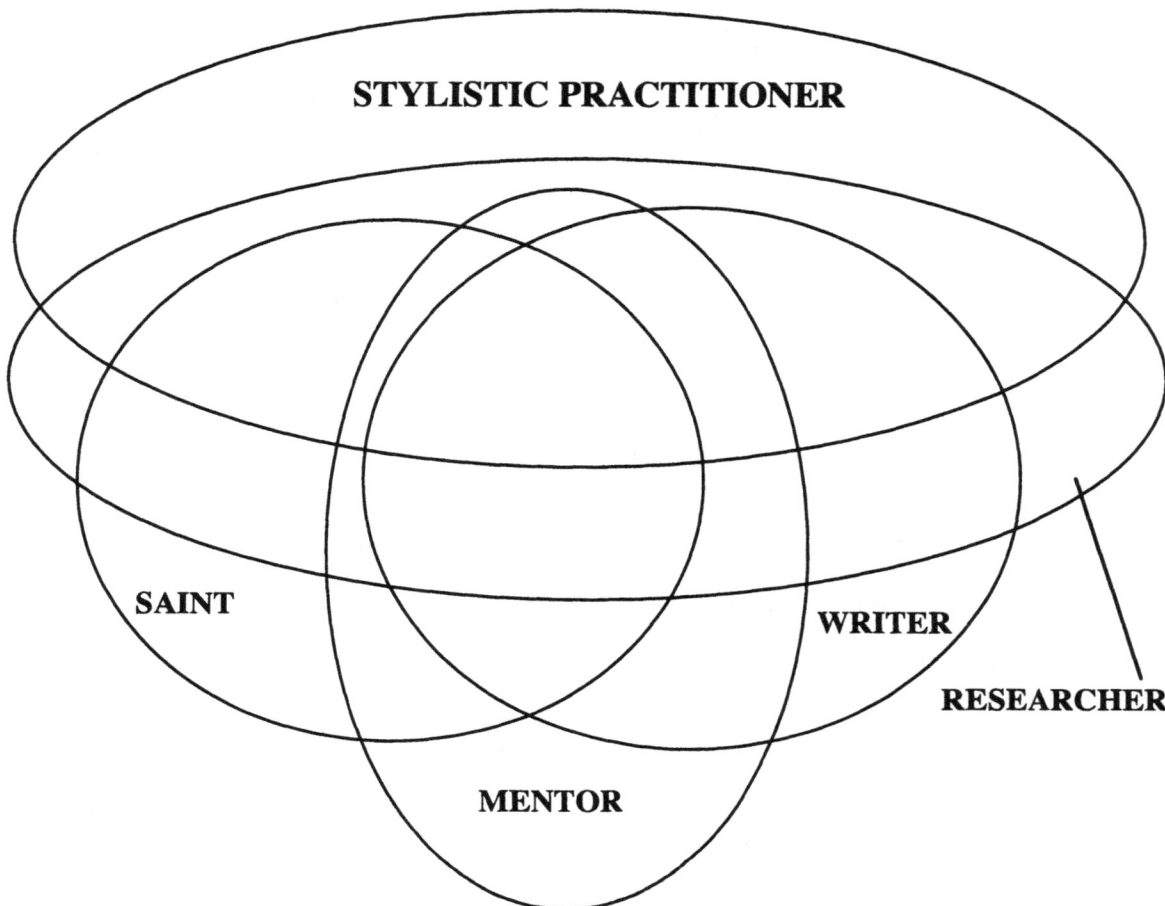

Proverbs 10:7  The memory of the righteous will be a blessing...

I have written goals for the research and writing components. I am proactively pursuing numerous goals for the mentoring component. I am openly modeling and sharing my findings concerning my view of ministry in my setting (stylistic practitioner).

### My Basic Mentoring Procedures for Age Group—30-40

Introduction      In my mentoring over the past year I have had occasion to work with several mentorees in the various age brackets as they explore these focused life concepts. Below is a summary of some of the things I have done. I have many individual sessions with the mentoree and assign basic projects about analyzing himself or herself which will give me information to use with the following steps. For some mentorees I met weekly. For others, I met a-periodically—whenever they finished the next information gathering project.

| Age | Approach/ Activities |
|---|---|
| 30-40 | 1. Construct time-line and note critical incidents. |
| | 2. Analyze critical incidents for indications of various focal life issues, mostly life purpose; some ministry insights. |
| | 3. Have the mentoree construct a destiny log. |
| | 4. Probe the destiny insights for more detailed information and in order to sense the life purpose indications. |
| | 4. Synthesize a rough draft life purpose introductory paragraph. Get the mentoree to interact and modify the life purpose paragraph. |
| | 5. Have the mentoree construct a ministry insights log. Probe the ministry insights for possibilities of effective methodologies and for suggestions of other ministry insights that I know of that may supplement and add to the skill set of the mentoree. |
| | 6. Anticipate a set of skills and a tentative major role that the mentoree could be working toward—this is about 5 years down road. |
| | 7. Construct some alternate possible time-line scenarios toward the 40 year age--for singles this involves future marriage possibilities and a possible social base pattern. It also involves future non-marriage. This usually works out to be 4 or more possible time-line scenarios for the next 5-8 years. |
| | 8. Working back on these time-lines I identify the common time available before the scenarios will branch into the different options. This common time allows for setting training that can be common to all the scenarios. |
| | 9. I then suggest possible goals that will move toward the 40 year hypothetical role and honor the common time available. |
| | 10. I constructed a rough draft Personal Life Mandate which had a life purpose paragraph, some possible role intents, some future training. The mentoree then massaged the Personal Life Mandate statement and arrived at a working draft. |
| | 11. I found that simply pointing out the possible scenarios and having a role out their for which skills were being developed brought hope. |

Comment      The problem with mentor counseling in this age bracket is that there is still so much uncertainty. And remember this is the age bracket with the most frustration when thinking about the focused life. What the mentoree needs is some clarity and some hope. One cannot give absolutely certain answers about how the life will flow. But you can give strong affirmation in terms of what God has shown. And you can point out possible alternative. And you can impart hope by suggesting developmental goals that will help the mentoree no matter which of the alternatives happen. Encouragement, hope, and possibility of some progress are the components that you are seeking to instill at this point.

### My Basic Mentoring Procedures for Age Group—40-50

Introduction    In my mentoring over the past year I have had occasion to work with several mentorees in this age bracket as they explored these focused life concepts. Below is a summary of some of the things I have done. I have many individual sessions with the mentoree and assign basic projects about analyzing himself or herself, which will give me information to use with the following steps. Because the mentoree is much older there is more data. Usually that means more time between sessions. It also means that I have to pore over more material. The synthesizing is more difficult for me. For most mentorees I met about monthly. For others I met a-periodically—whenever they finished the next information gathering project—as long as two months between meeting times.

| Age | Approach/ Activities |
|-----|---------------------|
| 40-50 | Steps 1 through 5 of the 30-40 age bracket were also done.<br>6. I had the mentoree do a solid giftedness analysis and construct the giftedness set Venn diagram.<br>7. I probed giftedness set for potential future role possibilities that would enhance it. I also probed past ministry activities that were satisfying and in which the giftedness set was allowed to operate.<br>8. I helped the mentoree outline several major roles that would somewhat fit.<br>9. We explored the possibilities of adapting the present role to any of these.<br>10. We explored the possibilities of leaving the present situation altogether and moving to other new roles.<br>11. I firmed up the life purpose and explored possible alternative multi-thrusts.<br>12. In one mentoree's case I started sponsoring the person in ministry situations so that giftedness and potential could be seen.<br>13. I had the mentoree construct a life purpose paragraph and major role paragraph as part of a draft Personal Life Mandate. I interacted with and modified a bit and added some future intents.<br>14. I also had the mentoree study the Ultimate Contribution Paper and come up with a tentative Venn diagram.<br>15. We finalized a working draft for the Personal Life Statement by adding some intents and developmental goals and projects that could move them further down the road to achievement of the major role that was envisioned. |

Comment    In this age bracket there is much information to analyze. Some mentorees in this age bracket have as much as 20-25 years of ministry experience (with exceptions for delayed patterns). The major problem is not visualizing the major role but finding a way to have an economic base to support such a role. Most major roles differ from present roles. The economic support base comes from these kind of roles—roles which do not necessarily enhance movement toward focus. A major component is how to encourage the mentoree in this bracket to trust God to bring about the role and to trust God to economically meet needs. There is a tendency to want to give up and settle for what is because a known safe secure situation is better than an unknown uncertain future. The danger, however, is to plateau and never move on to focus and a satisfied life. Much wisdom is needed here. In fact, I often ask God for a word of wisdom in my one-on-one times with mentorees in this age bracket. It takes such a breakthrough from God to encourage the mentoree to step out toward the major role envisioned.

## My Basic Mentoring Procedures for Age Group—50-60

Introduction      In my mentoring over the past year I have had occasion to work with several mentorees in this age bracket as they explored these focused life concepts. Below is a summary of some of the things I have done. I had about 6 sessions with one in this bracket and am part way through the process with two others. It looks as if with a 50-60 year old who already is experiencing implicitly much of the focused life and who has so much material about God's processing that 3-6 months is not an unreasonable time to expect to complete the activities that are described below. For the one I have completed it took about 4 months. Others are already that long in process with the end not yet in sight. For most mentorees I met a-periodically—whenever they finished the next information gathering project—as long as two months between meeting times.

| Age | Approach/ Activities |
|---|---|
| 50-60 | All the activities of the previous age groups were done in part or in whole. In addition I also had the mentoree do more reading in leadership emergence concepts. The differences that I found in mentoring in this age bracket were:<br>1. The mentorees are much more certain of themselves—what they are, what they are becoming and what they can do.<br>2. They are not concerned so much with ministry—they already have tasted of success in it. They know they have ministered well.<br>3. They are more concerned with learning what they should narrow down to. That is, they want to learn how to say NO and how to say Yes.<br>4. I helped in clarifying the multi-thrust life purpose and in looking at what a major role must contain in terms of various components.<br>5. I found that I had much data to look at and synthesize. But I also found that I could give assignments which had the mentoree help me synthesize the data.<br>6. I completed one complete Personal Life Mandate for one mentoree in this bracket and am partially on the way with several others.<br>7. The Personal Life Mandate was a back and forth operation. I would do something; the mentoree would do something. We would come together and compare. Where we differed each went back and tried to incorporate the others helpful views. We then came together again and again compared the reworked documents. We finally agreed on a working mandate.<br>8. We spent much time on talking about maximizing focus and how to select the most pressing opportunities that would lead to focus.<br>9. Both the mentoree and myself found the process stimulating and helpful. I believe such a process is a worthwhile thing to do at about age 50. That will allow the generation of a document that will enhance decision making for focus in the coming decade. |

Comment      There is an exhilarating feeling in working with a person in this age bracket— especially when you are convinced that this person is going to contribute much to the kingdom as focus is enhanced. And God is giving you the privilege of being a part of that process. Because of long experience and usually a strong personality one has to work carefully in terms of relational skills and change dynamics to get ideas to the person. You do not dictate to mentorees in this age bracket. It is more of a peer stimulation thing. But it is fulfilling and helpful for both parties.

## Scattered or Focused — Which For You?

Introduction        Well, let me warn you! In my observations on leaders, especially those contemporary with my own generation I have found only a few who are living focused lives but many who manifest other symptoms. *When it is all over—what can you say?* Here is what I would say about 5 types of lives.

1. **Disasters.** I have seen some start out apparently well but bomb out due to a variety of reasons: giving into sinful temptations and being eventually overcome or addicted to them, worldly pressures especially to succeed (see Mark 4 Parable of sower), break-up of families, financial impropriety, major problems due to abuse of power in ministry eventually leading to major conflict which dethrones, inordinate pride which can lead to any number of sins and eventually a major fall. Now they are out of the race. Many were very effective for different lengths of time in their lives. Now they are out of it—some even non-professing Christians. It is a sad thing to recruit many into the fray and then to drop out—one of Paul's fears (1 Corinthians 9:27ff). *When it is all over—what can you say?* **They not only didn't finish well—but they disappointed many and perhaps even caused them to finish poorly.**

2. **Meandering Lives.** There are people who never find it. They move from one thing to another always hoping and perhaps naively thinking that the next thing will do it. The next fad will satisfy. The next seminar will pull it together. And over a lifetime they meander from thing to thing and never operate with any kind of focus. *When it is all over—what can you say?* **If only they had ... they might have been.**

3. **Mediocre Lives.** Some leaders never produce. Very early they plateau. They have a sort of easy going focused life all right, but it is called a rut. They accomplish nothing significant. These leaders become lukewarm. They never find a life purpose—something around which they can get excited. So life becomes more of the same, continuing to do what they have been doing and never moving toward effective, focused lives. *When it is all over—what can you say?* **They lived. They did some things. But in essence it will be as if they never lived.**

4. **Cluttered Lives.** Many leaders I have observed lead busy cluttered lives. They are into so many things. They are driven by activities, perhaps even addicted to them and the affirmation they get in doing them. These activities both determine what is being done and provide reward. But is only temporary. Sooner or later it catches up to them. Their over involvement in so many things precludes their reflection on what is really happening to them. They are too busy to take time to assess personal leadership development. Usually this kind of life results in bombing out altogether, or burn out followed by mediocre involvement or plateauing. In any case, frequently there is no lasting fruit. *When it is all over—what can you say?* **They just simply ran out of steam. There were plenty of activities—at least for a time. But many of these activities were done without real depth in any of them. If they had it to do all over again they would say—I wish I had slowed down and assessed and then prioritized what I did.**

5. **Focused Lives.** Frequently this kind of life contains much of clutter symptoms and busy life symptoms. But as the time-line, the pilgrimage, unwinds, the clutter begins to drop away. Focused activities are prioritized over non-focused activities. There is a deliberate choosing of priority things. There is the sense of doing what one was made for and developing toward the being that God wanted. *When it is all over—what can you say?* **Two words sum it up— satisfied and fulfilled. Those are words worth hearing.**

**Scattered or Focused—Which For You** continued

Comment        Apart from category one, disastrous lives, all the rest can be summarized
               under two broad umbrella labels: Scattered lives or Focused Lives.  In real
               life, it will not be quite so simple.  We will all, most always, have some
               scatter and some focus.  But if you could choose an ideal, which would it
               be? I hope it would be toward focus.  Read again the definition of a
               focused life.

>    A <u>focused life</u> is
>    • a life dedicated to exclusively carrying out God's unique purposes
>      through it,
>    • by identifying the focal issues, that is, the **life purpose**, **effective
>      methodology**, **major role**, or **ultimate contribution** which
>      allows
>    • an **increasing prioritization** of life's activities around the focal
>      issues, and
>    • results in a **satisfying life** of being and doing.

Comment        Now read again the thesis with which I began this manual.

**Leaders, must make decisions about life and ministry which flow from
their understanding of who God has made them to be and for what
God is shaping them.  These decisions will lead them to full effective
purposeful lives which in retrospect will be seen to have been focused
lives.  But it is not a self-seeking individualistic choice of life but a
seeking of what a SOVEREIGN GOD is doing—His purposes.  All of
the focused life thinking must be done in light of a strong
understanding of the Sovereignty of God.**

Comment        What will it take to move you toward the focused life?  Let me suggest.  It
               is a matter of the will.  If you decide and if you trust God and if you look
               for the focal issues[34] **God will lead you into a focused life**.  He desires
               even more than you do for you to reach those unique purposes for which
               He created you and toward which He will shape you.

**For we are God's specially crafted work, created in Christ
Jesus to do good works, which God prepared in advance for
us to do.  Ephesians 2:10**

---

[34]Not all personality types are analytical in nature nor do they need to be.  But if they are willing, God will
reveal to them, possibly by others, what they need to know to focus.  They may not need explicit
identification of these focal issues I have labeled as life purpose, effective methodologies, major role, or
ultimate contributions.  What they need is to operate along those lines whether or not they ever know them
very well cognitively.

### Final Commentary

Comment          Remember these 6 important observations on Focused Life and Focal Issues:

1. **Life Purpose** without any other focal issue will die on the vine.
2. **Life purpose** + any one of the other three, **Effective Methodologies**, **Major Role**, or **Ultimate Contribution** can lead to a focused life.
3. **Effective Methodologies** without a life purpose becomes faddish and will fade or lead to a sense of so what and finally cynicism.
4. **Major Role** without a life purpose simply becomes self-serving.
5. **Ultimate Contribution** without a life purpose becomes self-glorifying.
6. The more **focal issues** there are to supplement a life purpose the more focused is the life. Synergism operates here.

Comment          I should put in a slight disclaimer here. I orininally defined the **Personal Life Mandate** as a one page description of limits and challenges that a leader can basically use for tactical and strategic decisions in ministry. Actually most Personal Life Mandates are one to three page documents. Each of the focal elements usually take more than one paragraph to describe. And almost everyone adds the Ultimate Contribution Set Venn diagram as an added page. They also frequently derive some goals that lead toward that Venn diagram so that the expanded Personal Life Mandate can be 1 to 4 pages (if a goal page is added) though the first two pages contain the essentials of the mandate.

Comment          Mentoring with people in all the different age brackets has given me a range of experience and a variety of views toward focus. Some just honestly don't think it is possible for them. Others have become cynical because of their past experience and are in the position of sort of wanting it but not believing they will move toward it. Some are extremely hopeful and sense they are moving toward it. Others are energized by the concepts and have begun to apply them in their lives. Everywhere we have taught on focus life concepts, it has generated excitement and hope. I have concluded that the notion of a focused life is a valid one. However, an ideal focused life will be rare. Practically speaking there will be many setbacks and compromises, especially in major roles. Never-the-less, we need ideals that will motivate us. Though we may never totally reach them we will find that even movement toward them and partial accomplishment will be satisfying.

Comment          Where are you in this process? Is there hope? Is there some possible movement for you toward focus? Always remember that it is God (Ephesian 2:10) who has uniquely made your for unique purposes in His plan. He alone is the one who can move us toward focus. If we obey Him and move with him in strategic guidance it does not matter whether we fulfill these concepts of focus. **Serving Him is the goal. A focused life is a by-product.** May the God of hope give you hope so that you may overflow with hope and know the powerful presence of the Holy Spirit as you increasingly minister to fulfill that for which you were created.

Final Word       Read this favorite paraphrase of mine from the Apostle Paul. When he had been in ministry about 21 years and had seen it all, he was still determined to apply disciplines to his life, because he wanted to finish well.

I am serious about finishing well in my Christian ministry. I discipline myself for fear that after challenging others into the Christian life I myself might become a casualty. 1 Corinthians 9:24-27

# Annotated Bibliography

**Adizes, Ichak**
 1988     **Corporate Life Cycles: How and Why Corporations Grow and Die and What To Do About It.** Englewood Cliffs, N.J. : Prentice Hall, c1988.

Comment:    This ministry insight, how to view where an organization is in its development, became for me a skill I could use when talking to organizational leaders. I have used this structural time paradigm about organizations more than any other single paradigm, when dealing with my understanding of an organization.

**Bertelsen, Walter**
 1985     "When God Gives A Sense of Destiny." Unpublished research paper, School of World Mission, Fuller Theological Seminary, Pasadena, CA.

Comment:    Was the first basic work on studying the scriptures for sense of destiny concepts. This was done as a research paper for ML530 Life Long Development.

**Brengle, Samuel**
 1890     **Hints To Holiness.** Atlanta: Salvation Army.

Comment:    Brengle was laid low by an injury for two years. During that time he wrote this first of many popular treatments of theological concepts he exhorted in his public ministry. This is an example of sphere of influence, providential use of sickness, and an early indication of ultimate contribution. Writing popular treatments of what he believed and taught and preached on became for Brengle an effective methodology.

**Carver, John**
 1997     **Boards That Make a Difference—A New Design for Leadership in Non-Profit and Public Organizations.** San Francisco, Calif. : Jossey-Bass.

Comment:    This was ministry insights breakthrough for me as to how boards ought to work. I was on two parachurch boards at the time and studied how to apply these concepts to the boards. I brought about change on both of these boards.

**Claude, Jean**
 n.d.     **Essays on the Composition of a Sermon.** Out of Print.

Comment:    Charles Simeon's discovery of this important work opened up for him an important effective methodology (a structured approach to homiletics) which involved his public rhetorician ultimate contribution. This was an example of a literary process item—in fact, a pseudo divine contact. It demonstrates also how a classical work can have effect on others long after we ourselves are gone.

**Clinton, Bobby (J. Robert)**
 1989     **The Making of A Leader.** Colorado Springs: NavPress.

Comment:    This is the popular treatment of leadership emergence theory. It gives an introduction to all three major variables of the theory (processing, time, response). It spends more time on the processing variable, hence stressing *spiritual formation*. **Unlocking Giftedness** stresses *ministerial formation*. This manual, Strategic Concepts, stresses *strategic formation*.

Clinton, J. Robert
    1989        **Leadership Emergence Theory**.  Altadena, Ca: Barnabas Publishers.

Comment:        This is the more academic treatment of leadership emergence theory. It goes into detail on all three formations: spiritual, ministerial, strategic.

Clinton, J. Robert
    1995        **The Mentor Handbook.** Altadena: Barnabas Publishers.

Comment:        This handbook was developed along with the Connecting book for use in classes teaching about mentoring.

Clinton, J. Robert
    1995        **Focused Lives, Inspirational Life Changing Lessons From Eight Effective Christian Leaders Who Finished Well**.  Altadena, Ca: Barnabas Publishers.

Comment:        This is the book detailing the research into 10 lives of effective Christian leaders who finished well (8 of them were written up). It was this research that forms the basis for findings given in **Strategic Concepts**.

Clinton, J. Robert
    2005        **The Leadership Emergence READER**.  Altadena, Ca: Barnabas Publishers.

Comment:        This contains many articles about important concepts of *Leadership Emergence Theory*. Many of these were research papers done after the manual Leadership Emergence Theory was written. Hence, this READER contains the on-going findings of the sixteen years following the initial publication of the manual.

Clinton, J. Robert
    2005        **The Focused Life READER.** Altadena, Ca: Barnabas Publishers.

Comment:        This reader contains articles that were written about the focused life during the ten years following the research, which produced the book, **Focused Lives**.

Clinton, J. Robert and Clinton, Richard W.
    1991        **The Mentor Handbook : Detailed Guidelines And Helps for Christian Mentors and Mentorees**. Altadena, Ca: Barnabas Publishers.

Comment:        Ministry insights in terms of personal ministry with others is captured in terms of nine mentoring types.

Clinton, J. Robert and Clinton, Richard W.
    1993        **Unlocking Your Giftedness — What Leaders Need to Know to Develop Themselves and Others** Altadena, Ca: Barnabas Publishers.

Comment:        This manual contains the detailed 10 year research into giftedness of leaders — 1983-1993). It gives expanded teaching into ministerial formation — how God shapes a leader's giftedness to produce ministry results.

Clinton, J. Robert and Stanley, Paul
    1992        **Connecting — The Mentoring Relationships You Need To Succeed In Life.** Colorado Springs: NavPress.

Comment:      This book was a joint effort. I was learning about the various relationships that Paul Stanley had seen in his Navigator ministry in Europe. I had also seen the importance of people shaping leaders in my leadership emergence theory research. This writing clarified for me what I was seeing.

Covey, Stephen
    1989        **7 Habits of Highly Effective People — Restoring The Character Ethic**. New York : Simon and Schuster.

Comment:      Covey's research corroborates many of the findings of my own focused lives studies. Though Covey is studying secular leaders, many of his findings are also seen in Christian leaders. His basal principle, "Begin with the end in mind," is a fundamental confirmation of my own major lesson, "Effective leaders view present ministry in terms of a life long perspective." My research into life long development of leaders has this basic underlying ideation.

Keirsey, David and Bates, Marilyn
    1984        **Please Understand Me**: Character & Temperament Types. Del Mar, CA: Prometheus Nemesis.

Comment:      This book is referred to in chapter 2. Essential Concepts About the Focused Life. It is mentioned in conjunctions with one of the two 2 Beingness Factors, Personality. This is a self-study manual with a simple test to help one figure out the Myers-Briggs profile. I use the Myers-Briggs profile to help me adjudge personality of leaders. For example, I assess the 8 leaders studied in **Focused Lives** as follows:  Charles Simeon — E/I STJ; A.J. Gordon — ESTJ; Samuel Brengle — ENF J/P; G. Campbell Morgan — I/E S/N TJ; Robert Jaffray — E/I STJ; R.C. McQuilkin — I/E S/N TJ; Henrietta Mears — E N/S F P/J; L.E. Maxwell — I/E STJ. Many web sites can help you determine your own profile. Just Google Myers-Briggs.

Hall, E. T.
    n.d.        **The Silent Language**. Out of print — not available.

Comment:      Shows the importance of surfacing implicit assumptions and making them explicit so that we can more deliberately use them, change them if they need that, or abrogate them if they are not helpful or healthy. As long as they remain implicit, they control us without us knowing it.

Mintzberg, Henry
    1983        **Power in And Around Organizations**. Englewood Cliffs, N.J. : Prentice-Hall.

Comment:      Mintzberg is one of the most insightful organizational gurus that I have studied. His grounded theory research develops insights that can be applied. This particular book looks at power in organizations — how it is structured and what needs to be done if change is to be brought about.

Mintzberg, Henry
    1983        **Structure In Fives : Designing Effective Organizations**. Englewood Cliffs, N.J. : Prentice-Hall.

Comment:      Mintzberg is one of the most insightful organizational gurus that I have studied. His grounded theory research develops insights that can be applied. This particular book identifies five basic structures that need to be in any organization.

# BARNABAS PUBLISHERS

## BARNABAS PUBLISHER'S MINI CATALOG

*Approaching the Bible With Leadership Eyes:* An Authoratative Source for Leadership Findings — Dr. J. Robert Clinton

**Barnabas:** Encouraging Exhorter — Dr. J. Robert Clinton & Laura Raab

**Connecting:** The Mentoring Relationships You Need to Succeed in Life — Dr. J. Robert Clinton

**Fellowship With God** — Dr. J. Robert Clinton

*Finishing Well* — Dr. J. Robert Clinton

**Figures and Idioms** (Interpreting the Scriptures: Figures and Idioms) — Dr. J. Robert Clinton

**Having A Ministry That Lasts:** By Becoming a Bible Centered Leader — Dr. J. Robert Clinton

**Hebrew Poetry** (Interpreting the Scriptures: Hebrew Poetry) — Dr. J. Robert Clinton

A Short **History of Leadership Theory** — Dr. J. Robert Clinton

**Isolation:** A Place of Transformation in the Life of a Leader — Shelley G. Trebesch

**Joseph:** Destined to Rule — Dr. J. Robert Clinton

**The Joshua Portrait** — Dr. J. Robert Clinton and Katherine Haubert

**Leadership Emergence Theory:** A Self Study Manual For Analyzing the Development of a Christian Leader — Dr. J. Robert Clinton

**Leadership Perspectives:** How To Study The Bible for Leadership Insights — Dr. J. Robert Clinton

Coming to Some Conclusions on **Leadership Styles** — Dr. J. Robert Clinton

**Leadership Training Models** — Dr. J. Robert Clinton

The Bible and **Leadership Values:** A Book by Book Analysis— Dr. J. Robert Clinton

**The Mentor Handbook:** Detailed Guidelines and Helps for Christian Mentors and Mentorees — Dr. J. Robert Clinton

**Parables—Puzzles With A Purpose** (Interpreting the Scriptures: Puzzles With A Purpose) — Dr. J. Robert Clinton

**Reading on the Run:** Continuum Reading Concepts — Dr. J. Robert Clinton

**Samuel:** Last of the Judges & First of the Prophets–A Model For Transitional Times — Bill Bjoraker

**Selecting and Developing Those Emerging Leaders** — Dr. Richard W. Clinton

**Starting Well:** Building A Strong Foundation for a Life Time of Ministry — Dr. J. Robert Clinton

**Strategic Concepts:** That Clarify A Focused Life – A Self Study Guide — Dr. J. Robert Clinton

**The Making of a Leader:** Recognizing the Lessons & Stages of Leadership Development — Dr. J. Robert Clinton

**Unlocking Your Giftedness:** What Leaders Need to Know to Develop Themselves & Others — Dr. J. Robert Clinton

**Webster-Smith, Irene:** An Irish Woman Who Impacted Japan (A Focused Life Study) — Dr. J. Robert Clinton

**Word Studies** (Interpreting the Scriptures: Word Studies) — Dr. J. Robert Clinton

# BARNABAS PUBLISHERS

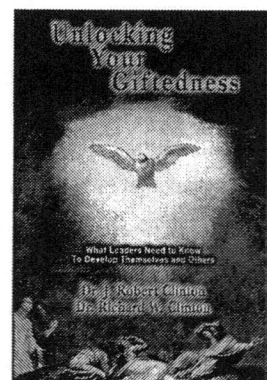

## BARNABAS PUBLISHERS
Post Office Box 6006 • Altadena, CA 91003-6006
Fax Phone (626)-794-3098